REBEL REEFERS

REBEL REEFERS

The Organization and Midshipmen
of the Confederate States Naval Academy

James Lee Conrad

DA CAPO PRESS

A Member of the Perseus Books Group

Designed by Reginald R. Thompson

Set in 11-point Bulmer MT by the Perseus Books Group

Library of Congress Cataloging-in-Publication Data
Conrad, James Lee.
Rebel reefers : the organization and midshipmen of the Confederate States Naval Academy / James Lee Conrad.—1st Da Capo Press ed.
    p. cm.
Includes bibliographical references (p.) and index.
  ISBN 0-306-81237-1 (alk. paper)
1. Confederate Naval Academy—History. 2. Patrick Henry (Ship) 3. Midshipmen--Confederate States of America—Biography. 4. Confederate States of America. Navy—History. 5. United States—History—Civil War, 1861-1865—Naval operations. I. Title.
V438.C66 2003
973.7'57--dc21

2003009888

First Da Capo Press edition 2003

ISBN 0–306–81237–1

Published by Da Capo Press, A Member of the Perseus Books Group
http://www.dacapopress.com

Da Capo Press books are available at special discounts for bulk purchases in the U.S. by corporations, institutions, and other organizations. For more information, please contact the Special Markets Department at the Perseus Books Group, 11 Cambridge Center, Cambridge, MA 02142, or call (800) 255-1514 or (617) 252-5298, or e-mail j.mccrary@perseusbooks.com.

1 2 3 4 5 6 7 8 9—07 06 05 04 03

Contents

❧❧

Acknowledgments

S OME HEAVY SPADEWORK WAS REQUIRED to unearth the often obscure and forgotten details of the Confederate States Naval Academy and its midshipmen; some of the material thus found appears herein for the first time in a published work. Several people helped me dig and deserve mention.

John Coski of the Museum of the Confederacy, in Richmond, Virginia, and author of *Capital Navy*, the definitive work on the Confederate Navy's James River Squadron, shared with me the results of his research and guided me through the museum library's holdings. His assistance was instrumental and greatly appreciated. William S. "Sam" Craghead of the Richmond Civil War Roundtable tracked down some obscure materials in the collections of the Library of Virginia and the Virginia Historical Society. Alice Creighton and Mary Catalfamo of the United States Naval Academy's Nimitz Library, in Annapolis, shared some of their treasures, including a privately published copy of Midshipman Willie Wilson's diary. Rod Clare of the Duke University Library, in Chapel Hill, North Carolina, and Brian J. Cuthrell of the University of South Carolina's South Caroliniana Library, in Columbia, assisted in obtaining valuable information from the collections of their institutions. Kimberly Ball of the Georgia Historical Society, in Atlanta, and Ann Hassinger of the United States Naval Institute, in Annapolis, supplied copies of past articles from the archives of the *Georgia Historical Quarterly* and Naval Institute *Proceedings*. The staff of the National Archives in Washington, D.C., were of particular service in combing their vast holdings for relevant information.

The Museum of the Confederacy and Diane Jacobs of the Virginia Military Institute archives, in Lexington, Virginia, supplied images from their collections. Ron Marlett graciously granted permission to reproduce for the dust jacket his original painting of the school ship *Patrick Henry*, currently on loan to the Port Columbus, Georgia, Civil War Naval Center. Mr. Chuck Peple, great-great-grandson of the Confederate States Naval Academy professor Augustus Peple, furnished a copy of a previously unpublished photo of his ancestor.

Special thanks are owed to John Coski, Dr. William N. Still, Jr., William C. "Jack" Davis, and Colonel Bernie Chachula, all of whom read the manuscript and furnished invaluable advice, comments, and criticism. Any errors remaining are mine and any opinions expressed herein are mine and not those of the Department of the Air Force or the Department of Defense.

Finally, loving thanks are owed to Susan, James Jr., and Kathryn, who made allowance for my extended absences whilst I set sail with the Rebel reefers.

Introduction

D EVISING A METHOD FOR TRAINING and educating professional junior offi-cers for service in its armed forces is a challenge every nation faces. Over the centuries military officer training has evolved from a haphazard system of "on-the-job" training involving the assignment of prospective officers to active regi-ments or warships to one that combines systematic study in a scholastic setting integrated with practical military training conducted and administered by a dedicated faculty unhampered by routine military duties. The United States Military Academy at West Point, New York, and its naval counterpart at An-napolis, Maryland, are the embodiments of the more structured approach to military officer training and education.

The Confederate States of America officially adhered to the old system in its army, assigning budding army officers as Confederate States cadets to active regiments for training, but it also obtained junior officers from several state mil-itary academies in the Southern states operating on the West Point system that remained open during the Civil War.

At the beginning of the Civil War, the education and training of Confeder-ate junior naval officers, or midshipmen, was still wedded to the traditional sys-tem of assigning midshipmen to warships to be trained and educated under the supervision of the ship's captain. By 1863, however, under the leadership of Secretary of the Navy Stephen R. Mallory, the Confederate navy moved to the more modern system of education and training when the Confederacy opened its sole national academy aboard the Confederate States Ship (CSS) *Patrick Henry,* anchored in Virginia's James River. There, until April 1865, a group of dedicated faculty educated these young men in basic academic courses such as mathematics, English, and foreign languages and trained them in specialized areas of naval warfare such as gunnery, seamanship, and steam engineering.

Confederate midshipmen saw more active service than would be expected for students at an academic institution. While their federal counterparts at the U.S. Naval Academy in Annapolis studied at a safe distance from the deadly fighting of the war, the midshipmen of the Confederate States Naval Academy, downriver from Richmond, bent over their books on the *Patrick Henry* constituted an element in the defenses of one of the Confederate nation's most strategic waterways. Their story, one of dedication and sacrifice, has scarcely been a subject of the historian's pen.

This book is an outgrowth of and companion to *The Young Lions: Confederate Cadets at War*, my study of the Confederacy's state military colleges and their cadets. The goal of this volume is to do for the midshipmen what I aimed to accomplish for the Confederacy's cadets—to provide the reader with an insight into the daily lives of the student-sailors and into the workings of Mr. Mallory's naval school. The academy's midshipmen and their state military-school counterparts were unique among Confederate military organizations. No other units were called upon to be students one minute and fighting men the next and few exhibited the exuberance and spirit of these young men. With the publication of this study I hope I have done justice to the memories of the Confederacy's "boy" sailors as well as its young soldiers.

1

"The Proper Education of Naval Officers"

T HE 290-TON BRIG *SOMERS* CUT A RAKISH FIGURE as she departed the Brooklyn Navy Yard on September 13, 1842. Since she was never expected to trade broadsides with an enemy vessel, her designer had graced her with very unmilitary, yacht-like, low and racy lines. She was armed with guns, to be used not in combat but in training her pupils—for the *Somers* had been specially built earlier that year as a school ship. Alexander Slidell Mackenzie, a "sanctimonious prig" whose literary pretensions were nevertheless admired by his fellow officers, had been appointed the ship's captain-schoolmaster.[1] His crew for this voyage consisted of a cadre of experienced sailors, apprentice seamen, and seven midshipmen—these being the most junior officers of the U.S. Navy, traditionally referred to aboard ship as the "reefers."[2]

Mackenzie's ship was an experiment that departed from a long naval tradition, which held "that the best place for a young man is at sea," where his training was conducted aboard ship with little or no instruction in matters not directly related to working a fighting vessel.[3] This traditional method of training future officers in "the school of the ship," involved assigning young men to an active naval vessel and placing them under the tutelage of officers or petty officers or, on larger ships, of a schoolmaster.[4]

The system had serious shortcomings. The assigned tutors often did not have time to adequately cover essential topics such as navigation, astronomy, and mathematics, so subjects that were seen as less "useful," such as history or

English literature, were rarely attempted. By 1842, the inadequacy of the traditional system caused Navy Secretary Abel P. Upshur to lament, "Little or no attention has hitherto been paid to the proper education of naval officers."[5] The practically unsupervised training of midshipmen aboard receiving ships (older ships that functioned rather like a naval boot camp) or cruising vessels carried on "in the midst of a thousand interruptions and impediments . . . render the whole system of little or no value," Upshur declared.[6]

Faced with a similar problem, in 1729 the British Admiralty had established the Royal Naval College at Portsmouth, on England's southern coast, in an effort to improve the education of the Royal Navy's officers. The college was a break with the tradition of exclusively shipboard training and was a laudable effort to raise the level of the generally scant formal education of the Royal Navy's officers, which, with the exception of practical seamanship and the mathematics necessary for navigation, was generally woefully inadequate.[7] Despite President John Quincy Adams's recommendation as early as 1825 that such an institution be established in the United States "for the formation of scientific and accomplished officers," the advocates of the "school of the ship" in the U.S. Navy were unwilling to bless anything so "radical" as a shore-based naval school along the lines of the Royal Naval College.[8] The *Somers*, a ship-based naval school, represented an experimental compromise blending thorough academic instruction with mastery of practical shipboard skills in a setting free of the myriad distractions present on an active warship. But the experiment went horribly wrong.

The *Somers* was a small ship, and was jammed with over 120 men, mostly young sailors-in-training cast off by the captains of other ships, for inexperienced trainees were considered more trouble than they were worth on a warship. One of the seven midshipmen she carried was to cause particular problems in the cramped, crowded spaces between decks.

Eighteen-year-old Midshipman Phillip Spencer was the undisciplined, arrogant son of Secretary of War John C. Spencer. Spencer had given up on disciplining young Phillip and instead obtained for him an appointment as a midshipman in hopes that the navy would perform that task. Phillip, however, resisted the navy's efforts to make him conform and already had been dismissed from two ships; he would have been expelled from the navy were it not for the intercession of Secretary Upshur. He was instead assigned to the *Somers*.

Once on board Mackenzie's ship Spencer went out of his way to make himself unpopular with both his fellow midshipmen and his pedantic skipper. Phillip, described by a former shipmate, William Harwar Parker, as a "tall, pale delicate-looking young man," found company among the apprentice sailors instead of with his fellow midshipmen, thus breaking the taboo against too much familiarity between those on the quarterdeck and the common sailors in the forecastle.[9] Spencer plied his newfound friends with food, tobacco, and liquor and regaled them with stories about turning pirate.

Unfortunately, these stories were reported to Captain Mackenzie, who had Spencer seized and searched. Hidden in his bandanna the searchers found a scrap of paper with Greek characters, allegedly a list of those of the crew to be killed and those who would join him in seizing the ship and turning pirate. Mackenzie clapped Spencer in irons on a charge of conspiring to mutiny and chained him to the quarterdeck, along with two other unpopular crew members, Boatswain's Mate Samuel Cromwell and Seaman Elisha Small, also implicated in the "conspiracy."

Over the next two days, the paranoid Mackenzie added eleven others to his collection of "mutineers." The *Somers* was already on a course for St. Thomas, Virgin Islands, where a U.S. consul—a diplomatic officer with the authority to take charge of the prisoners and return them to the United States—was stationed. Instead, over the following days Mackenzie browbeat his officers into consenting to summarily hang the three ringleaders as threats to the safety of the ship. The officers reluctantly gave their consent.[10] Having obtained the concurrence of his officers, Mackenzie gave Spencer, Cromwell, and Small one hour to make their peace with God and on December 1, 1842, two days' sail from St. Thomas, the three men were hanged from the brig's yardarm.[11]

In the ensuing controversy over Mackenzie's execution—or murder, depending upon one's point of view—of young Spencer and his mates, serious doubts were raised concerning the wisdom of sending young men to sea for their education and training subject solely to the whim of men such as the captain of the *Somers*. These doubts were hard to lay to rest, and it would take a new secretary of the navy to change the system and draw something positive out of Phillip Spencer's death.

On May 11, 1845, President James K. Polk appointed George Bancroft, a noted historian and educator, as secretary of the navy. Bancroft lost no time in addressing the issue of naval training and education and decided to establish a shore-based naval school along the lines of the army's West Point (founded in 1802). On May 1, Bancroft asked William Chauvenet, a navy schoolmaster and founder of the successful Philadelphia Naval Asylum School, to begin plans for creating a new government-sponsored, shore-based naval academy. By September 3, planning was complete and Bancroft chose Fort Severn, near Annapolis, Maryland, for the site of the new school, much preferring "the healthy and secluded" Annapolis to the "temptations and distractions" of Philadelphia.[12] On October 10, 1845, the Naval School began operations under Commander Franklin Buchanan with seven faculty and fifty midshipmen.[13]

Some sixteen years later, on March 16, 1861, the provisional government of the newly proclaimed Confederate States of America established a structure for the Navy Department it had created the previous month and a section of this act arguably "amply authorized" the creation of a naval academy.[14] In April, the Confederacy's President Jefferson Davis advocated establishing army and navy academies for the Confederacy along the lines of those of the United States and expressed his opinion that "to secure a thorough military education it is . . . essential that officers should enter upon the study of their profession at an early period of life and have elementary instruction in a military school."[15]

In December 1861, the Confederate Congress specifically required Secretary of the Navy Stephen R. Mallory to devise "some form of education for midshipmen."[16] Although authorized and required to develop a training and education program for midshipmen, Mallory was busily occupied with more important things—like building a navy for these future officers to command. It certainly was not that he was unacquainted with or opposed to the concept of naval colleges. Before the outbreak of war, Mallory had been a United States senator from Florida, and had served as chairman of the Senate's Naval Affairs Committee. He was therefore well acquainted with the old navy and its facilities, ships, operation, and naval academy. Indeed, his knowledge of naval affairs was one of the primary reasons Davis chose him for the naval portfolio. Although later blamed by the press, public, and some in the Confederate Congress for the various defeats suffered by Rebel naval forces, Mallory was an able administrator and was one of only two of Davis's cabinet to serve in the same post throughout the Confederacy's existence.

Although described as "not the type of man to whom come inspirations of genius," the somewhat portly, fifty-year-old Mallory was "incapable . . . of shirking a duty or a cause to which he had given his devotion," and he worked wonders.[17] He ordered the design of new warships, particularly the revolutionary ironclads. He dispatched procuring agents to Europe to negotiate contracts with shipyards in England and France for the construction of Confederate warships such as the famous commerce raider CSS *Alabama*. But he did not rely solely on European shipyards to create a Southern navy, and eventually eighteen shipyards throughout the South would also be working on naval vessels. Mallory's Navy Department established powder mills; engine, boiler, and machine shops; five ordnance works; and a ropewalk for the production of the miles of cable and rigging needed for the new warships. He also authorized revolutionary experiments with torpedoes, or naval mines, in an effort to even the odds with the much larger U.S. Navy.

Despite his tardiness in responding to Congress's direction to establish a training and education program for midshipmen, Mallory did recognize that the training of officers to command his navy's vessels and manage its shore establishments was important to the Confederate navy's long-term success. Those serving with them noticed the inadequacy of the navy's junior officers early in the war. Many of these inexperienced young men were characterized as being "officers in the navy without being naval officers."[18] One veteran officer observed that the Rebel navy particularly suffered from a "want of educated junior officers."[19]

Mallory certainly supported the establishment of a naval academy and noted the shortcomings of the existing system of training in a communication to President Davis on February 27, 1862, in which he recommended the establishment of a naval academy as the means of training midshipmen. In his message Mallory described his midshipmen as being, for the most part, young gentlemen "appointed from civil life and possessing generally but little knowledge of the duties of an officer and rarely even the vocabulary of their profession."[20] These neophytes were then posted "to vessels or batteries where it is impossible for them to obtain knowledge of its most important branches, which can be best, if not only, acquired by methodical study."[21]

Acting Midshipman St. George Tucker Brooke's recollection of his assignment for initial training to the receiving ship *Confederate States* anchored in Virginia's Elizabeth River illustrates Mallory's concern. Upon reporting aboard the "*States*," as it was called, young Brooke described how he was "given a book of instructions in heavy ship-gun drill and was required to learn the manuel [*sic*]. When I had learned it out of the book and from observation I was assigned with the other midshipmen, the duty of drilling the men at the heavy guns and sometimes at the Navy Yard."[22] Another young trainee, Acting Midshipman William F. Clayton, complained that he and his fellow middies "had no teachers . . . but were expected to fathom everything for ourselves, no lecturers to explain or elucidate."[23]

By the time the war began, in April 1861, Mallory had already obtained the services of many experienced senior officers, for although most of the U.S. Navy's "tars," or common sailors, were Northerners, many of its officers hailed from the Southern states.[24] By mid-1861, 24 percent of the U.S. Navy's officers, including ninety-five graduates of the U.S. Naval Academy, had resigned their commissions and "gone south."[25] Mallory also received the services of fifty-nine acting midshipmen who had resigned from Annapolis.[26] To facilitate the completion of the studies of these former Annapolis midshipmen and to ensure a continued supply of well-trained junior officers, the Confederate Congress passed an act on April 21, 1862, for the establishment of a naval academy with 106 acting midshipmen appointed thereto by members of the Congress from their respective states or districts and by the President from the Confederacy at large. Billets for twenty passed midshipmen were also authorized.[27]

While deciding how best to organize a Confederate States Naval Academy, Mallory had two shipboard establishments to study as models in addition to the shore-based U.S. Naval Academy.

In August 1860, the *Somers* experiment resurfaced in a modified form when "Old Ironsides," the storied by now sixty-year-old frigate USS *Constitution*, was pulled out of ordinary, refurbished as a school ship for fourth-class midshipmen, and anchored at the U.S. Naval Academy. Living and training aboard "Old Ironsides" protected the new midshipmen from the tender mercies of the upperclassmen while giving them shipboard experience under the watchful eye of the academy faculty.

Mallory also had a model of a shipboard naval school closer to home for inspiration. In May 1859, the Reverend William B. Yates, in association with the Charleston Port Society, opened the Charleston Marine School aboard the 200-ton brig *Lodebar*. Aboard the school ship, anchored off of White Point Gardens, Captain M. L. Aimar taught English, mathematics, and ship's handling and maintenance to forty-three poor boys "who had heretofore been wandering about the streets of Charleston."[28] The school had received some favorable national attention in an article in the December 1859 issue of *Harper's Weekly*.

As relations between the slave states of the South and the rest of the Union deteriorated throughout the 1850s and the prospect of South Carolina's secession drew closer (it seceded in December 1860), state authorities recognized in Reverend Yates's school a pool of homegrown naval talent. By 1860, the state of South Carolina began providing financial support to this "nursery for seamen" as the "proper counterpart of the State Military Academy."[29]

With the outbreak of the Civil War in April 1861, the *Lodebar* and its students transported troops to Confederate fortifications on islands around Charleston and for a time was armed and used to guard the Ashley River at Newton Cut. By the time Mallory turned his organizational talents to establishing a naval academy for the Confederacy, Charleston Marine School graduates and former students were already in service aboard the country's ironclads, blockade runners, and privateers.[30]

In carrying out the Confederate Congress's mandate, Mallory sought a compromise between an exclusively shore-based establishment and the older method of assigning midshipmen to active vessels. He also recognized military realities and the need not to weaken the nation's scant naval resources, and so on May 15, 1862, he ordered that the CSS *Patrick Henry,* flagship of the James River Squadron, be withdrawn from service for conversion to a school ship, "without interfering with her efficiency as a vessel of war."[31]

The CSS *Patrick Henry* had started life as the paddlewheel steamship *Yorktown* carrying passengers and freight between Richmond and New York City for the New York and Old Dominion Line. Two hundred and fifty feet long with a beam of thirty-four feet, a displacement of 1,300 tons, and carrying a brig rig in addition to her engines, she was "very beautifully modelled" and was considered a fast ship.[32] On April 17, 1861, the day Virginia seceded from the Union, the *Yorktown* and her sister ship, the *Jamestown*, were anchored in the James River and, along with other "enemy" property, were seized by the Commonwealth of Virginia. Ultimately the two vessels were sold to the Confederate States Navy for $280,000, but prior to the sale the smaller *Jamestown* was fitted with two thirty-two-pounder rifled cannon and was commissioned as the *Thomas Jefferson*, although that name was rarely used, while the *Yorktown* was sent to the Rocketts Navy Yard in Richmond, Virginia, for a more extensive refitting as a warship.[33]

Naval constructor Joseph Pierce supervised the transformation of the *Yorktown*, a tool of commerce, to the CSS *Patrick Henry*, a weapon of war. Pierce rearranged the ship's decks and strengthened or demolished much of her civilian superstructure. One-inch-thick iron plates bolted to her sides extended to two feet below the waterline to protect her engines and boilers, arguably making her the Confederate navy's first ironclad. To protect the crew from raking fire along the length of her deck and to guard the massive but exposed walking beam that drove her side-mounted paddlewheels, Pierce erected V-shaped iron shields on the fore and aft spar decks. Her offensive punch was provided by six eight-inch and two thirty-two-pounder cannon mounted in broadside augmented by a ten-inch pivot gun forward and a massive sixty-four-pounder pivot gun aft. Recommissioned as CSS *Patrick Henry,* and mustering a crew of 150 officers and men under the command of Captain John Randolph Tucker, a Virginian and veteran of the U.S. Navy, she was assigned to the Confederate Navy's James River Squadron in July 1861.[34] From then until the time she was withdrawn from active service for conversion to a school ship, the *Patrick Henry* served with distinction. Her captain and crew earned a resolution of thanks from the Confederate Congress for her part in the engagement between the ironclads CSS *Virginia* and USS *Monitor* at Hampton Roads, Virginia, in March 1862 and praise for her crew's role in the Confederate victory over Federal naval forces at Drewry's Bluff on the James River, downriver from the capital of Richmond, on May 15, 1862. During her service she earned the reputation among sailors of being, said her flag officer, a "'lucky ship' and her crew had unbounded confidence in her good fortune."[35]

Soon after the Drewry's Bluff engagement, the *Patrick Henry* was sent back to Rocketts Navy Yard to be converted in preparation for her new role as a school ship. Some of her guns had been removed and mounted in the fortifications at Drewry's Bluff in early May, but four others remained in place to be used for the training of midshipmen in gunnery and for her continued role as a James River defense ship. "Two little pine board recitation rooms" were constructed on the gun deck between the paddlewheel boxes.[36] To train the midshipmen in handling sails, an oversize fully rigged mast was stepped forward, giving the ship an odd, unbalanced look. A small launch mounting a twelve-pounder boat howitzer was also provided for training. So as not to diminish Richmond's defenses along the James, which was navigable up to the capital city, the school ship was to remain anchored by the Drewry's Bluff defenses.[37] Cabins were erected ashore at Drewry's Bluff in case the midshipmen were called in to man the batteries, but when on board the young men would sleep in hammocks sailor-style.

Mallory assigned the task of organizing the academy to Commander John Mercer Brooke, a graduate of the U.S. Naval Academy and head of the Confederate Navy's Office of Ordnance and Hydrography since March 1863.[38] Brooke, born on an army post near Tampa, Florida, in 1826, was the designer of the Brooke rifled naval cannon, one of the best of the Confederacy's home-grown ordnance, and was also the codesigner of the ironclad *Virginia*.

The academy was to be under Brooke's supervision as chief of the Office of Ordnance and Hydrography, but Lieutenant William Harwar Parker was chosen as superintendent of the Confederate States Naval Academy and given the task of writing its regulations and preparing "an estimate for books, apparatus, etc., necessary for the establishment of a naval school."[39]

A native New Yorker with a reputation for "high professional and scientific accomplishments," the distinguished-looking, heavily mustachioed, thirty-six-year-old Parker was the son of a naval officer and had entered the navy at the age of fourteen.[40] A gifted student, he graduated from the U.S. Naval Academy first in his class in 1848 and served on that academy's faculty for six years. In 1861 he cast his lot with his adopted state of Virginia and was soon commissioned as an officer in the Confederate navy. By the time of his appointment as head of the Confederate Naval Academy, he had seen extensive combat service in North Carolina and Virginia as commander of the gunboat *Beaufort* and in South Carolina waters as executive officer of the Confederate ironclad *Palmetto State* of the Charleston Squadron.

Brooke and Parker did not present Mallory with a final proposal for the organization of the school until July 23, 1863. Anticipating secretarial approval, however, the two officers began purchasing and scrounging the materials necessary for the academic mission of the school ship even before they submitted their formal proposal to Mallory. In early June, $57.50 was paid for nine copies of Hill's *Algebra*, ten copies of Greenleaf's *Higher Arithmetic*, and eight copies of Bullin's *English Grammar* "for the use of midshipmen on board schoolship."[41] This effort continued until autumn. In September, Brooke approved a payment of $40 for astronomy and English texts and another of $114 for textbooks and classroom supplies.[42] In November, he wrote to Thomas E. Martin, acting chief of the Lighthouse Bureau, asking him to transfer to the Office of Ordnance and Hydrography an "Azimuth Compass with tripod which would be of service for the instruction of Midshipmen on board the School Ship 'Patrick Henry'."[43]

The secretary did approve Parker and Brooke's proposal, and that summer the first midshipmen were received aboard the *Patrick Henry*, thus inaugurating the key aspect of Mallory's plan for the "proper education" of his Rebel reefers. A naval academy, the legacy of the unfortunate midshipman Phillip Spencer, had been brought to the Confederacy.

2

"A Floating Academy"

ONLY 52 OF THE 106 ACTING MIDSHIPMEN appointed in accordance with the law of 1862 reported in the summer of 1863 to the "floating academy" established on board the *Patrick Henry*.[1] The school ship could not accommodate more, so the remaining fifty-four acting midshipmen appointed to the Confederate States Naval Academy remained aboard various ships of the fleet or in service at shore installations and batteries until the time came for them to receive formal instruction on the school ship. And their time would come, for after the establishment of the academy, an acting midshipman was not eligible for his promotion examination unless in residence on the school ship.

Midshipmen pulled from active service to attend school were often disappointed with the order to report to the school ship. "These young gentlemen were, at first, very loth [*sic*] to come to the ship and take up their books," explained the superintendent, Lieutenant William Parker, "but when they found that it resulted in their returning to their ships as passed midshipmen, eligible to promotion to the grade of lieutenant, they became reconciled to it."[2] Midshipman James M. "Jimmy" Morgan's reaction to his assignment to the school ship was a case in point. "One can imagine my consternation and disappointment when I discovered that I was to be sent to school!" wrote Morgan years later. "I wondered if the Secretary of the Navy knew that I was all of 18 years of age, and that I was engaged to be married. I fretted and fumed, but now know that if there was one thing I needed more than another, it was a little schooling."[3]

"A little schooling" was just what young Mr. Morgan would get. "An exceptionally good corps of professors" greeted the first midshipmen to report to the Confederate States Naval Academy's school ship.[4] In addition to Superintendent William Parker, a theoretical as well as practical sailor who later would write a textbook entitled *Elements of Seamanship* for use on the school ship, an experienced group of navy and army veterans had been signed on as faculty.[5]

Lieutenant Wilburn B. Hall served as commandant and executive officer. Hall was a native of South Carolina who graduated from Annapolis first in his class, resigned his appointment as a passed midshipman in the U.S. Navy on March 7, 1861, and had seen wartime service with the Savannah, Charleston, and Mobile squadrons as well as on the Red River in Texas by the time of his appointment as commandant of the school ship and executive officer of the warship *Patrick Henry*. As commandant he was charged with the discipline and training of the students and as executive officer his primary duty was to keep the ship ready for active service—"in a word, he [was] to make the vessel a *model man-of-war.*"[6] Hall served as commandant and executive officer until the summer of 1864, when he was relieved of those duties by Lieutenant Oscar F. Johnston so that he could devote more time to teaching. In November 1864 Hall requested and was granted a transfer to the CSS *Chicora* at Charleston, South Carolina.

Johnston was a Virginian who had been a lieutenant in the U.S. Navy. Signed on initially as the academy's professor of astronomy, navigation, and surveying, he was also a veteran of the Savannah Squadron and had been aboard the navy blockade runner CSS *Oconee* when she foundered on August 18, 1863, while en route to England with a load of government-owned cotton.

Johnston transferred to the CSS *Virginia II* in November 1864 and was replaced by Lieutenant Benjamin P. Loyall, a native Virginian and an 1855 Annapolis graduate.[7] Loyall entered Annapolis on an appointment from Indiana and was serving as a lieutenant when he tendered his resignation from the U.S. Navy on October 5, 1861. As was the case with many Southern officers, Gideon Welles, secretary of the U.S. Navy, refused to accept his resignation and he was instead dismissed from the navy.

Before he could make his way south, Loyall was arrested and spent part of the war's first year imprisoned at Fort Warren, Massachusetts. After his release, he was promoted to lieutenant in the Confederate States Navy and assigned to the Gosport Navy Yard at Norfolk. February of 1862 found him assigned to the land defenses of Roanoke Island, North Carolina, with the rank of army captain. He was captured by Federal forces on February 8, but was paroled at Elizabeth City, North Carolina, thirteen days later.[8] His next assignment was to the James River Squadron's ironclad CSS *Richmond*, and he may have first been appointed commandant of the Naval Academy in May 1863, although he was reassigned to special duty prior to the arrival of the first midshipmen. In February 1864, after perhaps another short period as academy commandant, he was sent to command the CSS *Neuse*, then under construction near Kinston, North Carolina.[9] In August 1864, he returned to his former position on the school ship.

In late February 1865, First Lieutenant James H. Rochelle, a U.S. Navy veteran and officer with experience commanding vessels in the James River and the Charleston squadrons, including the ironclad *Palmetto State*, was assigned to the Naval Academy as commandant and executive officer of the *Patrick Henry*. Reporting to the *Patrick Henry* was sort of a homecoming for Rochelle, since he had been the ship's first lieutenant earlier in the war.

First Lieutenant Thomas W. W. Davies of Wetumpka, Alabama, served as the Naval Academy's assistant professor of astronomy, navigation, and surveying. Davies, a former Confederate Army officer, came to the school from the Charleston Naval Station and remained on the faculty until sometime in 1864, when he was transferred to the James River Squadron's ironclad *Virginia II*. Later that year he returned to his native Alabama, first to the naval station at Mobile and later to the Selma Naval Station.

First Lieutenant Charles Iverson Graves, an 1857 Annapolis graduate from Georgia and veteran of the Confederate navy's Mobile Squadron, taught the cadets seamanship.[10] Second Lieutenant James W. Billups served as Graves's assistant.[11] Both remained with the academy until its destruction.

The gunnery instructor was Second Lieutenant William Van Comstock. Appointed to Annapolis from Louisiana, Comstock resigned from the Naval Academy on January 30, 1861, and received an appointment as an acting midshipman in the Confederate navy on April 25, 1861. Prior to his assignment to the *Patrick Henry*, Comstock served at New Orleans on the receiving ship *St. Phillip* and on the CSS *Slidell*. In 1862 he was assigned to the Jackson, Mississippi, naval station and then to the receiving ship *Savannah*, probably as one of its cadre crew. In late 1864, Comstock left the *Patrick Henry* and returned to the Savannah Squadron, serving on board the steamers CSS *Macon* and CSS *Sampson*.

A core of professors, all army veterans, according to Superintendent Parker, who remained with the academy until its destruction, rounded out the academic team. The use of these veterans, who taught classic college courses rather than specialized naval courses, may have been due to these men's possessing some civilian teaching experience during the antebellum period, something not shared by most career naval officers. All of these men were carried on navy rolls as masters not in line of promotion, although at least one seems to have been promoted to lieutenant.[12] Two Virginians, George M. Peek and G. W. Armistead, taught mathematics and physics, respectively. Navy Lieutenant John P. McGuire served as Peek's assistant professor.[13] Gustave Adolphus "Gus" Peple, a native of Belgium, taught French and Spanish, and William B. Cox instructed the midshipmen in drawing and painting.[14] A Mr. Sanxey taught infantry tactics.[15] Louis N. Huck, another Confederate army veteran, served as professor of English literature beginning in June 1864. In early 1865, William B. Strange, then serving with the 9th Virginia Infantry Regiment, was also appointed to the faculty, but owing to problems in securing his release from the army seems never to have reported for duty.[16]

Since the school ship was a combatant vessel of the James River Squadron, she also shipped a permanent crew, who primarily performed the duties of their counterparts on other warships while also assisting in instructing the midshipmen in naval skills.[17] The health of those aboard was the responsibility of two warrant officer surgeons. Assistant Surgeon W. J. Addision had been commended for gallantry in battle at St. Charles, Arkansas, in June 1862. He remained with the *Patrick Henry* from 1863 until early 1864, when he was transferred to the Red River. He was captured in the sinking of the ram *William H. Webb* on April 24, 1865. The ship's other assistant surgeon was James G. Bixley. Assistant Paymaster William M. Ladd was responsible for paying the midshipmen and crew and keeping the ship's accounts. Assistant Paymaster John F. Wheless joined the crew in late 1864 after the destruction of his ship, the ironclad *Neuse*. First Assistant Engineer Elias Guy Hall tended the *Patrick Henry's* machinery as he had done since almost the beginning of the ship's naval service, except for brief assignments aboard the CSS *Harriet Lane* and CSS *Missouri*. Andrew Blackie, another former *Savannah* crewman, served as boatswain. Gunner E. R. Johnson tended the ship's great guns and magazine until 1864, when he was replaced by Gunner William F. Brittingham, a veteran of various ships of the James River Squadron and of Charleston's ironclad CSS

Chicora. The sailmaker, William Bennett, formerly of the receiving ship *Confederate States*, was responsible for the *Patrick Henry*'s sails and cordage.

The faculty and crew were on board and awaiting the first acting midshipmen in residence as they reported to the school ship in July and August 1863. Most of these young men had already seen active naval service. Acting Midshipman Samuel P. Blanc was a former Virginia Military Institute cadet who had trained army recruits at Richmond at the start of the war, but transferred to the navy in August 1861 and had seen extensive naval service. Some, such as Acting Midshipman Hubbard Taylor Minor, Jr., had served in the army.[18] All were young, between fourteen and eighteen years of age at the time of their appointment, of "good moral character," and from states throughout the Confederacy.[19] Most reported aboard having already undergone a physical examination during which the discovery of any of several infirmities could have resulted in denial of an appointment, such as

> . . . muscular tenuity; glandular sweatings; chronic cutaneous affections; severe injuries of the bones of the head; convulsions; fistula lachrymalis; deafness; copious discharge from the ears; impaired or inadequate efficiency of one or both of the superior extremities, contractions of a joint, extenuation, or a deformity; an unnatural excurvature or incurvature of the spine; impaired or inadequate efficiency of one or both of the inferior extremities on account of varicose veins, fractures, lameness, contraction or unequal length, bunyons [*sic*], overlying or supernumerary toes.[20]

A naval surgeon had examined each man at the time of his appointment, probably using the form prescribed by the navy for examining recruits to take a medical history based on the answers to questions such as "Have you ever had fits?"; "Are you in the habit of drinking?"; "Are you subject to the piles?"; and "Have you any difficulty in urinating?"[21] A physical examination followed with the surgeon beginning at the head and proceeding to the feet to check for those disqualifying extra toes.

Upon reporting to the school ship, those who had not already been examined underwent an entrance examination conducted by the academic board, which ensured that each student could read and write well and could add, subtract, multiply, and divide whole numbers.[22]

Physical and academic standards were rigidly enforced for the good of the service, but sometimes those standards were questioned. The father of Midshipman W. J. Claiborne, for example, wrote Secretary Mallory seeking the facts surrounding his son's resignation from the school ship. Commander John M. Brooke's reply to Mallory, in which he transmitted Superintendent Parker's explanation, noted "the importance of maintaining the present Standard of requirement by which fitness for the Naval Service [is] determined and the interests of the Country guarded."[23]

Those arriving who did not already possess uniforms had them made, usually by Richmond tailors. The regulation undress uniform for Confederate midshipmen was a frock coat of steel gray—a color unpopular with the sailors, who preferred the traditional navy blue—double-breasted with two rows of medium-sized navy buttons, three medium buttons parallel to the bottom of the cuffs, and a rolling collar. Midshipman Minor's uniform cost $100; he had to furnish the naval buttons, which were designed by Commander Brooke and featured "a ship under sail seen from the bow surrounded by stars in an arch over sea" sailing over the letters "CSN."[24]

The fatigue, or general duty uniform, was of the same cut and color as the regulation undress, but was made of "the coarsest materials."[25] When authorized, gray flannel jumpers and trousers, straw hats, and white jackets could be worn. In practice, this uniform was probably very similar to that of a common sailor, which by regulation consisted of a gray frock with white cuffs and collar and gray trousers for winter or a white frock and trousers for summer with a black neckerchief and a white or black hat.[26] The uniform trousers were bell-bottomed and made "tight at the knee and twenty-two inches in circumference at the bottom."[27] The naval regulations authorized a thick, flat, round gray cap without a visor for wear "at sea," although it is probable this traditional sailor's "porkpie hat" was worn at other times.[28] Those midshipmen designated as officers of crews or companies on the school ship were authorized to wear a distinctive insignia on their jackets.[29] Whether on board ship or on liberty in Richmond, the midshipmen were required to be in uniform. The officers of the school ship were required to wear the service dress uniform at all times, but were authorized to wear blue flannel uniforms instead of steel gray so long as Confederate naval buttons and insignia were worn.[30] During the summer months the officers could exchange their visored caps for cooler straw hats.

The school ship regulations also required the reefers to provide themselves with quite a lengthy list of personal items, including four pairs of drawers, six handkerchiefs, a mattress, a pillow, two blankets, two pairs of sheets, six towels, two pairs of boots, a hair brush, two combs, and a needle-and-thread case.[31] Acting Midshipman James O. "Olly" Harrison, after paying over $50 for his "bedding, blankets, and tableware" and $20 as his share of the mess bill, also discovered that he needed heavy shoes for "drilling on shore" and light shoes for "climbing amongst the rigging."[32] The former he asked his father to send, the latter he would have made by the government shoemaker at Drewry's Bluff. Each mess, made up of twelve to fifteen midshipmen, was to procure a "looking-glass," wash basin, water pail, and slop bucket for common use.[33]

The midshipmen who berthed on the ship (as opposed to some who later lived in the cabins at Drewry's Bluff) slept below decks in hammocks hung sailor-style on hooks from the deck beams overhead. Quarters were close. Morgan described the hammocks as "slung as closely together as sardines in a box."[34] The hammocks were also the subject of boyish pranks. "My sleep was a little interrupted last night," Hubbard Minor noted in his diary after his first night on board the *Patrick Henry*, "for the boys tied ropes to my hammock & swung me all night nearly."[35]

Rested or not, a reefer's day began with the firing of the morning gun at 7 A.M. Hammocks were taken down, rolled up, and stowed. By eight, the midshipmen were at breakfast summoned by the drummer playing the tune "Dixie." Hardtack, "generally infested with weevils and worms," along with "a tin cup full of hot water colored with chicory or burnt grains of ground corn . . . brevetted [as] coffee" made up the meal.[36] Breakfast was not the only meal subjected to criticism. Midshipman Morgan summed up the fare in general as "scanty and unappetizing."[37] Salt-junk, beef so heavily salted to preserve it that it had to be soaked in water before being eaten, was the staple meat and its toughness aroused suspicions that it had "been carved from very close to the horns of some half-starved animal."[38] Corn meal became "a staple article of diet" after the price of wheat flour rose to $1,200 a barrel in depreciated Confederate currency.[39] Complaints were usually left unvoiced, however, since all realized that the soldiers in the trenches not far away were no better off.

Occasionally a treat was served. "I feel . . . fin . . . today," Olly Harrison wrote in a letter home. "It is what the sailors call 'duff day' we draw 11 oz of flour & dried fruit enough to make 'duff' and molasses to the amount of a half pint to sweeten said 'duff' with."[40]

The midshipmen could supplement their diets somewhat by purchases in Richmond's markets or restaurants. But this was an expensive proposition, since food prices skyrocketed as time went on. Restaurants were especially pricey. Richmond's Oriental Restaurant charged $5 for a plate of oysters and $12 for a bottle of ale, although a drink of rye whiskey could be had for $2. A "Fine Havana" cigar to top off the meal set one back another dollar.[41] A midshipmen's pay of $500 per year would not support many trips to the Oriental, even if most of it had not been held on account by the paymaster.

Foraging was an option for midshipmen who could not afford Richmond's culinary delights. Midshipman William F. Clayton's shipboard mess was blessed with a slave named Bob, whose master, Clayton speculated, "probably hired him to the ship in the hopes that he would fall overboard, get drowned, or would desert to the enemy."[42] Bob had one redeeming quality, sticky fingers, and he was greatly attached to his midshipmen, and they, because of his ability at foraging, "loved him as a brother."[43] Bob ran risks for his messmates; after one raid on an army encampment he returned with three hams and a bullet hole through his hat.

Perhaps fittingly, immediately after breakfast at 8:45 the drummer rolled out "Surgeon's Call," and midshipmen feeling ill reported to the surgeon for aid and comfort. By ten o'clock, the surgeon presented to the superintendent a list of "names of those whose condition of health unfits them for any academic duty, or renders it desirable that they should be excused from employment as a means of recovering their health."[44] Being sick did not guarantee a place on the sick list, however. "[M]ost of us were sufferers from [chills and fever], and many . . . were also weakened from chronic dysentery brought on by the bad food, . . . " recalled a midshipman, "but simple chills and fever were never considered of sufficient importance to allow one to be excused from either duty, lessons or drills."[45]

A bugle announced assembly for the first forenoon recitation at 8:55. The midshipmen, with folding camp stools under their arms, formed in two ranks with their section on the port side of the quarterdeck. The reefer with the highest grades in the particular subject took attendance, marched his section to the assigned recitation room "in a military and orderly manner," and reported the names of any absentees to the instructor.[46]

To the extent that it focused on technical subjects, the curriculum of the Confederate States Naval Academy was based on that of the U.S. Naval Academy and followed the admonition of the respected U.S. naval hero Captain Thomas Truxtun, who wrote in 1797:

> Without presuming to dictate the studies which are most essential to [a midshipman's] improvement, we could wish to recommend such as are most suitable. . . . Astronomy, geometry, and mechanics, which are in the first rank of science, are the materials which form the skillful pilot, and the superior mariner. The theory of navigation is entirely derived from the two former, and all the machinery and movements of a ship are founded upon the latter. The action of the wind upon the sails, and the resistance of the water at the stem, naturally dictate an enquiry into the property of solids and fluids: and the state of the ship, floating on the water, seems to direct [the midshipman's] application to the study of hydrostatics and the effects of gravity. A proficiency in these branches of science will equally enlarge his views, with the regard to the operations of naval war, as directed by the efforts of powder, and the knowledge of projectiles.[47]

The course of study of the academy was organized into six departments and twenty-two branches, which could take up to four years to complete. The midshipmen were divided into four academic classes, each pursuing a different course of study. The fourth class, the most junior, studied practical seamanship, naval gunnery, artillery and infantry tactics, arithmetic, algebra, English grammar, and descriptive geography. The third class covered seamanship, gunnery, artillery and infantry tactics, algebra, geometry, plane and spherical trigonometry, physical geography, history, and French. The second class concentrated on seamanship, steam (not taught at Annapolis until 1864), gunnery and field artillery, astronomy, navigation, application of algebra to the measurement of planes and solids, political science, and French. Midshipmen of the first, or senior, class worked on seamanship and naval tactics, gunnery, infantry tactics, navigation, surveying, French, and Spanish.

Once all were assembled in the recitation room, the instructor called on the midshipmen to take their places at the blackboard to demonstrate their knowledge, or lack thereof, of the subject at hand. Hubbard Minor knew both success and failure at the board. Once he noted with pride that despite "quite a hard lesson in Algebra . . . I stood quite a good examination."[48] Ten days later, however, disaster struck. "On this day," he wrote gloomily in his diary, "while at the black board there was one of the strangest things happened to me I ever saw[.] I was unable to do anything at all & I could not reason one bit."[49]

The course of study was demanding. Minor repeatedly noted his academic efforts in his diary: "Studied hard all day. . . . [D]ay . . . spent in hard study & onerous duty. . . . Spent like most of my days here in Hard study & duty. . . ."[50] The instructors continually challenged their students. "We have fine teachers," Olly Harrison wrote his father, "who demand a reason for everything."[51] Harrison seemed to thrive on the challenge and reported to his father, "I have been the leader of the section to which I belong ever since I came on board, on the account of my marks."[52]

Some of the reefers felt too challenged. Acting Midshipman Clifton R. Breckinridge, son of John C. Breckinridge, a Confederate major general who was a former U.S. vice president, confessed to his father, "My marks for the past week are not satisfactory in some respects while some of them are moderately good . . . . I feel very bad when I see my marks so low & still all my time is occupied it is very disheartening to study hard and not meet your expectations."[53]

Despite the hard work and their impatience to be in the fight, the midshipmen seemed to understand the value of their undertaking. "I sometimes wish I were still in the army," Midshipman Minor admitted, "[but] when I think that here I am getting a good education & and at the same time serving my country I am content."[54] Only a month later, however, Minor's contentment was wearing thin and he wrote to his cousin, Lieutenant Robert D. Minor in Richmond, asking him to take him along to sea. Lieutenant Minor refused, advising his young cousin that there would be no sea service for him until he graduated.

Not surprisingly, the most important classes, accounting for a possible 430 points out of 1,000 on the annual examination, were those of the first department (seamanship, naval tactics, and steam) and the second department (gunnery, field artillery, and infantry tactics).

To teach seamanship, the instructors used Superintendent Parker's *Elements of Seamanship* and his *Questions on Practical Seamanship*.[55] Instruction in this most important of subjects was both practical and theoretical. Midshipmen were required to master various knots such as the "Spanish Fox," the "Knittle," and the "Turk's Head," and to be able to explain their uses aboard ship. He had to know what a "woolding" was as well as an assortment of stoppers—Deck, Dog, Bitt, Trip, and Ring.[56] The student was required to demonstrate how to stay the foremast and set up rigging, how to rig the bowsprit, get the tops over, rig and fid a topmast, and rattle down the rigging.

Hands-on instruction was a valuable and well-liked part of the course in seamanship. On one busy day, Hubbard Minor "went aloft as a Top sail yard man & liked the exercise very much," and continued to have "much more practical study today & learned how to signal[. P]ulled in the evening in the boats & I had charge of [the] launch[.]"[57]

To prepare him for future service as an officer at sea or on a river, a midshipman was taught a ship's routine and the orders necessary to carry out that routine, and was then quizzed on it all. He learned the duties of an officer upon "taking the deck" in port, the orders for piping down and stowing hammocks, hoisting and lowering boats, squaring yards, airing bedding, sending up and sending down various masts and yards, hoisting in and serving out provisions, clothing, and small stores, and a myriad of other necessary orders. There was much to learn, one example being the lengthy series of orders to loose sails by hauling up by the buntlines: "Beat the call—aloft sail loosers; man the boom tricing lines—trice up—lay out and loose—man the clew-jiggers and buntlines—stand by to let fall at the third roll [of the drum]—roll off—let fall—haul up—lay in and lay down from aloft."[58] There was yet another set of orders if the sails were to be hauled out by the bowlines.

The boys were trained in the evolutions, or set of prescribed movements, that are necessary to sail a ship, such as tacking by the wind on starboard tack, under all plain sail; wearing under close-reefed main topsail, fore main, and mizzen storm staysails in a gale; trimming a ship with the wind hauling aft and trimming a ship with the wind hauling forward. The orders to accomplish these tasks had to be memorized and the midshipmen had to be "prepared to illustrate every evolution by a Diagram."[59] They were taught to rate chronometers and find the deviation of compasses, instructions for which were included in books such as "Hints for Young Masters." [60]

And there were questions, always questions: "What is meant by 'holidays'?" "What is a 'euphroe'?" "What is a 'Timenoguy'?"; "What are 'Slops'?" "Who is the Jack of the Dust?" "If the crew wish to complain of any part of the ration, how should they do it?" "What is meant by goose-winging a foresail?" "By the wind under top-gallant sails, courses, jib, and spanker, [the] wind freshens and ship begins to gripe. What do?" "How do you 'start' whiskey?" And so on and on.[61]

The most important course of the second department was gunnery. To carry its great guns to within range of the enemy was the reason a warship existed, and a thorough knowledge of the theory and practice of utilizing these lethal weapons was therefore essential for a midshipman.

Every Saturday at 9 A.M. "an Exercise of Great-guns" was to be held.[62] Time was also set aside during the week, but this time might instead be used for cutlass or boat howitzer drill. To facilitate instruction on the great guns, the midshipmen were organized into gun crews, each crew composed of seventeen to twenty-one young men. Two captains were selected for each crew; a first captain, who was generally a first classman, and a second captain, drawn from the second class. As much as possible the other members of the crew were to be from the same class. Each crew was given a number, number 1 crew being made up in whole or in part of firstclassmen, counting down to a crew composed in whole or in part by fourthclassmen.

Upon its conversion to a school ship, the *Patrick Henry*'s larger ordnance was removed and mounted in the Drewry's Bluff fortifications. But some of the eight-inch cannon may have remained on board in broadside to be used in the training of the midshipmen and also to fulfill the vessel's role as a man-of-war.[63] A fairly large piece of naval ordnance, these guns weighed 6,300 pounds and used a normal combat charge of sixteen pounds of gunpowder.

The midshipmen were called to the drill by the drum and quickly fell in on either side of the cannon. Closest to the muzzle on the left stood the first loader and behind him, the second loader. To the right was stationed the first sponger and behind him, the second sponger. Moving along the left side toward the cascabel at the rear of the gun were stationed the first shotman, first side tackleman, first port tackleman, first train tackleman, first handspikeman, first captain, and powderman. Across the barrel from each stood his counterpart of the second section ending with the second captain.

Firing a muzzle-loading cannon was a dangerous business, and the steps involved were well choreographed.[64] At the first captain's command of "Silence!" the crew snapped to attention and turned toward him to watch and listen for the next order. It came quickly: "Cast loose and provide!"

Under the watchful eye of the first captain, the first loader and first sponger made sure that the gunport in the ship's bulwarks was open and removed the gun's tompion. At the same time the second loader hooked the side tackle to the gun's left side training bolt, while the second sponger did the same on the right. The train tacklemen hooked the gun's train tackle to its eyebolt in the deck behind the gun, collected the sponges and rammers from their racks, and placed them along the right side of the gun. The side tacklemen and shotmen assisted the others in loosening the ropes that held the gun tight against the bulwarks.

The powderman returned from the magazine with a cartridge in his wooden tin-lined passing-box, which he carried under his left arm with his right hand on the lid. The gun captains removed the sight covers, strapped on waist belts carrying a box of fifty friction primers, put on their heavy leather thumbstalls or covers, and supplied themselves with priming wires. The crew, their tasks completed, stood at attention awaiting the next command, which was, "Load with cartridge!"

The powderman moved up to the first loader, removed the cover of the passing-box, and tilted the box toward the loader. The first loader took the red cartridge bag from the box, put it in the gun's muzzle, and with his left hand shoved it "well down."[65] Once the loader pushed the cartridge as far down as he could reach, the first sponger stepped up with a rammer and, assisted by the first loader, shoved the cartridge firmly down the gun tube until a mark on the rammer showed that it was "home." The first captain, who stood with his leather-covered thumb over the vent hole, inserted a priming wire down the vent to puncture the cartridge bag and ensure that the cartridge was seated. If all was well he called, "home."

Next a solid round shot or explosive shell would be loaded, but since this was a practice the captain gave the command, "Prime!" Removing a primer from the box on his belt, the first captain placed it into the vent hole and commanded, "Point!"

On this command the crew sprang into action to manhandle the gun onto its target. All except the first train tackleman grabbed hold of the side tackle ropes and with the help of the handspikemen pulled and pushed the gun and its carriage from side to side. The first captain connected his lock-string to the primer, adjusted the breech site, and, standing out of the gun's recoil path, sighted down the barrel. Heavy wooden wedges called quoins were hammered between the cascabel and carriage to provide needed elevation. When the first captain was satisfied with the lay of the gun, he cried, "Well!" and, stepping back with his left arm raised and the lock-string held taught in his right hand, commanded, "Ready!" The crew dropped the side tackle and the train tacklemen prepared to check the gun's recoil by taking in the slack of the train tackle at the moment of firing.

The captain let his left arm fall, shouted "Fire!" and pulled the lock-string sharply. The friction primer sent a spark into the powder in the cartridge bag and a cloud of smoke and a jet of flame belched from the cannon's mouth. The great gun bucked and recoiled and strained against the ropes of the tackle.

The smoke had yet to clear when the first captain commanded, "Serve, vent, and sponge!" As the captain removed the lock-string and cleared the vent with a priming wire, the first sponger and first loader repositioned themselves on either side of the muzzle. The captain covered the vent with his thumb and the sponger took a wet sponge and rod and with the help of the first loader shoved it down the hissing barrel. When it struck home, they twisted it so the worm on the end of the sponge could free any smoldering residue. The sponge was withdrawn and the sponger rapped it sharply on deck to loosen any pieces of unburned cartridge bag that may have been dragged out.

At the command "Run Out!" the first and second captains took handspikes and with the assistance of the crew guided the gun to the center of the port. Once done, the command "Secure!" was given. The powderman returned his passing-box to the magazine and the chocks were inserted under the carriage. The second captain took the breaching rope and ran it from starboard to port through the jaws on the cascabel and secured it. The sights were covered, the tompion replaced, and the ports closed. The "exercise on the Greatguns" was completed for another Saturday.

All of this learning, both academic and practical, was crammed into four forenoon recitations before dinner at 2 P.M. Afternoon recitations began promptly at 3:25 and concluded at 4:35, when exercises on the great guns, small arms, or cutlass were held. Evening roll call took place at sunset, and supper immediately thereafter. Evening study period began at 7:55 and lasted until tattoo and lights out at 9:30. Taps ended the day at 10:00 o'clock. Every Sunday an inspection parade took place at which each reefer was to "appear dressed in his best uniform suit, and clean and tidy in every respect."[66] All formations were called by the drum, except for the morning and evening call to study and the call to assemble for recitations, which were heralded on the bugle. It was a busy, challenging day. "You have no idea how fully our time is occupied," Olly Harrison wrote home. "The majority of my Section rise at 4 in the morning and are busily engaged until 10 at night."[67]

Classwork was not the only thing that consumed a midshipman's day; the fulfillment of myriad other duties was required. Aboard ship, midshipmen stood watches and attended to other shipboard duties. Special details were also performed. On September 12, 1863, for example, Midshipman Minor was put in charge of a boat to ferry Secretary and Mrs. Mallory out to the school ship for a visit.

The students also filled various positions of responsibility. Each week a midshipman was appointed superintendent of his mess. He was held responsible for "the cleanliness and general neat arrangement of the room; the preservation of public property in it; and for the strict observance there of all the regulations of the ship."[68]

Each day the commandant appointed a midshipman as superintendent of steerage.[69] In exchange for being excused from all recitations, drills, and exercises during his twenty-four-hour tour of duty, this young gentleman was responsible for the cleanliness of the steerage, the good order of its occupants, the safety of the public property therein, and for the lighting and extinguishing of all lamps in the steerage and study rooms. He was to be ready at all times for boat service and was in charge of "the opening of the Spirit-Room, and serving of grog."[70] All this responsibility had a price; the superintendent of steerage was liable for punishment for "violations of regulations and orders, occurring in the steerage, which cannot be traced to others."[71] He could "relieve himself of this dilemma" only by a satisfactory excuse or by turning in the guilty party.[72] Since turning in a shipmate was against the unwritten code of conduct among reefers and could be hazardous to one's health and reputation to do so, it is likely that superintendents of steerage without a gift for persuasive speech accumulated more than their fair share of demerits.

Another time-consuming duty was serving as officer of the deck. This midshipman's duty station was on the starboard side of the quarterdeck, the captain's traditional post, except when the officer of the deck was supervising work being performed forward or was attending parades, roll calls, and formations. He was strictly charged "not to sit down or lounge while on deck, but [to] *walk his watch*."[73] The officer of the deck was responsible for ensuring that the orders of the ship were carried out and that the ship's routine as established by the executive officer was followed. He received all visitors to the ship "with courtesy" and met all boats coming alongside.[74] He was responsible for seeing to it that the drummer and bugler sounded the proper calls at the proper time. He received the absentee reports from the section leaders and was required to search out those missing and order any not excused to join their sections. At taps, the officer of the deck was required to visit steerage and report to the officer in charge that the midshipmen were "in their hammocks."[75] He was also required to keep the "Liberty Book," which documented the comings and goings of midshipmen on leave, as well as the log, in which were recorded the weather conditions, the activities on board during his watch, "in short, all matters pertaining to the school or ship."[76]

Presiding over all of this activity was a lieutenant or master, designated the officer in charge, who did a twenty-four-hour tour of duty beginning at 8 A.M. daily; the superintendent of steerage and the officer of the deck reported to him and were under his supervision. He commanded the midshipmen at morning and evening roll calls and parades and inspected the recitation rooms and steerage during his tour of duty. He was the superintendent's and executive officer's representative and as such was to "consider himself as in charge of the ship during his tour of duty" and was strictly charged to be "particularly attentive to the proper and man-of-war like carrying on of duty about the ship."[77] He was a most important and, from the midshipmen's point of view, most dangerous man, for he was also required "to maintain good order among the students, and enforce the regulations and orders which apply to them."[78]

For a midshipman, given the sheer number of those regulations and orders—rules and regulations permeated their entire existence on the school ship—violating them was not difficult. A midshipman could not play a musical instrument on Sundays or during study hours. He could smoke only on the hurricane deck or in the gangways. No midshipman could post any "map, picture or piece of writing" on the bulkheads without the permission of the executive officer.[79] Reefers were specifically forbidden to "wear their hands in their pockets" and so were the ship's officers, to "exhibit a good example."[80] Lounging about the quarterdeck was prohibited. In general the students were admonished to "abstain from all vicious, immoral, and irregular conduct, [and] are enjoined to conduct themselves upon every occasion with the propriety and decorum which characterize the society of gentlemen."[81]

Chapter 10 of the *Regulations for the Confederate States School-Ship Patrick Henry*, entitled "Discipline," listed eighteen specific offenses. Six of these were particularly serious and could result in dismissal, not just from the school ship but from the navy. These offenses were intoxication or the possession or use aboard ship of any "spirituous, vinous, fermented, or other intoxicating drinks"; absenting oneself from the ship without permission; conduct unbecoming an officer and a gentleman; failure to submit to a first- or second-class punishment; and commission of any "immoral or disgraceful act" while away from the ship.[82] Malingering, feigning illness to avoid duty, could also result in a dismissal from the naval service.[83] Lesser offenses included the use of "profane, obscene, or vulgar" language; introducing gunpowder or fireworks on board; combinations or assemblies to challenge authority under any pretext; assembling to present a complaint to a superior officer in groups larger than three (a rule aimed at preventing potentially mutinous assemblies); answering for another at roll call; and use of "reproachful or provoking speech or gestures" toward or striking or attempting to strike another midshipman.[84]

As members of the Confederate States Navy, midshipmen were subject to trial by court-martial for violations of the Naval Code or of the naval regulations.[85] However, under the school ship's regulations the superintendent punished most infractions. For infractions not considered deserving of severe punishment, demerits were awarded. Demerit offenses were divided into six classes: first (ten demerits), second (eight demerits), third (six demerits), fourth (four demerits), fifth (two demerits), and miscellaneous (one to ten demerits at the discretion of the superintendent).[86] Two hundred demerits during the course of the academic year resulted in a midshipman's dismissal from the academy and his being dropped from the rolls of the navy. The superintendent had the authority to "reduce or remit recorded demerits upon satisfactory explanation in writing being made in reference to a particular case, or upon satisfactory assurance in writing, or well-grounded hopes of future conduct."[87]

More serious violations of the rules led to more serious punishments. The regulations provided for three classes of punishment. The first class included "confinement to the limits of the ship; private reprimands; deprivation of recreation within the ship; confinement to room or apartment; reprimand to be read on parade; suspension from recitations and from all drills and exercises."[88] The sole punishment of the second class was "confinement in-guard room" and that of the third class was dismissal, unless the offender resigned if given the opportunity.[89]

Confinement, or quarantine, as the midshipmen called it, varied in the degree of restriction and duration. Confinement to the guard room was to be imposed only "upon those who . . . shall be guilty of highly insubordinate, riotous, or mutinous conduct" or when lesser forms of confinement had been disregarded by the offender.[90] This was the closest form of confinement and was limited to one week's duration.[91] Breach of this confinement was treated as the court-martial offense of breach of arrest.[92]

Of those first-class punishments involving quarantine, confinement to the limits of the ship was the least onerous. It could be of any duration and during its term limited the offender to the confines of the ship unless ordered off the ship by a superior officer to perform duty.[93] Next in severity was deprivation of recreation; those sentenced to this first-class punishment were restricted to their quarters except when attending recitations, meals, parades, and exercises and "to answer the calls of nature."[94] This punishment was limited to a maximum of twenty days.[95] Confinement to room or apartment was not limited in duration. A miscreant so punished could not leave his quarters except to take meals and attend to "the calls of nature." The closest form of quarantine, with the exception of confinement to the guard room, was "suspension from recitations and all drills and exercises," which meant confinement to room or apartment for not more than fourteen days with trips abroad limited to those necessary to answer nature's calls.[96]

Quarantine was not just an idle threat. Midshipman William Clayton and his classmates received thirty days' confinement for making fun of the accent and mannerisms of a Prussian army officer detailed to the school ship to teach swordsmanship. The Prussian endured the midshipmen for a week and then left the ship after telling Superintendent Parker that "were it not for the climate and scarcity of water, he would rather be in h—l than teaching them d—m [*sic*] midshipmen."[97]

Hubbard Minor was no stranger to quarantine either. He spent one day on confinement for fighting with another midshipman and later received ten days' quarantine for an unspecified offense for which he felt unjustly singled out by Commandant Hall, after which Minor's respect for Hall was diminished:

> I fear that I will be at eternal war with Lt. Hall . . . as long as he or I
> remain on board for I was bound by duty to report him one day &
> he has taken outrage at my having done so & now looks for every

opportunity in his power to get me into trouble. He has a contemptible disposition & no Chivalric feeling or he would not use such petty revenge. I feel almost at times like it would do me good to humble his mean spirit.[98]

Fortunately for both him and the lieutenant, Minor did not give in to his urges.

All was not books and boats for the reefers—there was time for fun. William Clayton described his class as one that "had no societies, neither did it engage in the usual collegiate sports, yet a jollier, more dare-devil set never lived; for fun or pranks they were ever ready, and took hardship or pleasure with equal indifference."[99] And fun and pleasure could be had seven miles up-river in Richmond.

The school ship had a fairly liberal leave policy that allowed one half of the students to visit Richmond and vicinity for up to twenty-four hours each Saturday. Therefore, unless on quarantine or restricted to the ship for duty reasons, each midshipman had an opportunity to visit the capital every other Saturday. And if they could not visit the capital city, the city often came to them in the form of excursions downriver to see the Drewry's Bluff defenses. Midshipman Clayton described the bluff as "a regular picnic ground for the young people of Richmond and Petersburg, which we middies greatly enjoyed."[100] Familiar faces were sometimes among the visitors. Olly Harrison spotted among one excursion party a family friend he had last seen in New Orleans and noted, "Mrs Jeff Davis was among the party."[101] The midshipmen reciprocated for these visits on December 28, 1864, with a "Midshipman's Hop" held on board the *Patrick Henry*, then docked at the Rocketts Navy Yard, to which the young ladies of Richmond were invited.[102]

Visitors from Richmond were common since many of the midshipmen came from prominent families. Joseph Davis Howell, a brother of the first lady, Varina Davis, Daniel M. Lee, a nephew of General Robert E. Lee and son of Captain Smith Lee, Clifton R. Breckinridge, a son of Major General John C. Breckinridge, Buddy Mallory son of Secretary Mallory, and Raphael Semmes, Jr., the son of Admiral Raphael Semmes of *Alabama* fame, as well as "many other scions of the most prominent families in the South," passed through the school ship.[103] It was to be expected that many midshipmen had family or friends in Richmond.

Richmond, the center of the Confederacy's public life, was an exciting town, a city bursting at the seams with refugees and, even though subdued by the war, boasting a thriving nightlife. In addition to restaurants such as the Oriental, Richmond offered the theater as a diversion, although sometimes the high-spirited reefers stole the show. Midshipman Clayton attended the theater after a "few drinks" with some friends from his previous service aboard ship.[104] At the performance they had the misfortune of sitting behind a man Clayton surmised from his elegant dress to be a "blockade runner or a beneficiary of that trade," for he sported an expensive, and tall, beaver hat.[105] After being asked to "douse his glim" by one of Clayton's companions and refusing to "take in his royals," the worthy gentleman received a blow to the top of the hat, which forced the brim unto his shoulders.[106] The police were summoned, a chase ensued, an escape was made. Clayton's trip to the theater even made the papers. The next day's edition of the Richmond *Examiner* reported the disturbance under the headline "Some More Ruffianism of the Navy."[107]

More sedate dinners with friends offered pleasant evenings and refreshments not available in the midshipmen's messes. The city's prostitutes also offered a variety of "horizontal refreshments." Whether the young men availed themselves of this particular diversion is unknown, but there were ample opportunities for those so inclined. The Ballard and Exchange hotels were centers for the "sporting life." In the area nearby were no less than forty gambling establishments serving the finest foods Richmond had to offer in the most opulent surroundings with a choice selection of "soiled doves" in the rooms upstairs to console the losers and cheer the winners from the gaming tables. Locust Alley, between Main and Franklin streets, was home to many high-class prostitutes. Much cheaper, but far more risky, was Screamersville in the western suburbs. Screamersville, so named because of the cries of men caught in the hell of the delirium tremens, was a place where "sallow-faced, dope-drugged, booze-sotted harlots of the most desperate sort served . . . clientele" not much better than they.[108] Frolic in some of Richmond's seedier areas could be dangerous; James Kelley of the *Patrick Henry's* crew was robbed one night and murdered the next in the "house of two white women of easy virtue."[109] Safer and closer to home were two young sisters, Amanda and Carrie, both "rentable for riding," who visited Drewry's Bluff and the nearby naval batteries where midshipmen were often posted.[110]

Certainly young women were on the minds of these young men. Hubbard Minor's thoughts revolved around his lost love, Rosalie. During one of his midnight watches while thinking of his "first boyish love & its object[,] my love returned with full force & I resolved to write Rosalie & ascertain my fate."[111] However, after this initial burst of passion, he recalled a writer who opined that absence does not necessarily make the heart grow fonder and prudently decided to "await until I had again seen Rosalie before I in any way committed myself."[112] But, he admitted, "how long that resolve will last I do not know."[113]

Love smote even the faculty. Thirty-six-year-old "Gus" Peple journeyed to Richmond each week to tutor fifteen-year-old Miss Sarah Arabella Loundes in French. After each lesson he returned to the school ship wearing an ivy leaf on his lapel, courtesy of Miss Loundes. The reefers would chase him around the deck trying to pluck the ivy from his coat, but Peple "loyally kept it until the next visit when he got a fresh one in its place."[114]

Mail from home was an eagerly anticipated diversion from school-ship routine. When mail was not forthcoming the folks at home heard about it. "Please write to me as soon as you get this letter," one reefer wrote his father. "Tell Ma to write to me, seems a long time since I have received a letter from any of you."[115] "You all must write more frequently & not wait for me," another busy middie wrote, "for actually this is the only day in the week that I have a half an hour spare time."[116]

Other leisurely pursuits included letter writing, sailing on the James River in the school ship's launch, and, as the war closed in along the banks of the river, touring Richmond's defensive lines. Midshipman Morgan along with Acting Midshipmen J. A. Carter, William K. Hale, and Joshua C. Wright received permission to tag along with Major General Robert Hoke's Division as it crossed the James on a pontoon bridge not far from the *Patrick Henry*'s anchorage on its way to assist in efforts to recapture Fort Harrison on Richmond's outer defensive line.[117]

Morgan and his mates got to see General Robert E. Lee and witnessed three unsuccessful assaults on the fort. After the third repulse, however, the Confederate soldiers "broke and fled in disorder."[118] Morgan was carried along in the rout and declared, "I may have been a web-footed sailor but I did not notice any infantrymen pass me on the way back."[119] Having had enough spectacle for one day, the middies made their way back to the ship, losing one of their number along the way to an army surgeon, who impressed the young sailor into grisly duty: holding a soldier's leg while it was amputated.

Welcome though these diversions were, if a midshipman hoped to see his hard work, patience, and endurance rewarded, he needed to stay focused upon the examinations administered to every midshipman each June and December. The academy's academic board, the department heads, and the course instructors conducted the examinations aboard the school ship.[120] At least five persons might also attend the examination at the invitation of the secretary of the navy for the purpose of "witnessing the examination of the several classes, and of examining into the state of the police, discipline, and general management of the institution."[121] On November 30, 1863, Commander Brooke, at Mallory's direction, "respectfully" invited sixteen Congressmen to "attend an examination of Acting Midshipmen on the first proximo on board the C. S. Steamer "Patrick Henry" at Drewry's Bluff, James river Va."[122]

The school-ship regulations required that the examination "be sufficiently thorough to enable the board to decide upon the proficiency and the relative merits of the members of the several classes . . . and it shall embrace all the studies, theoretical and practical, pursued by the several classes during the year."[123] Superintendent Parker proudly declared that "all who attended our examinations spoke highly of the school."[124]

Writing an unsatisfactory examination—"bilging," in midshipman slang—resulted in the student's name being placed on a list forwarded to the secretary of the navy, who would make a decision as to whether the student "shall be dropped from the Navy List and returned to [his] friends, or be allowed to continue on board the school-ship for further trial."[125] Bilging was the fate of Olly Harrison, despite his promising start. Harrison failed his December 1864 examinations and there was some controversy surrounding his failure. As his father described it, only eight of Harrison's class "came up to the standard required—Olly stood no 9—now the injustice to Olly is just this; three youths *below him* in scholarship are to be retained . . . . The boys who passed have joined in a letter to Olly expressing their regret at his failure & their belief that injustice was done to him."[126] Although "Olly's case is under consideration," explained the elder Harrison, "I am satisfied Olly must leave the school," and he would therefore seek a commission in the army for his son.[127]

A satisfactory examination resulted in advancement one or more classes or graduation with a certificate, which entitled the midshipman to the warrant and the single gold shoulder braid of a passed midshipman.[128]

The academy was proving its value, and those responsible for its administration praised its success. Superintendent Parker declared that "the behavior of the young men has been all that he could have expected."[129] Commander Brooke reported to Mallory: "The Naval School, under the superintendence of Lieutenant Parker, is conducted in a most satisfactory manner and its importance can not be overestimated."[130] Mallory in turn reported to President Davis: "The satisfactory progress already made by the several classes gives assurance that the Navy may look to this school for well instructed and skillful officers."[131]

Brooke, no doubt with an eye toward obtaining a share of the Confederacy's dwindling resources, noted that "as the efficiency and tone of the Confederate Navy will hereafter depend chiefly upon the early training of its officers, it is most important that this establishment should be carefully fostered."[132] Unfortunately, as the military situation worsened, support for the academy became a low priority. For example, the inability to accommodate all of the navy's acting midshipmen was a constant source of frustration to the Navy Department and led to several unsuccessful efforts to obtain additional billeting space. In December 1864, the Confederate Congress did authorize and appropriate $6,000 "for the erection of an additional number of houses, similar to those now at Drewry's Bluff, for the accommodation and instruction of the acting midshipmen of the navy."[133] Additional space was essential to the success of the academy, Mallory informed the president, since rotating midshipmen between the school ship and active service was "disadvantageous to the officer, who thus loses, or fails to acquire the habit of methodical and continuous study" required to master his profession.[134]

That same month, Commander Brooke forwarded to Major General Jeremy F. Gilmer, chief of the Army Engineer Bureau, Superintendent Parker's request that two schooners, the *North Wind* and the *James Buchannan*, formerly employed as part of a pontoon bridge near Drewry's Bluff, be turned over to the Naval Academy "in view of the large number of Midshipmen expected next year and the impossibility of quartering them all aboard [the *Patrick Henry*]."[135]

Brooke's anticipation of large numbers of midshipmen was not ill founded. In June 1864 a midshipman wrote, with some exaggeration, "Every man who has a son who has just arrived at the conscript age, or . . . who has a child old enough to walk, sends him to the 4th class, with a letter to the Capt.

requesting him to keep his son free from all harm. . . . Consequently the 4th class is divided into innumerable Sections."[136] However, neither the money to build the cabins nor the schooners ever appeared. The space problem was never solved and those young men not aboard the school ship continued to learn at sea.

3

⚓

"The Best Place for a Young Man Is at Sea"

A S AN ACADEMIC INSTITUTION, THE ORGANIZATION of the Confederate States Naval Academy can be likened to a modern-day university with a "main campus"—the school ship *Patrick Henry*— and dozens of "branch campuses." These "branch campuses" existed wherever an acting midshipman was assigned either before or after his time at the school ship. In keeping with the university analogy, in many respects these branches also provided a sort of "postgraduate" education to passed midshipmen. To be sure, the school ship was an essential and required part of a midshipman's education, but it was on board a warship that the reefer received his most practical, albeit dangerous, education in accordance with the time-honored philosophy that "the best place for a young man is at sea."

A passed midshipman fresh from his final exams or an acting midshipman preparing for his first exam could find himself assigned to one of the Confederate navy's fourteen or so naval stations, where he might serve on the station commander's staff—as did William F. Clayton, who served as "flag midshipman" to Flag Officer William F. Lynch at Wilmington, North Carolina—or find himself posted to one of the naval squadrons for service afloat.[1]

At the apex of its power, the Confederate navy had approximately 130 ships in commission ranging from tiny, swift torpedo launches to huge, ponderous ironclads; from small wooden coastal gunboats to sleek raiders of commerce on the high seas.[2] Midshipmen served on all but the smallest of these vessels.

The common denominator of all naval vessels, regardless of size or mission, was the ship's routine. This routine was essentially identical to that practiced in the U.S. Navy and was rarely strayed from, since it was believed that keeping to the routine reduced disciplinary problems and added a measure of predictability and stability to sailors' lives. That it probably also added a measure of boredom was not of consequence.

About dawn, a marine bugler—on the very few Confederate ships with a marine corps contingent—or a drummer sounded or beat out reveille. The master-at-arms or the boatswain's mate of the watch ran noisily through the berth deck shaking the hammocks of the sleeping sailors. Once awakened, the tars took their hammocks down, rolled them tightly, and stored them in rope netting along the berth deck bulwarks for airing and for added protection against enemy gunfire and shell and wood splinters from shots hitting the ship. Rolling and stowing hammocks was to be accomplished in seven minutes, but rarely was.

After the hammocks were stowed it was time to clean the ship, and brooms, sand, buckets, and holystones were broken out and issued to the crew. The berth deck received a washing and the spar deck was holystoned under the direction of a boatswain's mate. Other crewmen polished brass, cleaned cannon, and on sailing ships inspected the sails, rigging, halyards, ropes, and blocks.

Cleaning the ship was to be finished by 7:30, and the men washed, dressed, and lined up for inspection by the master-at-arms. At 8:00 the boatswain blew his whistle to pipe the crew to breakfast, each man reporting to his mess, which was normally made up of eight to twelve sailors who had similar duties such as firemen, coal heavers, or gun crews. Each member of the mess took a turn at being cook or mess orderly. The cook or mess orderly unlocked the mess chest containing the mess's cooking gear, tableware, and the food issued by the ship's cook or paymaster. Breakfast was usually salt junk—hard, heavily salted beef—and one pint of coffee.

At 9:30 the men were called to quarters. The guns and rigging were inspected by the captain or one of his lieutenants and the sick reported to the ship's surgeon for examination and possible inclusion on the ship's binnacle, or sick, list. Once at their duty stations, the sailors could relax and read letters from or write letters to family and friends, although the sighting of an enemy vessel or new orders from the captain quickly changed the calm to a bustle of activity.

The ship's day officially began at noon. The ship's bell was rung, the midshipmen appeared with their sextants to take a sighting of the ship's position and note it in their logs, as did the master or captain. The main meal of the day was also served: beef or pork, vegetables, and coffee. The captain was required by navy regulations to "adopt suitable precautions to prevent the use of improper quantities of fruit" and ensure that the men did not drink the fresh water stowed in casks aboard until "the mud and other impurities it may contain shall have time to settle."[3]

The men of the Confederate navy generally ate better than their army comrades—so much better that it became a source of embarrassment, and Paymaster John DeBree, chief of the navy's Office of Provisions and Clothing, recommended in April 1864 that a board review the navy ration and perhaps reduce it. As the war progressed, certain items such as tea and coffee and flour became scarce, but even so the quantity of food was such that one sailor remarked that he "had plenty to eat and little to do."[4]

It was undisputed that sailors, who were generally "well-clothed and always had a dry hammock at night," had it better than soldiers.[5] The contrast between life in the navy and mere existence in the army became more pronounced as the war continued. The envy felt by the soldiers was experienced by one of the academy faculty, a man with a reputation for impeccable appearance, while riding a train from Charleston to Richmond. The splendidly attired naval officer found himself seated with a ragged soldier returning to Lee's army who eyed his well-dressed companion suspiciously and questioned him concerning his rank and regiment. Upon being told that his companion was a naval officer, the infantryman ruminated on that bit of information awhile and finally declared, "I'll tell you what it is, if things don't soon look better, I'll be dogged if I don't try to navy it a little while too."[6]

After the noon meal the men returned to their stations and performed duties until 4:00, when a light meal was served at the change of the watch. The time after the meal was sometimes used by the captain for morale-building activities such as concerts or boxing matches. At 5:30 the men were again called to quarters and inspected. After the inspection the boatswain piped the call for "string hammocks" and the men not on watch were free to sling up their hammocks and lounge and relax in them. Checkers and dominoes were popular games among the sailors (cards were forbidden aboard ship). Or the men could use the time to mend clothing, tell stories, or listen to music provided by a banjo- or fiddle-playing shipmate. The smoking lamp was lit in the forecastle or galley and the men could indulge their tobacco habit with pipes or cigars. Matches were forbidden aboard ship because of the risk of fire and the men lit their tobacco with tapers ignited from the lamp.

At sunset, usually between eight and nine, tattoo, a signal for all to return to quarters, was sounded, all fires were extinguished, and the men not on watch moved to the berth deck and climbed into their hammocks. Reading in bed by lamp or candlelight was forbidden.

On Sundays ships with chaplains aboard rigged for church and on all ships the captain was charged by regulation to "take care that no duty but such as is absolutely necessary be carried on during Sunday."[7] Once a month the crew assembled, with hats removed, for the reading of the Navy Code and the taking of roll.

Aboard ship the men were divided into four divisions. The master's division was charged with the operation, navigation, and steering of the vessel; the engineer's division stoked, operated, and maintained the engines; the surgeon's division treated the sick and wounded; and the powder division was responsible for opening the magazine and supplying the powder boys with the proper powder charges, shot, and shell.

Since the ship operated twenty-four hours a day, seven days a week, the crew was normally divided into two watches, port and starboard, to ensure that the men still obtained regular periods of rest while the ship was kept continuously manned. The ship's day was divided into five four-hour watches and two two-hour watches, called dogwatches, and the port and starboard watches alternated standing each watch.[8]

Life on a Confederate warship was generally hard and unglamorous. Since the Rebel navy was primarily a "brown-water" force, operating on the South's rivers and coastal waters, Confederate sailors had little opportunity to "see the world." There were, therefore, few opportunities for a Confederate tar to contemplate the wake of his ship disappearing into a crimson sunset on the high seas. Living conditions on board Confederate warships varied from the comparative openness of a foreign-built high seas commerce raider to the stifling, ovenlike heat of a home-built ironclad baking in the Southern sun. Granted, little attention was paid to creature comforts in any warship's design, but life aboard these ironclads was particularly severe. Confined for the most part to rivers and harbors, rarely venturing forth to challenge the enemy, ironclad crews languished aboard their ships. The ship's iron casemates absorbed the heat of the sun and the dampness of the surrounding air and water. Forced-air blowers were never fitted to these ships, and since the ventilation otherwise provided was inadequate, crews were often sick with respiratory ailments caused by the damp, stale, air thick with the noxious fumes of the engines. "Intense thirst universally prevailed," wrote Surgeon Daniel B. Conrad aboard the ironclad *Tennessee* in Mobile Bay, and many men crept "out of the ports on the after deck to get a little fresh air."[9] The CSS *Atlanta* leaked constantly, was sluggish to respond to her helm, and was "dark, wet, and unventilated" below decks.[10] So bad did conditions become aboard many of the ironclads that the crews were billeted ashore.

Engagements with the enemy might have provided some excitement, but little action came the ironclad sailor's way. "We are living the same monotonous sort of life here as usual, nothing to eat scarcely, and no amusements," wrote Master James C. Long from the ironclad *Albemarle* to his friend Hubbard T. Minor.[11] Even the prospect of relieving boredom with action raised a sense of foreboding, since the ironclads were sluggish, and plagued with faulty engines and machinery that often broke down. Long described his ship as "the poorest ironclad in the confederacy" and warned Minor, "[Y]ou must not expect too much of the 'Albemarle.'"[12]

Poor living conditions were not peculiar to the ironclads, however. Sixteen-year-old Acting Midshipman William F. "Willie" Wilson described his quarters aboard the side-wheel steamer CSS *Savannah* as "the damndest place" and declared with disgust "a person cannot sleep for the mosquitoes and cockroaches."[13] After four months at the school ship, his dedication to education gone, Midshipman Minor finally wangled an assignment to the Savannah River Squadron. He reported just before Christmas of 1863 and, like his friend Long, he too was assigned to an ironclad—the squadron's flagship, *Savannah*, Captain Robert F. Pinkney commanding. Minor, however, would not be doomed to the usual boring life of a sailor aboard an ironclad.

Minor enjoyed his time away from the *Patrick Henry* and took advantage of many opportunities to visit Savannah. He was particularly friendly with Miss Annie Lamar, "one of the wealthiest [ladies] of Savannah," and became her regular companion.[14] Monday, May 30, 1864, however, he spent on board the *Savannah*, noting, "[N]othing of importance has occurred."[15] But the following day was much different, for while standing his watch, Minor received orders "allowing me to be one of the officers who were to go on expedition."[16]

Assembling their crews of twenty armed seamen, Minor and Acting Midshipman John D. Trimble, an academy comrade from Maryland, steered their boats from the *Savannah* over to the anchorage of the ironclad floating battery, CSS *Georgia*, where they rendezvoused with the expedition commander, Lieutenant Thomas P. Pelot, and boats and crews from other ships in the squadron. Lieutenant Pelot was a veteran of the U.S. Navy from South Carolina who had begun the war as captain of a privateer and moved on to command of the navy steamers *Oconee*, *Resolute*, and *Georgia* with the Savannah Squadron. His orders from the squadron commander, William W. Hunter, were to capture any Federal blockaders who ventured close inshore. The USS *Water Witch*, a 370-ton side-wheel steamer that often patrolled alone in Ossabaw Sound, south of Savannah, was a particularly tempting target. This ship was one of the U.S. Navy's favorites, having taken part in the Paraguay War of 1855 and the battle at the Head of the Passes to the Mississippi in October 1861. To capture the *Water Witch*, or any other Yankee ship he might find, Lieutenant Pelot had seven boats, fifteen officers, and 177 men at his disposal.

After mustering his command near the *Georgia*, Pelot and his men boarded the steamer *Firefly*, which, with his boats in tow, transported him and his men down the Savannah River and St. Augustine Creek to the Isle of Hope Battery. From there, the crews rowed to Battery Beaulain on the Vernon River and camped for the night.

The next day, Pelot, his second-in-command, Lieutenant Joseph Price, a North Carolinian and former officer in the U.S. Revenue Service, and the surgeon, C. Wesley Thomas, took a boat and crew out on a reconnaissance mission. Midshipman Minor was left in command of the camp. Pelot returned about noon having left Lieutenant Price and Surgeon Thomas on Green Island to keep an eye on a Federal vessel spotted in Ossabaw Sound. Minor was ordered to prepare the boats for launching and the expedition got under way about 7:30 P.M. Price and Thomas were taken aboard and Pelot began vainly searching for the intended target. Unable to find the enemy, Pelot ordered two men ashore near Ossabaw Sound to keep watch and returned with his force to Battery Beaulain.

On Thursday, June 2, the boats got under way at 8:30 P.M. One of the lookouts on the beach had discovered a target that he said was anchored in the Little Ogeechee River near Racoon Key not more than three miles away. The expedition's pilot, a black man named Moses Dallas, determined that they could reach her. Pelot ordered the boats up the Vernon River to conceal them in the marshes while he devised a battle plan with his officers.

Pelot's plan was to attack the Federal vessel from both sides simultaneously. In the port column were boats one, three, five, and seven and in the starboard column were boats two, four, and six. Pelot commanded boat one, Price boat two, Minor boat three, and Trimble boat four. They shoved off after midnight in the dark and rain.

Occasional lightning bolts illuminated the whitewashed boats as the crews pulled them quickly but silently through the water. Around two on the morning of June 3, a ship's light was sighted and a flash of lightning illuminated the target over a thousand yards away. It was the *Water Witch*. The Confederates closed the distance. At 300 yards, Midshipman Minor said a prayer asking God "to prosper our undertaking to shield us from harm & to make us do our duty."[17] At eighty yards they were hailed from the enemy ship. Pilot Dallas answered, "Runaway Negroes," but Lieutenant Pelot quickly shouted, "We are Rebels. Give way boys!"[18]

The boats sprang forward as the men pulled mightily on the oars. Pelot's boat bumped up against the *Water Witch* first and Minor's boat touched immediately thereafter. Price's starboard column was delayed by having to row to the far side of the Yankee vessel. Two boats' crews failed to get fully on board because the quartermaster of the *Water Witch* began to move the paddle wheels back and forth to deter the boarders.

As Pelot's men began to cut away the antiboarding netting, the *Water Witch*'s officer of the deck, Acting Master's Mate E. D. Parsons, panicked and abandoned his post without giving orders to slip the cable, start engines, or repel boarders. The *Water Witch*'s commanding officer, Lieutenant Austin Pendergrast, was awakened by the commotion and led his officers and some of the crew from below up on deck, where they poured punishing small arms fire down on the Confederate sailors hacking through the defensive netting.

It was not enough to stem the assault, and soon Pelot was on deck with some of his men. Master Charles W. Buck tried to fire a howitzer into the boarders but was cut down before he could pull the lanyard. Hand-to-hand fighting with pistol and cutlass raged along the deck. Pelot and Pendergrast crossed cutlasses at one point and the Federal commander was felled by a gash that knocked him senseless. A flash of lightning lit the deck and by its light the Federal paymaster, Billings, shot Pelot through the heart. Minor also made it on deck despite being slightly wounded. Price too was wounded by a cutlass blow to the head. He later commended Ordinary Seaman E. D. Davis for saving his life by "having cut down every opponent when I was sorely pressed by them."[19]

The Confederates quickly gained the upper hand, in large part because the off-duty watch of the *Water Witch* cowered below decks. When Price led his men below, the ship's engineers all surrendered at the first appearance of a Rebel officer. Only one Federal crewman escaped death or capture, a black man named McIntosh who in the confusion of the fighting jumped overboard and was picked up by a Federal ship later that day.

The fifteen-minute battle to capture the *Water Witch* cost the lives of Pelot, Pilot Moses Dallas, Quarter-gunner Patrick Lotin, Coxswain W. R. Jones, and Ordinary Seaman J. M. Stapleton.[20] In addition to Price and Minor, ten others were wounded. Federal losses were two dead, twelve wounded, and seventy-seven captured. Enlisting the services of the ship's captured pilot by means of a cocked pistol held to his head, Price brought the *Water Witch* to safety. She served her new masters under the same name as part of the Confederate Savannah River Squadron until her destruction at the capture of Savannah in December 1864.

But opportunities for such swashbuckling adventure were rare for those assigned to a home-water vessel, and service aboard one of the wide-ranging, glamorous Rebel cruisers was in many ways much to be preferred. Exotic ports, frequent though relatively safe actions against unarmed enemy merchantmen, and the promise of generous shares of prize money awaited the reefer assigned to one of the commerce destroyers such as the *Alabama* or *Shenandoah*.

Midshipman Jimmy Morgan shipped out on the cruiser *Georgia* in the spring of 1863, an unusual assignment for an acting midshipman and one obtained for him by his future father-in-law, Secretary of the Treasury George Trenholm.[21] A converted merchantman, the cruiser was, in Morgan's words, "absolutely unfitted for the work."[22] She was slow under either sail or steam—or both—and her engines, which had cogs of lignum vitae wood turning iron cogs on the propeller shaft, were unreliable. "[F]requently the wooden cogs would break," Morgan recalled. "When they did it was worse than if a shrapnel shell had burst in the engine room . . . endangering the lives of every one within reach."[23]

Morgan's cruise lasted from April to October 1863 and took him from Greenock, Scotland, to Bahia, Brazil; Trinidad; Cape Colony, Africa; Tenerife;

and finally Cherbourg, France. Along the way his ship took nine prizes, including the U.S. merchant ship *Dictator*. As the *Dictator* had been captured far from any friendly port to which she could be taken, Morgan was placed in charge of burning the vessel. The *Dictator* was valued at $86,000, one half of which was by law to be paid to the crew of the *Georgia* as prize money, which was shared out by a formula according to rank. Morgan, as the only acting midshipman aboard, should have received a one-twentieth share, and years later noted ruefully, "[T]he amount of prize money (still due me) which I should have received would have almost equaled the share of the captain."[24]

During this cruise, Morgan also became the cause of the Confederacy's only foreign "war" when he was roughed up ashore by some Moroccan "troglodytes." Upon the return of Morgan's shore party to the *Georgia*, Captain William L. Maury ordered the ship's guns to fire on the Moors, who, according to a satisfied Morgan, "stood not upon the order of their going but disappeared."[25]

Along with these excitements, Morgan got to enjoy a more peaceful sailor's reward off the coast of Brazil in "the golden splendors of the most gorgeous sunset it has ever been my good fortune to behold."[26]

Service aboard one of the navy's smaller gunboats, though not as glamorous or potentially lucrative as service aboard a cruiser, had the advantage of conferring greater responsibility, for there the midshipman was a bigger fish in a smaller pond. Prior to his *Georgia* adventure, Jimmy Morgan was one of only two officers and eight men aboard the tiny one-gun gunboat *Beaufort*. The captain, First Lieutenant William Sharp, was often absent from the ship attending other duties and left "Captain" Morgan in command.

The Navy Regulations did provide guidelines for the normal utilization of midshipmen aboard ship. Passed midshipmen were to "be preferred to midshipmen who have not passed their examination for the more responsible duties," but were required to perform "whatever duties pertaining to that class of officers may be assigned to them."[27] During quarters, or battle stations, midshipmen could be found on the quarterdeck as captain's aides or assisting the master's, engineer's, or surgeon's divisions. A passed or other competent midshipman might direct the powder division, which consisted of "all those stationed below the gun decks" except for the surgeon's division and the paymaster and his clerk.[28] Midshipmen might also be found assisting the lieutenants in command of the guns.

Sometimes midshipmen found themselves entrusted with duties far beyond those normally assigned to someone of their rank. When Captain Raphael Semmes laid up the commerce raider CSS *Sumter* at Gibraltar, Spain, in April 1862, he placed Passed Midshipman Richard F. Armstrong in command of the ship and her ten-man skeleton crew. In July, Passed Midshipman William Andrews succeeded Armstrong. In October, Andrews was suspiciously murdered aboard the *Sumter* by his second-in-command, Acting Master's Mate J. T. Hester.[29] Acting Midshipman James A. Peters, a prisoner of war released in September 1864 from Fort Warren, Massachusetts, after fifteen months' internment, found himself temporarily "in charge" of the ironclad CSS *Virginia II* on the James River in early 1865.[30]

A midshipman had an additional duty not shared by his fellow officers—he was to study and learn his trade. Navy Regulations required both passed and acting midshipmen to keep journals recording "important occurrences on board and all observations made by them, their remarks relative to ports or anchorages, and everything worthy of record, or that may be useful to navigators."[31] Passed midshipmen's journals were subject to inspection at the commander's discretion, while those of acting midshipmen were to be presented to the commander for inspection the first of each month. To sharpen their skills, each acting midshipman was required to ascertain the position of his ship each day and report his findings to the captain. Navy Regulations stipulated that acting midshipmen were responsible for furnishing themselves with a sextant or octant and a copy of Nathaniel Bowditch's *New American Practical Navigator* or some other approved navigation treatise, as well as a treatise on marine surveying.

That service aboard ship was deemed an integral part of a midshipman's education was reflected in the Navy Regulations' admonition that a reefer "at all times embrace every opportunity of acquiring useful information which may be applicable to their profession as seamen and officers."[32] One source of useful information was the ship's officers.

At the top of the organizational pyramid aboard ship stood the commander—traditionally called "captain," although his actual naval grade could be anything from master to captain—who was the undisputed authority aboard ship. According to Navy Regulations he was responsible "for the whole conduct and good government of the officers and others belonging to the vessel . . . and must himself set an example of respect and obedience to his superiors, and of unremitting attention to his duties."[33] The captain was also responsible for the instruction of the ship's midshipmen, ordinary seamen, and boys. He was the supreme authority on board and had ultimate responsibility for everything pertaining to his ship.

The ship might belong to the government, and the captain might command it, but the next senior officer, the first lieutenant or executive officer, ran it. This officer was charged with "the superintendence of the general duties to be performed" under the direction of the captain.[34] Among other duties he was to inspect the ship daily; receive the reports of the master, boatswain, gunner, carpenter, and sail maker twice daily; control the expenditure of the ship's stores; superintend the officer of the deck; be familiar with the capabilities of each man aboard; personally supervise the opening of the magazine; maintain order and see that the sick and wounded were cared for in the event the ship was abandoned; and act for the captain in his absence. His sole reward was that he did not have to stand watch unless there were less than three other qualified officers on board.

The master was the officer in charge of the actual sailing of the ship. He superintended the loading of the ship's stores and the ship's cables, chains, and rigging. His division was responsible for steering the vessel and he was responsible for its navigation. The master's duties included taking soundings when the ship approached land or shoals, examining all charts and noting any errors, and inspecting the ship's compasses, time glasses, lead lines, and log. He was to ascertain the ship's position each day at noon and report his findings to the captain. All "nautical books, instruments, charts, national flags and signals" as well as the ship's log and the keys to the spirit room were in his care.[35]

In addition to these officers, several other officers ranking below midshipmen in order of precedence for command could be found aboard ship. The boatswain (pronounced "bosun") was the naval version of the army's first sergeant. In the military vernacular of today the boatswain's job was to "kick ass and take names." In the more tempered, official language of the regulations he was "with his mates, to see that the men go quickly upon deck when called, and that when there they perform their duty with alacrity."[36]

The bulk of the duties of the gunner were set forth in the *Ordnance Instructions for the Confederate States Navy* and primarily involved the taking aboard, stowage, and safeguarding of powder, shot, shell, small arms, and ammunition. He was also in charge of the ship's anchors and lifebuoys and, on sailing ships, the lower- and main-yard rigging.

The carpenter was responsible for the general maintenance of the ship. He was to ensure that the hull, deck, masts, and yards were kept in good repair along with the pumps, ship's boats, ladders, and gratings. In the event of damage to the hull, he and his mates were the primary damage-control party responsible for quickly plugging the leaks.

On sailing vessels, the maintenance, repair, replacement, and stowage of the sails were the responsibility of the sail maker and his mates.

On ships with steam engines—most Confederate ships—good engineers were essential. Highly trained specialists, chief engineers were examined and recommended for commissions by the Navy Department's Office of the Engineer-in-Chief, headed by Chief Engineer William P. Williamson. The three warrant-officer engineer grades—first, second, and third assistant—were filled by appointment of Secretary Mallory or by other officers, subject to the secretary's approval.

The senior engineer aboard ship was in charge of the engineering department. This department concerned itself solely with the maintenance and operation of the ship's engines and stood its watches in the engine room. A competent engineer could make or break a warship since the jerry-rigged engines of Southern-built warships seemed to have the uncanny ability to break down at the worst possible moment. More than once, engine failures resulted in the capture or scuttling of Rebel warships. Work in the engine room was hot, dirty, and dangerous. Accidents could and did occur. For example, on May 27, 1863, eighteen men died when an improperly tended boiler on the CSS *Chattahoochee* exploded near Bloutstown, Florida.

In addition to one or more engineers, the engineer's division consisted of firemen who tended the furnaces and boilers and coal heavers, often slaves hired out to the navy by their owners, who fed the furnaces with coal. The engineer was to report to the captain at noon daily concerning the quantity of coal consumed and the amount remaining in the bunkers and the average revolutions per minute of the engines over the previous twenty-four hours. Any defects in or conditions that placed undue stress upon the engines were to be reported to the captain immediately.

The ship's surgeon, responsible for the medical care of the crew, was appointed by and remained under the medical supervision of Surgeon-in-Charge W. A. W. Spotswood's Office of Medicine and Surgery. Navy doctors were rated as surgeons, passed assistant surgeons, and assistant surgeons. All of the surgeons and the majority of the assistant surgeons of the Confederate navy were veterans of the U.S. Navy and followed that navy's practices until 1864, when Spotswood issued *Instructions for the Guidance of the Medical Officers of the Confederate States Navy*.

The surgeon was the keeper of the ship's medical stores, which included such nostrums as asafetida, *chloriformi, extratici belladon*, and *strychniae*, and equipment such as splints, stomach pumps, trepanning sets, glass penis syringes, tourniquets, thermometers, urinals, bandages, basins, boxes, and brushes.[37] Whiskey was also a medicinal item in the surgeon's charge. Prior to the *Water Witch* expedition, Lieutenant Pelot felt it was necessary to "go well provided with Whiskey, as it was important to have more than would probably be required in the Medical Department."[38] Accordingly, Assistant Surgeon W. C. Jones purchased four bottles of whiskey at $25 a bottle from the provisioners Claghorn & Cunningham of Savannah, Georgia.

The ship's surgeon supervised any assistant surgeons aboard and maintained the binnacle list and the list of those in hospital. He was also required to keep a log of daily practice in which he detailed the maladies treated and the names of the patients. His floating practice was busy. The daily journal of the surgeon of the Mobile Squadron's CSS *Gaines*, for example, contained over 720 detailed entries between May 1, 1862, and January 31, 1863.[39]

The ship's paymaster was a combination accountant and storekeeper. Paymasters were supervised by the navy's Office of Provisions and Clothing and were required to be bonded. All of the originally appointed paymasters in the Confederate States Navy had been pursers in the U.S. Navy. The paymaster might have an assistant paymaster and clerk under his supervision. The paymaster received, safeguarded, and disbursed the crew's pay as well as ordering, receiving, and issuing food, clothing, and small stores—items of personal comfort for the crew such as knives, tobacco, needles, and the like. Although dismissed as "just a sea-going clerk" by some line officers, paymasters—from the head of the Office of Provisions and Clothing on down to those of the smallest vessels—performed small miracles by keeping Confederate crews well fed and supplied despite severe shortages.[40] On payday, the paymaster was a reefer's favorite person aboard ship and received blessings for his "munificence," as when Midshipman Willie Wilson noted fondly in his diary, "Mr. Kelly (God save his old soul) paid us off about two months ago."[41]

Another source of useful information for the midshipmen were the ship's "tars," its common sailors.

Midshipman William F. Clayton described a midshipman as the "connecting link" between officers and sailors and noted that there was, therefore, "a familiarity between the sailor and the midshipman. The midshipman learns from the sailor much of seamanship, how to knot and splice, and the one looks after the interest of the other, both afloat and ashore."[42]

Sailors in the Confederate navy—graded as petty officers, seamen, second class firemen, ordinary seamen, coal heavers, landsmen, and boys—were a varied group of individuals. In the U.S. Navy, many of the officers were Southerners and were free to resign and offer their services to the new Confederate States Navy. Federal seamen were mostly Northerners, many from New England, where maritime traditions ran deep. Those seamen who were from the South were not free to resign as officers were and had no means short of desertion to offer their services to the Confederacy. Consequently, experienced Southern seamen were in short supply. Even when experienced men were found, they were often unsuited for service aboard a man-of-war, having previously been merchant sailors unschooled in gunnery and strangers to naval discipline.

Men of foreign birth were common among the experienced sailors the Confederate navy did recruit. France, England, Holland, Ireland, Italy, and Spain were all represented on the cruiser *Alabama*, but even ships in home waters had a large percentage of foreign seamen. In one transfer of sailors from the army to the Savannah Squadron in March 1864, 25 percent of those rated as seamen were English by birth and 29.6 percent of the able seamen were Irish. It is estimated that of the approximately 5,000 officers and men of the Confederate navy, 845 were born in Ireland.[43] One Englishman at Norfolk, Virginia, in 1862 described the Confederate tars he saw there as "truly magnificent specimens of bone and muscle—mostly foreign-born, from the merchant navy; [who] reminded me much of what I had seen in the British navy in American waters—bronzed and rosy fellows, active as cats and fit to fight a frigate at any odds."[44]

Unfortunately, Flag Officer William W. Hunter, commander of the Savannah Squadron, seems to have missed out on the "magnificent specimens" of foreign seamen seen at Norfolk. "I find that no reliance whatever can be placed on the shipped men of foreign birth who are with this squadron," he complained. "Without an exception, all the men who have been and are being tried by the naval court-martial here for mutinous conduct are Irish and English."[45]

Many foreign-born sailors joined the crews of Confederate commerce raiders on the high seas after their own ships fell prey to them. These men were lured by the promise of prize money and had no great love for the Southern cause. Consequently, when they were bored or the work became too dangerous or they were fed up with naval discipline, these men deserted. Sometimes, though, sailors who volunteered from captured merchantmen "proved to be among the best men."[46]

A midshipman might very well serve with black sailors. Free blacks could join up with squadron commander or navy department approval and slaves could serve with the permission of their masters. How many blacks served as sailors in the Confederate navy is uncertain, but their numbers may have been in the hundreds.[47]

Black or white, American or foreign-born, the seamen exerted a strong influence on the reefers—so strong that Captain Thomas Truxtun warned years earlier that a midshipman coming aboard his first ship might be taken in:

> No character, in their opinion, is more excellent than that of the common sailor. Blinded by these prepossessions, he is thrown off his guard, and very soon surprised to find, amongst these honest sailors, a crew of abandoned miscreants, ripe for any mischief or villainy. If the midshipman, on many occasions, is obliged to mix with these . . . he ought to resolutely guard against this contagion, with which the morals of his inferiors may be affected. He should, however, avail himself of their knowledge.[48]

The navy, like the army, was home to many hard cases, and occasionally a reefer might fall under their bad influence and breach the discipline of the ship. If he did, the academy regulations no longer governed his punishment; he was now subject exclusively to the Navy Code and the Navy Regulations.

Discipline in the navy was always swift and sometimes severe. The captain of a ship, particularly one on the high seas, was the closest thing to God on earth that one was likely to meet, and soldiers were sometimes shocked at the swift severity of naval justice in action. James Morgan's brother Gibbes, an army officer, visited him on board the *Beaufort* on one of the occasions when young

Jimmy was in command in the captain's absence. While the brothers were visiting, a crewman named Jurgenson came back to the ship from liberty drunk. When he failed to obey Midshipman Morgan's command to be silent, Morgan had him put in double irons and bucked and gagged. Gibbes Morgan was incredulous that "a little boy . . . had authority to order such a severe punishment."[49] Morgan explained that little boy or not, he was the senior officer aboard, that he was not being cruel, that Jurgenson was an old sailor and one of his personal favorites, but knew he was in the wrong and expected punishment for his disobedience of orders and would have lost all respect for Morgan as an officer had he not done so. Brother Gibbes was still unconvinced and left shaking his head saying, "I must go back and tell my boys what I have seen this day."[50]

The punishment of flogging had been abolished in the U.S. Navy by Congress on September 28, 1850, and although Stephen Mallory as chairman of the U.S. Senate Naval Affairs Committee had championed its return, he did not press for its institution in the Confederate States Navy. The following punishments, however, were recognized as lawful in the Rebel navy: death, cashiering (dismissal from service) of officers; dismissing from command (called in the Code "dismissing on command"); suspension of command, pay, and emoluments; and other minor punishments such as confinement or confinement in irons. Twelve articles of the Navy Code carried the death sentence as their maximum punishment for noncompliance and four articles provided for cashiering of officers. Any crime not specified in the Navy Code was "judged and punished according to the laws and customs in such cases at sea."[51]

The most serious offenders and all officers charged with violations of the Navy Code were tried before a general court-martial composed of not less than five or more than thirteen officers convened by the President, the secretary of the navy, or the commander of a fleet or squadron operating outside the limits of the Confederate States. Petty officers and sailors were tried before summary courts-martial convened by the commander of a vessel and composed of not less than three officers of the grade of passed midshipman or higher. A summary court-martial had jurisdiction over offenses that the captain could not punish himself, but did not require trial before a general court-martial. Punishments that could be meted out by the commander without trial were carried out at the "captain's mast," at the foot of the ship's mainmast, the traditional place for receiving the captain's discipline.

In today's navy, midshipmen are held to the same standards as other officers, but this was not entirely the case in the nineteenth century, and some particularly peculiar punishments were reserved for midshipmen. For example, a
midshipman on a sailing ship might be "mastheaded," a punishment consisting of a "fatherly lecture" from the first lieutenant followed by a trip "to the
masthead or foretopsail yard to spend six or seven hours and ruminate over the
bad luck of having been caught."[52] Midshipman William Clayton, a masthead-
ing veteran, did not give this punishment much credit for deterrence, since a
midshipman at the masthead had "no thought of remorse or repentance, . . .
and with schemes for more secrecy in the future, he sits out his punishment
and counts the minutes when the first officer of the deck will hail the foretopsail yard and order him down."[53]

Even though they were young, midshipmen were nevertheless expected to
conduct themselves as officers and gentlemen, and unseemly conduct was
quickly dealt with, as Midshipman Willie Wilson discovered while serving
aboard the Mobile Squadron's CSS *Morgan.*

Wilson had taken exception in the most profane way to an order given
him by Lieutenant Charles I. Graves and then took it upon himself to report
the matter directly to the squadron commander, Admiral Franklin Buchanan.
The crusty old admiral, wise in the ways of midshipmen, responded with a
stern lecture for young Wilson, noting that "gentlemen should be guarded in
their expressions of their superiors and not commit themselves by violating the
law in speaking disrespectfully of them in the presence of servants or officers so
as to be overheard."[54] The admiral told the midshipman that in his opinion,
Lieutenant Graves was remiss in not suspending him from duty "for your curs-
ing and swearing and reported you to me," and the lieutenant would be directed to "be governed strictly by the law hereafter in such cases."[55] As for
young Mister Wilson, the next time he had a complaint about a superior's conduct he would be wise to follow the regulations and report him to the officer's
superior "and not to commit himself by being disrespectful in so doing he in-
jures his own cause."[56] Midshipman Wilson would later meet Lieutenant
Graves as one of his professors aboard the school ship; whether the lieutenant
held a grudge is not recorded.

Often his very youth would save a midshipman from serious punishment.
Acting Midshipman John T. Scharf, when serving aboard the Savannah River
Squadron's CSS *Water Witch* after her capture, ran afoul of his commander,

Master Henry L. Vaughan, himself a graduate of the Confederate States Naval Academy, for some unspecified offense. Vaughan wrote to Flag Officer William W. Hunter, the squadron commander, requesting that Scharf, whom he relieved of duty, be punished. Hunter replied that without a complete investigation, "I am not prepared to take official action . . . especially as it so seriously involves the career of a young officer, who has acted with distinguished conduct in this war on more than one occasion."[57] Instead Hunter appealed to Vaughan's "magnanimity, judgment, and generosity touching this matter, and if possible consistent with your sense of duty rather reclaim young Scharf if possible."[58] Since he had no officer available to replace him, Hunter recommended that Scharf be returned to duty.

After a spirited fistfight across the *Georgia*'s deck with Passed Midshipman John T. Walker, Jimmy Morgan found himself placed under close arrest by Captain Maury. But Morgan's status as the only acting midshipman aboard meant there was "a great deal of unpleasant work which some officer had to attend to during my incarceration, such as boat duty, acting as master's mate of the berth deck, and superintending the issuing of the grog ration, besides my regular watch on the forecastle."[59] After a week of this, the other officers prevailed upon the captain to restore Morgan to his duties.

Breaches of discipline were serious matters and had to be dealt with quickly. Captains also needed to remove the potential causes of disciplinary problems rapidly, for if left unaddressed they could lead to problems that might very easily destroy the effectiveness of the crew and the vessel. One such potential source of problems that was beyond the power of the captains to completely remove was the spirit, or grog, ration.

In 1794, the U.S. Congress established a daily ration of one half pint of distilled spirits or one quart of beer for the sailors of the navy. In 1861, the Confederate navy adopted the spirit ration of the U.S. Navy and even established whiskey distilleries in Georgia and South Carolina to supply the fleet. The sailors' spirit ration was usually issued in the form of grog—whiskey diluted with water to temper the effect of the alcohol.

The spirit ration was controversial and was abolished in the U.S. Navy in July 1862, but the Confederate navy, probably partly out of a sense of tradition and partly to maintain morale, continued the practice, over the objections of commanding officers, who worried about its potential impact on good order and discipline, and paymasters, who fumed over its cost. Surgeons generally supported the ration for its perceived beneficial health effects, particularly when issued first thing in the morning. The unease of Confederate naval authorities with the spirit ration was reflected in the Navy Regulations, which charged the captain with convincing his men to "relinquish the spirit part of their ration . . . for not less than three months, or for the remainder of the cruise" in favor of a three-cents-a-day payment in lieu thereof.[60] Few men did so, though the numbers of men who did agree to forgo the ration probably increased somewhat when the payment was raised to twenty-two cents a day in 1864. The captain was also authorized to withhold the ration without compensation from any crewman who was guilty of drunkenness.

Midshipman Morgan on the *Georgia* witnessed the mischief possible from mixing thirsty sailors and a room full of whiskey within the confines of a ship at sea. When some coal heavers discovered that only a thin bulkhead separated a coal bunker from the spirit room, they proceeded to bore a hole through the bulkhead into a keg of whiskey and run a pipe to dispense from the keg through the hole into their waiting cups. They distributed drinks from their makeshift pub throughout the ship and soon a drunken brawl was raging on the berth deck that the master-at-arms could not quell. The executive officer persuaded the ringleaders to come up from below and assemble at the foot of the mainmast and ordered the master-at-arms to place them in irons in the brig on bread and water. The "biggest bully" on the ship refused to submit, whereupon Morgan jumped on his back and forced him to the deck, where he was manacled.[61] "The other mutineers," boasted Morgan, "quietly extending their arms in sign of submission, were placed in irons, and confined below."[62]

Though not subject to the academy's disciplinary rules and regulations when at sea, the young gentlemen were not forgotten by that institution. Indeed the Navy Regulations provided, "The admission, continuance and examination of midshipmen for promotion, shall be according to such rules as are or may be established by the Navy Department, in connexion with the Naval Academy."[63]

The academy had a long reach. In November 1863, Commodore Samuel Barron, commander of Confederate naval forces outside of home waters with headquarters in Paris, received a communication from Commander Brooke:

> By direction of the Secretary of the Navy, I enclose you twelve
> copies of examination papers and forms of reports of examination

for the 1st, 2d and 3d classes of midshipmen in the Confederate States Navy, for distribution to the commanding officers of vessels abroad when an opportunity offers. Please inform the commanding officers . . . to have the midshipmen under their respective commands examined.[64]

The examination papers contained questions on seamanship and steam; gunnery, artillery, and infantry tactics; and navigation and astronomy. Commodore Barron was directed to return the examination reports to the school ship so that the academic board could determine the relative rankings of the midshipmen in accordance with academy regulations.

The distances involved and the problems inherent in communicating with the captains of cruisers at sea delayed Commodore Barron's compliance with Commander Brooke's direction. In June 1864 Navy Secretary Mallory wrote to Barron, "I have received the report of the examination of the midshipman on board the *Florida*, and you are requested to forward the report of examination of those now in Europe which was directed some time since."[65] Barron reported from Paris almost two months later, "All the midshipmen except the *Alabama*'s have been examined, and the reports sent to the Navy Department."[66] Sometimes the Navy Department wasn't even sure where the reefers were stationed. "If your brother and midshipmen Anderson and Maffitt are still in Europe," Chief Clerk of the Navy E. M. Tidball wrote to Captain James D. Bulloch, the navy's purchasing agent in Europe. "[P]lease ask Captain Barron to have them examined . . . and send the report to the department."[67]

The quality of the education received by midshipmen not on board the school ship was a cause for concern by the Navy Department. Too often they were allowed to neglect their studies and other requirements regarding their training were ignored. To ensure that the reefers with the fleet would be prepared for the rigorous academics of the school ship, the Navy Department, "deeming it of the first importance that no opportunity be neglected for the advancement of the midshipmen in their studies and deportment," issued a directive on February 4, 1864, to all commanders of vessels in Confederate waters.[68] Henceforth, the "sunset regulation" requiring midshipmen to return from liberty by sunset would be strictly enforced and commanders were to "insist upon their pursuing their studies as prescribed by the regulations of the school ship."[69] Journals were to be kept as required by the Navy Regulations and were to be presented by each midshipman to the board at his December examination, along with letters from their commanding officers "certifying to their good conduct and studious habits."[70]

Even prior to the formal establishment of the Naval Academy, acting midshipmen stood for examination by roving boards of officers at locations throughout the South. The lads aboard ship did not welcome such attention. "Today orders came from Mr. Holloway that all the Midshipmen were to prepare for examination," Midshipman Willie Wilson noted in his diary on June 24, 1862. "There is a good many scarred [*sic*] youngsters just now."[71]

Midshipman Clayton recorded that his class was examined three times; the first at Richmond in 1862, the second at Charleston in 1863, and the last on board the *Patrick Henry* in August (more likely July) 1864. Clayton's fourth-class examination began in Richmond in the basement of the Jewish Synagogue on Mayo Street near the Exchange Hotel on Thursday, July 17, 1862. He and his classmates appeared before an examining board composed of Commanders Robert Thoburn and Charles McBlair and Lieutenants William H. Parker and Lubian Myers and presided over by Flag Officer George N. Hollins.[72]

The examination proper began the following day and, after an overnight break, continued until 11:35 on the morning of the nineteenth. All was not good news. Acting Midshipman Neil H. Sterling failed mathematics and his examination was not continued. Acting Midshipmen James Dyke and James Pinckney exhibited the same inadequacy. Midshipmen Daniel M. Lee, Thomas Pinckney, and Clayton "withdrew by permission" from the mathematics exam.[73]

Acting Midshipman Morgan stood for his examination to advance to the third class before the same board on July 16. By his own admission he "had not opened a schoolbook since I had left Annapolis."[74] It showed; he was found deficient in mathematics and was "put back to [the] 4th C[lass]."[75] His classmate Jefferson Phelps was "put back" with him, as were James G. Baldwin and T. G. Ganett who performed unsatisfactorily in their examinations at Mobile.[76]

Acting Midshipman Robert Crawford failed even to show up for his examination at Richmond in 1863, but he must have had a good excuse since he was given permission to attend the examinations at Wilmington, Charleston, or Mobile. He did and he passed.[77]

Some apparently decided to dispense with the formality of exams and promoted themselves. Captain French Forrest, commander of the James River Squadron, alerted Brigadier General John H. Winder, provost marshal of Richmond, that a man named Joiner "is parading the streets here and passing himself off as a passed midshipman—that he has forged the name of Commander Mitchell of the Navy" on a document showing he had passed his examination.[78]

Examinations were a high-pressure time for the reefers and it was understandable that they would need to let off steam after the exams were over. Unfortunately, these celebrations sometimes led to ungentlemanly conduct. Acting Midshipman James Wilson and his comrades from Drewry's Bluff finished their examinations in Richmond on April 10, 1863. Afterward, Wilson admitted, they went on a general "Bust," Ralph J. Deas "got very drunk, & smashed the crockery in Pizzini's confectionary store. After raising things generally we turned in."[79]

The young men training at sea often went into harm's way and sometimes morbidly predicted their potential fates. "Here lies the body of W. F. Wilson," Willie Wilson self-eulogized in April 1862, "who died defending his loved South against the fanatical hordes of the North."[80] Sometimes the eulogies were real and the midshipmen were forced to recall the price paid by the dead. In November 1864, the midshipmen and crew of the *Patrick Henry* were mustered on deck. The ship's ensign and jack were lowered to half-staff and a general order from the Navy Department was read:

> Information has reached the Department of the death of Passed Midshipman W[illia]m B. Sinclair, late of the *Florida* at sea, on the 10th of July last.
>
> In passing from a prize ship to the *Florida*, his boat was swamped and he, the only one of the crew lost, perished in rescuing a seaman who could not swim.
>
> On this and many previous occasions, this young officer displayed that courage, coolness and conscientious devotion to duty and to right, which ever marked his brief career.[81]

William B. Sinclair, Jr., son of a navy surgeon, had graduated from the naval academy in July 1864, seventh in his class.

4

⚜

The Exhibition of "Good Discipline, Conduct, and Courage"

AT 6 A.M. ON APRIL 21, 1861, AS MARYLAND WAS ENGULFED by a rising tide of secessionist fervor and rumors of Rebel plots to seize for the Confederacy the venerable USS *Constitution*, berthed at Annapolis, Captain George S. Blake, the U.S. Naval Academy superintendent, ordered "Old Ironsides," already loaded with the academy's library, trophies, and memorabilia and with her faculty and midshipmen aboard, to set sail for Fort Adams at Newport, Rhode Island. Here, safely away from the war, the academy's work continued until 1865—though in the end Maryland did not secede.[1] The fine unoccupied brick buildings at Annapolis were converted into the United States General Hospital, divisions one and two.

No similar safe haven was chosen for the Confederate States Naval Academy. Indeed, the academy and its school ship were part of the naval linchpin linking the land defenses of Richmond on either side of the broad expanse of the James River, and after the spring of 1864 the war was never very far away. "One always associates a collegiate institution with peace and quiet," observed Acting Midshipman James Morgan, "but this naval college was located in the midst of booming guns."[2]

The *Patrick Henry*'s usual anchorage was in the James River at the foot of Drewry's Bluff, a precipice towering ninety feet above the southern bank of the James River and commanding the waters below. The river between the bluff and the opposite bank was obstructed by sunken vessels and huge wooden cribs filled with stone. A passage for smaller Confederate vessels remained open through the obstructions and it was in this breach that the school ship was to be scuttled if that became necessary. Below the fortifications at Drewry's Bluff along the south bank, or southside, as it was known, were the naval batteries Brooke, Semmes, and Wood. Even farther downriver was an unfinished battery near Howlett's farm. On the northside of the James, the Confederate fortified lines began at Chaffin's Bluff, a mile downriver from Drewry's, and stretched inland through formidable Fort Harrison and into Richmond's Outer Line.

By the summer of 1863 when the school ship first anchored there, the fortifications of Drewry's Bluff had already been described as a "second Gibraltar" with the extensive earthworks at Fort Darling holding over twenty heavy guns manned by army artillerists and navy and marine gunners—a joint service arrangement rare in the Confederate armed forces.[3] The complex at the bluff was also the site of Camp Beall and its three companies of Confederate States Marines, the largest contingent stationed anywhere in the South. In 1863 the installation was commanded by the navy's Captain Sidney Smith Lee, Robert's elder brother. Captain Lee assumed command from Commander Ebenezer Farrand in May 1862 and remained in command until March 1864, when he was replaced by Major George H. Terrett of the Confederate marines. Drewry's Bluff also served as de facto headquarters of the James River Squadron, since its vessels were usually anchored in the river nearby.

Even had some acting midshipmen from the academy not been stationed there, the sprawling installation atop Drewry's Bluff would have attracted them. Acting Midshipman Hubbard Minor viewed the post for the first time in October 1863 and was "charmed with the place."[4] "There is quite a little village here now," he noted in his diary.[5]

Minor did not exaggerate. By mid-1863, in addition to the wooden barracks constructed for the marines and midshipmen, neat log houses had been built for the families of the garrison and refugees from Norfolk and Portsmouth, Virginia. A hotel was in operation, as was a post office. A Masonic lodge was formed in October 1863 and two churches served worshippers. A village cemetery adjoined one of the chapels, and one of the graves there contained the body of a child whom her sailor father had patriotically named

Rebellion Virginia Chicora Davis Johnson. But for all its appearance as a normal, bustling village, Drewry's Bluff was also the largest, most important Confederate defensive installation on the James River, and those stationed there had an important duty to perform: defend the Confederate capital.

Attending classes in the midst of the distractions offered by Drewry's Bluff, the comings and goings of the James River Squadron, and the ever-present threat of an ascent upriver by Federal forces was a challenge for the middies. Even so, Superintendent William Parker felt that the exposed location of the school ship offered at least one benefit: it curbed the midshipmen's desire to see more active service, for "the officers and men feel that they were not withdrawn from active service. It was not like being in a bomb-proof, for their vessel was performing the same duty as the others."[6] The academy students' impatience to see action could not be entirely curbed, however, since the *Patrick Henry* was filled with "lads, between the ages of 14 and 18, who were restlessly champing at the bit because they wanted to take a more active part in the fray which was going on around them."[7] Acting Midshipman John Mason's lament was typical. Writing a naval officer cousin, he confessed, "I do feel dissatisfied with myself for remaining in such a snug, lazy berth in these times."[8]

However, the fray around them often impinged on the execution of the educational mission of the academy. As the war moved closer, it was not uncommon for a professor to begin a lesson by summoning one of the reefers to the blackboard, but, as Jimmy Morgan recalled,

> [He] frequently got no farther before a crashing of great guns aroused his curiosity and he would request one of the young gentlemen to step outside and see which one of the batteries was using a particular rifle gun or heavy smoothbore. Having received the information, he would attempt to resume the recitation, when he would again be interrupted by a message from the captain to send two or three midshipmen to assist in working the guns of some battery which was short of officers. After the artillery duel was over those boys would return to the ship and continue their studies.[9]

Such interruptions were not conducive to good scholarship, particularly when they cut into the already limited time the reefers had for study. After comparing himself and his classmates to famous men who studied and persevered under adverse conditions, Acting Midshipman William Clayton nonetheless concluded that those men were fortunate, since "they had the time, however inauspicious to study," while the midshipmen, "had to snatch what we could get, and when we had done our duty mighty little of the twenty-four hours remained."[10]

The toil duty took on studying time often adversely affected scholastic achievement. "I was on deck and missed two days," Clifton Breckinridge explained to his father the general, "but the days I did not in History I led the class, but in those two days the[y] caught up with me and three or four passed me."[11] Often the midshipmen were taken from their studies for details not to their liking. One of these was guard-boat duty. "[G]oing down with the guard boat has ceased to be fun," Olly Harrison confessed. "From the point in the river where the guard boat usually lies we can plainly see the yankee pickets on Aiken's house. But they never fire at us: *they might wake up Quarles.*"[12]

Irksome or not, and regardless of the cost to their studies, the reefers readily volunteered for service away from the school ship—so much so that asking for volunteers became futile. Every young man raised his hand high when volunteers were called for, so the officers took to selecting midshipmen for details as rewards for good grades and behavior. One call for volunteers came soon after the new year in 1864.

Since the capture of Roanoke Island, North Carolina, in 1862, Federal forces had tightened their grip on that state's strategic sounds and the towns controlling the rivers that flowed into them. New Bern, at the confluence of the Trent and Neuse rivers, was such a town and the Federals constructed strong earthworks and stationed a flotilla of gunboats nearby to deny the Confederacy two of the river connections to the trade with the outside world upon which the Confederate war effort depended. Commander John Taylor Wood wanted to change that.

Wood, the nephew of President Jefferson Davis, grandson of former President Zachary Taylor, and son of Federal General Robert Wood, had already garnered a well-deserved reputation for skill and daring during the war, and the plan he discussed with General Robert E. Lee in the waning days of 1863 exhibited those qualities to the fullest. Although some thought had previously been given to wresting New Bern from the Yankees, Wood argued that the time was particularly favorable for a joint army-navy effort against the town. While the CSS *Neuse*, under construction for the express purpose of challenging Federal control of her eponymous river, was still not ready to be used in such an attack, the lack of her guns could be compensated for by capturing one or more of the Yankees' gunboats near New Bern. Those guns could then be turned upon the Federal fortifications in support of an army land assault. Wood felt that one or more of the enemy vessels, after losing their combat edge to months of dull, routine patrolling, could be surprised and captured.

Lee saw merit in Wood's proposal and wrote President Davis on January 2 recommending approval of an assault upon New Bern and proposing Major General George E. Pickett to command the army forces involved. The plan was approved by the President and orders for its execution began to fly.

One of these orders landed on the desk of Flag Officer French Forrest, commander of the James River Squadron. Forrest was directed to furnish forty-five men from the vessels under his command for "special service with Commander John Taylor Wood."[13] The men were to be outfitted with "rifles, cutlasses . . . revolvers . . . 40 rounds of ammunition, cooked rations for three days, cooking utensils, and axes," peajackets and blankets.[14] Similar orders went to Wilmington, North Carolina, and Charleston, South Carolina.

The order to Forrest also directed that Acting Midshipmen Richard Slaughter, Paul H. Gibbs, and John B. Northrop be detailed to the expedition. On board the *Patrick Henry*, Lieutenants Parker and Benjamin P. Loyall, assisting Parker on the school ship, picked five more reefers for the venture: William F. Clayton, Henry S. Cooke, Daniel M. Lee, John T. Scharf, and Palmer Saunders. Loyall was to command the James River contingent of four ship's cutters gathered from various vessels in the squadron, each with a crew of ten sailors and two midshipmen, one to command the boat and one to steer. From Drewry's Bluff came twenty-five Confederate marines armed with Enfield rifles under the command of Captain Thomas S. Wilson. Surgeon Daniel B. Conrad was detailed as medical officer for the expedition. Only Loyall and Parker knew the destination and purpose for which the men had been chosen, although others, knowing that the swashbuckling Wood would be in command, expected "nervous work."[15]

Loyall's orders were to rendezvous with Wood and the force from Charleston under Lieutenant George W. Gift and the Wilmington contingent, commanded by Lieutenant Phillip Porcher, upriver from New Bern at Kinston, North Carolina. Loyall, who was to be Wood's second in command, took his flotilla of four boats down the James and then up the Appomattox River, and arrived at the rail center of Petersburg, Virginia, before daylight on January 29. A train was waiting and Loyall had the cutters hauled out of the water and loaded upon flatcars before the sleeping townspeople awakened. The boats were lashed upright on the cars and "it was a novel sight to see a train like that—Jack [Tar] sitting up on the seats of the boats and waving his hat to the astonished natives, who never saw such a circus before."[16]

En route to Kinston the boat train stopped frequently to take on wood and water for the locomotive and at every stop Surgeon Conrad watched with amusement as "the young midshipmen swarmed into the depots and houses, full of their fun and deviltry, making friends of the many pretty girls gathered there, who asked all manner of questions as to this strange sight of boats on cars filled with men in a uniform new to them."[17] The boys boasted that they were going "to board, capture and destroy as many of the enemy's gunboats as possible" and the girls begged them to bring captured flags or other trophies with them when they returned.[18] After extracting promises of a kiss per flag, the smiling reefers reboarded their boats vowing to return with the spoils of war, and waved and cheered as the train pulled away.

The boat train reached Kinston around 2 A.M. on January 31 and Wood was waiting. The contingents from Charleston and Wilmington had been de-layed by a lack of railway cars and did not arrive until almost noon. In addition to cutters, Lieutenant Gift brought two large flat-bottomed launches from Charleston, each one armed with a twelve-pounder boat howitzer. Anxious to be off, Wood ordered the twelve lighter boats into the water. Gift remained be-hind with orders to catch up as soon as he could get the unwieldy launches un-loaded.

As they rowed toward New Bern, almost sixty miles downriver, Wood di-vided his force into two divisions, one to be commanded by him and the other by Loyall. En route to New Bern the river alternately widened to the size of a lake and narrowed to the point where the trees on either bank seemed almost within reach. "Not a sign of life was visible," recalled Midshipman John T. Scharf, "save occasionally when a flock of wild ducks startled at the approach of the boats, rose from the banks. . . . No other sound was heard to break the stillness save the constant, steady splash of the oars and the ceaseless surge of the river."[19]

They finally reached New Bern at four on the morning of February 1. Wood and his men rowed up and down in front of the town through a dense fog in a futile search for a suitable target, but approaching daylight forced a re-treat back up the Neuse to Bachelor's (or Batchelder's) Creek to rest the men, await Gift's arrival, and hide "among the reeds and rushes."[20] While the men rested, Wood and Loyall rowed back toward New Bern and near the town sighted an enemy gunboat at anchor in the river between the guns of Forts Stevens and Anderson, both held by Union forces. Wood also used the time to communicate with General Pickett, whose men were fighting the Federals fur-ther inland along Bachelor's Creek; the exchange of fire could be plainly heard by Wood's sailors and marines.

Back in Kinston, Gift, with the assistance of his eighty-five men and two mules "borrowed" from a local resident, got his ungainly launches into the water, mounted the howitzers, and rowed furiously to catch up with Wood. Gift and his launches reached the Bachelor's Creek hiding place around sunset on the first of February.

With Gift's arrival Wood finally revealed the full extent of the audacious mission to the men and the "grand scheme . . . was received by the older men with looks of admiration and with rapture by the young midshipmen, all of whom would have broken out into loud cheers but for the fact that the strictest silence was essential."[21] The men were instructed to tie strips of white cloth around their left arms as a means of identifying friend from foe in the dark, a prayer was said, and the watchword "Sumter" given. Captain Wilson's marines were distributed among the boats to act as sharpshooters.

The midshipmen, excited by the prospect of combat, were "gaily chatting about what they intended to do—joyous and confident, and choosing each other for mates to fight together shoulder to shoulder."[22] But as they entered the boats at around 10 P.M., a seventeen-year-old midshipman, Palmer Saun-ders, contemplating the stars rapidly disappearing behind thickening clouds, said to his friends, "I wonder, boys, how many of us will be up in those stars by tomorrow morning?"[23]

By the time Wood set out against the ship he and Loyall had spotted, Pickett's land assault on New Bern had already failed. Pickett marched from Kinston around 1 A.M. on February 1 with the infantry brigade of Brigadier General Robert F. Hoke and portions of the brigades of Brigadier Generals Montgomery G. Corse and Thomas L. Clingman, a total of 4,500 men. Pickett sent another force under Brigadier General James Dearing across the Neuse to attack Fort Anderson while Brigadier General Seth Barton's cavalry was dispatched to cut the Atlantic and North Carolina Railroad line and prevent reinforcements from reaching New Bern's Yankee garrison.

Pickett engaged the Federals commanded by Brigadier General Innis M. Palmer along Bachelor's Creek and drove them back to their New Bern fortifications after inflicting about 100 casualties and capturing 293 officers and men, 2 cannons, 300 stands of small arms, several wagons, 2 flags, 14 Negroes, and 2 ambulances complete with surgeons who had been sent out by Palmer to treat smallpox sufferers in the countryside.

Having pursued the Federals to within range of New Bern's heavy guns, Pickett now found himself pummeled by shot and shell. No word had been received from Barton all day, and not until two trainloads of reinforcements chugged into the Yankee garrison did Pickett discover that Barton and his cavalry had failed him. Reluctantly Pickett ordered a retreat, having lost thirty-five killed and wounded; he also took with him twenty-two Confederate deserters in Federal uniform whom he had captured, and who, after a drumhead court-martial in Kinston, were all hanged.

Wood, not knowing the outcome of Pickett's assault, started his boats toward their target in two columns. He gathered the boats together a short distance downriver from Bachelor's Creek, issued his final instructions, and offered up a final prayer. "It was a strange and ghostly sight," Scharf, in charge of the boat howitzer on one of Gift's launches, recalled, "the men resting on their oars with heads uncovered, the commander also bareheaded standing erect in the stern of his boat; the black waters rippling beneath; the dense overhanging clouds pouring down sheets of rain, and in the blackness beyond an unseen bell tolling as if from some phantom cathedral."[24] The unseen bell ringing out two o'clock was aboard the expedition's target, the USS *Underwriter*.

A 325-ton side-wheel steamer, the *Underwriter* was the largest Federal gunboat on the river. She was armed with two eight-inch guns, one thirty-pounder rifled cannon, and one twelve-pounder boat howitzer. On this night, she and her seventy-two men were under the command of Acting Master Jacob Westervelt.

Taking their bearings from the pealing of the *Underwriter's* bell, Wood's boats pulled slowly and cautiously toward her, arms at the ready. When they were 300 yards from the ship her hull suddenly loomed up out of the darkness and her bell tolled five times, marking half past two. Hard upon the final strike of the bell a nervous voice on board called "Boat ahoy!" Wood did not reply, and again the challenge came, "Boat ahoy! Boat ahoy!" Not until the battle rattle sounded calling the *Underwriter*'s men to battle stations and figures could be seen running about the deck, did Wood break his silence to shout to his crews, "Give way, boys, give way!" The men put their backs into rowing and the boats sprang forward, rapidly covering the remaining distance to the gunboat's side, although it seemed to take a lifetime to the Confederates, who expected the ship's great guns to open up at any minute and smash their small boats to splinters. At 100 yards the enemy began a withering small-arms barrage, for the big guns on deck were unable to be depressed enough to hit the rapidly oncoming attackers. The marines stationed in each boat returned fire with "great coolness."[25]

On Wood's boat, Surgeon Conrad watched as the Federal musketry took its toll: "Our coxswain, a burly, gamy Englishman, who by gesture and loud word was encouraging the crew, steering by the tiller between his knees, his hands occupied in holding his pistols, suddenly fell forward on us dead, a ball having struck him fairly in the forehead."[26]

Before someone could grab the tiller, Wood's boat swerved and instead of striking by the *Underwriter*'s gangway hit the paddlewheel housing. The following boat, commanded by Lieutenant Loyall, struck where intended, and the bow oarsman, James Wilson, caught the gunboat's rail with a grapnel. Loyall and his men poured out of the boat and up the *Underwriter*'s gangway. Loyall, nearsighted and without his spectacles, tripped at the top of the gangway and the four men following him took the blast of gunfire intended for him. Riddled with bullets, they fell on top of the hapless lieutenant. Federal sailors were firing from a position near the ship's armory and men inside passed out loaded muskets to the marksmen outside, so that they could keep up an almost ceaseless, deadly fire. Engineer Emmet F. Gill also fell dead on the gangway in this hail of lead.

Loyall had shed his load of bodies and Wood was boarding over the wheelhouse, when Lieutenant Gift in his launch noticed that the *Underwriter* was trying to get under way. He ordered Midshipman Scharf to open fire with his howitzer. Scharf sent a shell through the ship's pilothouse, but before he could reload, the crowd of Confederates on deck made further fire impossible without hitting his own comrades.

As their numbers increased, the Confederate boarders pushed the Federal tars aft along the hurricane deck. Palmer Saunders, praised by Wood as "a most promising young officer," was at the forefront.[27] As young Saunders at-tacked a huge Federal sailor, this "giant of the forecastle" brought his cutlass down on the young reefer's head striking a powerful blow.[28] As he fell to the bloody deck, Saunders was also shot in the stomach.

Midshipman Daniel Lee jumped from his boat into the hand-to-hand combat on the *Underwriter* and tackled a Yankee sailor, but the Yankee gained the upper hand and pinned Lee to the deck. As they struggled, several of Lee's mates ran to his aid and one put a loaded pistol to the Federal's back. From be-neath his opponent, Lee shouted, "Don't shoot, you fool! Can't you see how thin this man is? I am under here!"[29]

Midshipman Scharf, now in the thick of the fight, charged along as "down the companionways [the defenders] were driven pell-mell into the wardroom and steerage, and even to the coal bunkers" before surrendering.[30]

The force of more than 200 Confederates began to overwhelm the de-fenders. Loyall was in front as the enemy "fell back under the hurricane deck before the steady attack of our men . . . [who] came along from forward with cutlasses and muskets, . . . clubbing and slashing."[31]

After about fifteen minutes of fierce fighting, Surgeon Conrad waiting in his boat heard "a strange synchronous roar," which he at first did not under-stand, but whose meaning became clear as soon he made out the cries of "She's ours!" from the gunboat.[32] His job just now beginning, Conrad jumped up on the *Underwriter*'s deck with his medical supplies and slipped in the mixture of blood and rainwater covering it. As he fell he grabbed hold of a nearby officer, who promptly put the muzzle of a cocked pistol against his ear. Conrad instinctively knocked the weapon aside and was somewhat amazed that the officer who had come just short of blowing his head off, First Lieu-tenant John Wilkinson of the Wilmington contingent, said only, "I'm looking for you doctor; come here."[33]

Wilkinson led the doctor to where Palmer Saunders lay cradled in the arms of another reefer. The doctor examined the young man and "in feeling his head I felt my hand slip down between his ears, and to my horror, discovered that his head had been cleft in two."[34] Conrad directed that Saunders and the other dead be laid out on the quarterdeck and went in search of wounded. In the ship's wardroom he found an additional half dozen sailors with slight pistol wounds.

In addition to Saunders and Gill, Seamen Hawkins and Sullivan and Ma-rine Bell had also been killed. Another fifteen to twenty men were wounded.

Federal losses were, by Confederate reports, nine dead, eighteen wounded, and nineteen captured. Thirty more of the *Underwriter*'s crew escaped by jumping overboard and swimming ashore. Captain Westervelt was wounded and either fell or jumped overboard, although there was some evidence that he deserted his ship early in the fight and was shot while hanging on to a hawser.[35]

The ship now his, Wood turned his attention to moving her from under the guns of the Federal forts. But the fires in the furnaces were banked and not enough steam was in the boilers to move her. To make matters worse, the gunners in Fort Stevens, alerted by the noise of the fight and by members of the *Underwriter*'s crew who had made it ashore, began firing upon the gunboat. One shell disabled the walking beam that operated the paddlewheels, passed through a chicken coop on deck near where Captain Wilson had his marines drawn up in ranks—silencing many of the birds, which had been cackling madly during the fight—before finally punching its way through the hull. With her machinery disabled and under intensifying fire from shore, Wood reluctantly decided to destroy his prize. Surgeon Conrad was directed to move the Confederate dead and the wounded from both sides to the boats and Lieutenant Francis L. Hoge was ordered to burn the ship. "[T]he guns were loaded and pointed towards the town," Midshipman Scharf recalled, "fire was applied from the boilers, and in five minutes after the boarders left, the *Underwriter* was in one mass of flames from stem to stern, burning with her the dead bodies of those brave antagonists who had fallen during the action."[36]

Federal Brigadier General Innis M. Palmer first reported the loss of the *Underwriter* on February 2, adding his opinion that "without venturing to fix the responsibility for her capture, I may say that it appears utterly inexcusable."[37] Admiral David Dixon Porter described Wood's success as "rather a mortifying affair for the navy."[38]

As commander, Westervelt was singled out for responsibility for the loss of the *Underwriter*. On February 15, with the captain still unaccounted for and presumed captured, Secretary of the Navy Gideon Welles forwarded to Rear Admiral Samuel P. Lee, commander of the North Atlantic Blockading Squadron, a letter from the superintendent of the North Pennsylvania Railroad demanding an inquiry into Westervelt's "derelictions from duty."[39] Lee acknowledged receipt, but noted, "The capture of the commanding officer and most of the other officers renders a satisfactory court of enquiry difficult."[40] But Commander Henry K. Davenport, Westervelt's superior, defended the vanquished crew: "The *Underwriter* was overpowered. She fought well. I am not ashamed of the Navy."[41]

Westervelt would not have to defend his actions, however. On February 25, Davenport reported to Lee, "I have just recovered the body of Captain Westervelt. I shall have it interred with all the honors of war tomorrow at 11 o'clock."[42]

The one bright spot for the Federal navy in an otherwise gloomy situation was the action of Acting Third Assistant Engineer George E. Allen, who overpowered the two Confederate soldiers who were guarding a boat that was taking Allen and twenty of his comrades to an uncertain future in a Rebel prison camp. For his actions Allen was promoted by Secretary Welles to acting second assistant engineer.

As the *Underwriter* blazed in the distance, the middies in Wood's boats pulled hard for Swift Creek, about six miles upriver. Here General Dearing had an encampment and the most seriously wounded were entrusted to his care. The dead were buried in the afternoon with the funeral service read by Lieutenant Loyall. "It was a very solemn scene," Scharf remembered. "The boats crews were formed in a square around the graves, with the officers in the centre. After the funeral services, Lieut. Loyall offered up a beautiful prayer, thanking God for their victory and safe return."[43]

To the victors go the spoils and although the destruction of the *Underwriter* was a disappointment, praise of Wood and his men was unstinting. "To Lieutenant Loyall . . . the success of the expedition is greatly due," Wood reported to Secretary Mallory. "I recommend him most heartily to the notice of the Department for promotion."[44] On February 10, 1864, Loyall was duly rewarded with a promotion to commander and with command of the ironclad *Neuse*, then under construction along the banks of its namesake river. "Of all the other officers," Wood continued, "I can only say they were ever zealous and prompt. I do not believe a finer body of young officers or men was ever brought together. They are a credit to any service."[45]

Wood himself was lionized. "I am all admiration for Wood," Lieutenant George Gift wrote of his commander. "He is modesty personified, conceives boldly and executes with skill and courage."[46] Wood "is surely one of our rising men," a fellow officer declared, "and I say Godspeed to him."[47] Wood typically downplayed his accomplishment. "Many thanks for your kind expressions and wishes," he wrote in response to a friend's congratulatory letter. "I hardly deserve them. As regards promotion, I have opposed it. . . . [T]he affair does not deserve it."[48] On February 5, the Confederate congress did take notice of Wood's accomplishments and passed a joint resolution of thanks for, among other exploits, "the capture from under the guns of the enemy's works of the U.S. gunboat *Underwriter*."[49]

The men from the James River Squadron waited for orders at Kinston until February 10 before loading their battle-scarred boats, each with an average of fourteen plugged bullet holes, aboard the flatcars for the trip home. The midshipmen, recalling the promises extracted from the young ladies en route to North Carolina, fashioned miniature "captured" Federal flags. "We old ones purposely stopped at all the stations we had made coming down in order to see the fun," Surgeon Conrad recalled:

> The young ladies were called out at each place, and after the dead were lamented, the wounded in the cars cared for, then the midshipmen brought out their flags, recalled the promises made to them, and demanded their redemption. Immediately there commenced a lively outburst of laughter and denials, a skirmish followed by a slight resistance, and the whole bevy were kissed *seriatim* by the midshipmen, and but for the whistle of [the] train warning them away, they would have continued indefinitely.[50]

Eight reefers left with Wood and seven returned to the school ship, where classwork continued despite the distractions caused by the details of students to temporary duties away from their studies, the signal station on the roof over the recitation rooms, and the *Patrick Henry*'s use as a receiving ship for exchanged prisoners of war. Welcoming back these ragged, gaunt Southern warriors was part of the duties of the officer of the deck, often assisted by a midshipman. One day when Midshipman Morgan had this duty, while he endeavored to keep the gangway clear as ordered he was approached by a much disheveled, very gloomy former prisoner who politely asked who was in command of the *Patrick Henry*. Morgan impatiently and somewhat sternly replied, "Pass forward, 'My Man;' don't block the gangway!" The man's eyes blazed with indignation and he drew himself erect and growled, "Mr. Morgan, I will apply for you when I get a ship, and I will show you, sir, who goes forward!"[51] Morgan's "man" turned out to be Commander Beverly Kennon, whom

Morgan had last seen struggling in the Mississippi River after his command, the CSS *Governor Moore*, had been sunk from under him at the Battle of New Orleans in 1862. "If the deck had opened and let me drop into the coal bunkers . . . I would have been grateful," confessed a mortified Morgan.[52]

As the Confederacy's military situation worsened, the calls upon the midshipmen became more and more frequent. In early April 1864, Acting Midshipman William Clayton and nine other academy midshipmen were detailed to participate in another joint army-navy effort in North Carolina. Lieutenant Robert D. Minor, superintendent of the Richmond Naval Ordnance Works and veteran of the CSS *Virginia*, was to take ten ship's boats and crews from the James River Squadron to operate in support of an attack on Plymouth, North Carolina, on the Roanoke River by troops under Brigadier General Robert F. Hoke. The primary naval support would be the recently completed ironclad CSS *Albemarle*.

Minor used a boat train to move his boats and men from Petersburg to a launching point on the Meherrin River at Hicksford, Virginia. From the Meherrin, Minor's little flotilla made its way to the Chowan River, thence to Edenton Bay and through the Cashie cutoff to the Roanoke River above Plymouth.

As Minor and his men threaded their way to the Roanoke, the attack on Plymouth went ahead without them. Commander James W. Cooke took the *Albemarle* downriver on Sunday evening, April 17. Plagued by serious machinery problems on the recently completed vessel and having floated stern first most of the way, Cooke reached a point three miles above the city at ten the following evening.

After a reconnaissance by Gilbert Elliott, the *Albemarle*'s builder, revealed that high water in the river would allow the ship to float over the Federal obstructions, Cooke shoved off at 2:30 A.M. on April 19. After running past Federal shore batteries, the *Albemarle* descended upon the USS *Southfield* and rammed and sank her; then Commander Cooke turned on the USS *Miami*, which was badly damaged and her captain killed by one of her own shells ricocheting off the *Albemarle*'s armored casemate sides. Having cleared the river of Federals, Cooke remained off Plymouth all night shelling enemy positions in support of the army's assault. Plymouth surrendered to Hoke at noon on Wednesday, April 20.

Minor attempted to contact Cooke on April 28, but was informed by Lieutenant Albert G. Hudgins, captain of the CSS *Bombshell*, that Cooke had gone downriver a few hours before Minor's note arrived. It appears that Minor's mission, of which no details are known, was not going well. "If everything goes well I think you will receive cooperation," Hudgins explained. "The *Pare* has not been raised yet, but I hope to have her ready when you want her."[53]

Judging by his reply to Minor, Hudgins was clearly frustrated by his orders to cooperate with Minor. He wrote testily, "I do not wish to complain, but would respectfully request speedy orders" and swore, "If I can help it I will not have anything to do with launches again."[54]

Hoke continued his offensive after the fall of Plymouth. In preparation for an attack on New Bern, Loyall started the CSS *Neuse* downriver on April 22. The ship lacked her second course of armor plate, and her newly assembled crew was not impressed with the ship, which they christened the "Neusance."[55] And a nuisance she was to prove to everyone but the enemy; half a mile from her anchorage at Kinston she ran hard-aground. By nightfall the ship's bow was hanging in the air four feet above the water. She remained stuck there until mid-May.

Hoke went on to capture Washington, North Carolina, on the Pamlico River southwest of Plymouth, on April 30 after a brief siege. Despite the loss of the *Neuse*, Hoke was determined to strike New Bern and convinced the navy to order the *Albemarle* to take the stranded *Neuse*'s place. On May 3 Hoke also invited Minor and his boats to participate in the operation if Minor thought his orders from the Navy Department would permit it. Hoke suggested that Minor take his launches to "Free Bridge, on Trent River, 15 miles from Kinston on the Upper Trent road, where they can be crossed, and proceed down to the point where they may be wanted."[56]

Had Minor done this he would have been Hoke's only naval support, for the *Albemarle* never made it. To reach New Bern Cooke had to leave the Roanoke, cross Albemarle, Croatan, and Pamlico sounds, and sail up the obstructed *Neuse*—all in the face of Federal naval opposition. At noon on May 5, the *Albemarle,* accompanied by the gunboats *Bombshell* (a converted Federal transport captured at Plymouth) and *Cotton Plant* made the attempt. Federal gunboats under Captain Melancton Smith quickly intercepted the *Albemarle* and her consorts. After two hours of stiff fighting, the *Bombshell* was recaptured and the severely damaged *Albemarle* retreated to Plymouth to rejoin the *Cotton Plant*, which had taken refuge there earlier. Deprived of naval support, Hoke did not attack and Minor and his middies made their way home.

As the *Albemarle* retreated, Lee and Lieutenant General Ulysses S. Grant were locked in combat in northern Virginia's tangled Wilderness area while Major General Benjamin F. Butler's Army of the James came knocking on Richmond's "backdoor" on the southside of the river. On May 5, 1864, Butler landed at City Point and Bermuda Hundred Landing, twelve miles downriver from Drewry's Bluff. His coming ashore profoundly altered the operation of the Confederate States Naval Academy as an academic institution.

On the afternoon of May 5, Major Frank Smith of the Confederate States Marines, commanding Drewry's Bluff in Terrett's absence, boarded the *Patrick Henry* and asked to see Captain Parker, the senior naval officer on the river in the absence of Commander Robert Pegram, the acting squadron commander. Smith showed the superintendent dispatches from signal officers downriver reporting large numbers of Federal warships and transports moving upriver. While Smith and Parker pondered these reports, a messenger came on board reporting Butler's landing. Both officers recognized the threat to Drewry's Bluff, which was not sufficiently manned to withstand a land assault. Parker quickly drafted every spare sailor and midshipman he could find and along with Smith's marines manned the installation's inner defensive lines.

But Butler would not come in force until May 13, and by that time Confederate troops sent from North Carolina under the command of Lieutenant General Pierre G. T. Beauregard were in place. Although Butler managed to capture the outer works of Drewry's Bluff's land defenses, his penetration was contained and he was pushed back into the Bermuda Hundred loop of the James River. Using the Howlett's Farm battery, now completed and named Battery Dantzler, as the anchor on his left, Beauregard established a fortified line across the neck of Bermuda Hundred down to the Appomattox River on his right. Butler chose not to challenge Beauregard's line and stayed "bottled up" in Bermuda Hundred. Drewry's Bluff would not be threatened by land for the remainder of the war.

The day after Butler's landing, the James River Squadron received a new commander, Captain John K. Mitchell. Mitchell, commander of the defeated Confederate naval forces at New Orleans in 1862 and currently chief of the navy's Office of Orders and Detail, had succeeded French Forrest. He immediately faced two major threats.

First, with Butler moving along the southside of the James, a foray upriver to support him, by the Federal James River Flotilla, seemed inevitable. At three in the morning on May 5, Federal vessels had departed Newport News, Virginia, on just such a mission. But their ascent upriver was slow and cautious because of the threat posed by Confederate torpedoes or submarine batteries, known today as mines. The threat was real; in August 1863 the USS *Commodore Barney* had been blown up by a torpedo on the James River.

Commander Hunter Davidson's Submarine Battery Service was indeed waiting for the Federal ships. But slaves had alerted the Yankees to the locations of some of Davidson's shore stations for detonating the electric torpedoes hidden in the river, and as the flotilla advanced, ships bombarded the riverbanks, dragged the river with hooks, and landed parties of U.S. Marines to seek out and destroy these torpedo-detonating stations.

At Deep Bottom, where the James makes a sharp bend, Acting Master Peter N. Smith of the Submarine Battery Service, along with Jervies Johnson and John Britton, avoided detection and watched and waited for an opportunity to strike. On May 6, the USS *Mackinaw* and the smaller converted ferryboats *Commodore Jones* and *Commodore Morris*, preceded by even smaller vessels dragging for torpedoes, came into view of the Deep Bottom station. Despite orders to remain well clear of and behind the boats dragging for torpedoes, Lieutenant Thomas F. Wade of the *Commodore Jones* disobeyed and inadvertently placed his ship directly over one of Smith's "infernal machines." Smith crossed the wires leading from a galvanic battery to the weapon and watched in awe as hundreds of pounds of gunpowder did its work and the *Jones* "absolutely crumbled to pieces—dissolved as it were in mid-air, enveloped by the falling spray, mud, water, and smoke."[57]

At least sixty-nine sailors died in the blast, and Federal retribution was swift. Marines and sailors searching the Confederate-occupied left bank spotted John Britton running along the opposite shore and shot him dead. Crossing over, they quickly captured Smith and Johnson and interrogated them as to the locations of the river's torpedo defenses. Even when placed in the bow of the lead ship to ensure he would be the first casualty should a torpedo be hit, Smith refused to cooperate. Johnson, however, succumbed to the pressure and revealed the locations of several devices. The Federals continued upriver, but after the destruction of the *Commodore Jones* did so even more slowly.

On May 7 the advance slowed even more when the gunboat *Shawsheen* was ambushed and destroyed by a roving Confederate artillery battery. Shocked by the rapid losses of the *Jones* and *Shawsheen*, Admiral Samuel P.

Lee, superintending the navy's operations in support of Butler, informed the general on May 14 after the flotilla reached the bend in the river known as Trent's Reach where the right flank of the Army of the James lay, that unless Butler advanced and secured the southside of the river, Lee could advance no farther. But Butler was soon to be "bottled up" in Bermuda Hundred, and by early June the Federal navy gave up on any further advance and went over to the defensive, placing obstructions in the river at Trent's Reach between themselves and Mitchell's squadron, which left the river between there and Drewry's Bluff a watery no-man's land.

The glacial pace of the Federal flotilla gave Mitchell time to deal with his second major problem—a lack of manpower. To oppose the James River Flotilla's four monitors and over a dozen wooden gunboats, Mitchell initially had eight operational warships—one ironclad, the *Richmond*; six wooden gunboats; and the *Patrick Henry* with her four guns. In mid-May the long-delayed ironclads *Virginia II* and *Fredericksburg* also joined the squadron.

The addition of these two crew-hungry warships to the squadron aggravated an already critical shortage of officers and men. Soldiers from Lee's army and sailors from Drewry's Bluff were pressed into service and Mitchell was promised several hundred of the 1,200 men whose transfer from the army to the navy had been ordered back in March. Despite these efforts, by early May the two new ironclads were still undermanned and Mitchell was forced to cast about for other sources. One of these sources was the *Patrick Henry*.

Though technically not part of his squadron, the school ship's compliment of experienced officers, men, and enthusiastic midshipmen was too valuable for Mitchell to ignore. On May 10 Mitchell requested that the navy department transfer eleven sailors from the school ship to the squadron. One week later he requested the services of three midshipmen. Mitchell also needed a captain for the *Richmond* to replace Commander Robert B. Pegram, who had been transferred to command of the new *Virginia II*, and drafted Superintendent Parker as the ironclad's new captain. Parker took with him Acting Midshipmen George A. Joiner, Richard C. Slaughter, Henry H. Tyson, and Willie Wilson. Lieutenant Billups commanded the *Patrick Henry* in Parker's absence.

Parker was not the only academy officer to be pressed into service. Lieutenant Hall was assigned to command of the gunboat *Drewry* on May 19. Two days later he was reassigned, along with Lieutenant Oscar Johnston, to the *Virginia II* accompanied by Acting Midshipmen Clarence Cary, Algernon Doak,

John B. Northup, Roger Pinckney, Henry H. Scott, and Daniel B. Talbot. Boatswain Andrew Blackie was also transferred from the *Patrick Henry* to the *Virginia II*. Assistant Surgeon W. J. Addison and Assistant Paymaster William M. Ladd left the school ship to join the crew of the *Fredericksburg*. The reefers were also used aboard the squadron's gunboats: Frank Morehead and Thomas Pinckney on the *Nansemond*, Franklin B. Dornin and Paul Gibbs on the *Roanoke*, and Ferdinand Hunter aboard the *Hampton*. Other midshipmen were sent to man the guns at Drewry's Bluff as well as a battery on the Mechanicsville Pike three miles from Richmond.

The summer of 1864 saw the middies doing "more fighting than studying" as "constant drafts were made upon the school."[58] Those remaining aboard the school ship assisted in laying torpedoes and patrolling the river and took part in "several interesting skirmishes with . . . Federal sharpshooters."[59] The reefers tried with varying degrees of success to balance the call of duty with the call of the books. "I have been continuously engaged lately between guard boat duty and my studies," one reefer reported to the homefolk.[60]

Prior to Butler's containment at Bermuda Hundred, Secretary Mallory pressured a reluctant Mitchell to strike a blow with his ironclads against the Federal flotilla. To do so a path large enough to allow the passage of the deep-draft ironclads had to first be cleared through the Confederate's own obstructions at Drewry's Bluff. Army engineers under Captain Charles T. Mason began the job, and on May 15 Mitchell sent Parker in the *Richmond* to gauge the engineers' progress. Parker reported that none of the ironclads could pass except at high water and he identified to Mason the additional work necessary to clear a more usable passage through the obstructions.

Not until May 23 did Mitchell get all of his ironclads through the obstructions and not until June 21 did he attack the Federals. The strike took the form of a long-range bombardment of the Federal vessels at Trent's Reach from an anchorage almost two miles away, beyond the effective range of the Confederate guns. A disgusted Parker, whose *Richmond* had entangled her propeller in her own broken steering chain and could not take part in the operation, characterized it as "a *fiasco*."[61]

On June 25, Mitchell was directed to return Boatswain Blackie and all of the midshipmen serving with the squadron to the *Patrick Henry*. He protested the order, complaining, "The loss of these officers to the squadron will be seriously felt, as the vessels are now deficient in watch officers to take charge of the deck."[62]

Mitchell was also ordered to return to the school ship the ship's cutter and a "metallic boat" requisitioned from it. Mitchell was displeased with this order also, explaining to the Navy Department that the squadron lacked a sufficient number of small boats for guard duty and that the *Patrick Henry*'s boats were "engaged in important examinations and reconnoissances [*sic*] near the enemy."[63] Whereas he had great need of them, he could "see no special necessity or use for such boats to the *Patrick Henry*."[64]

It is not known whether Mitchell managed to hold on to the boats, but he did lose Blackie and the midshipmen. By July Parker and enough of the faculty were reassembled on the school ship to conduct the midyear examinations. On July 30, the Navy Department published a special order with the names of twenty-six graduates, among them William Clayton, Willie Wilson, Dan Lee, and William B. Sinclair, Jr.[65]

Assignments for some of the newly passed midshipmen quickly followed. Clayton headed for Savannah and the gunboat *Pee Dee*. Willie Wilson received orders on August 3 to report aboard the CSS *Virginia II*. Dan Lee went to the cruiser CSS *Chickamauga*, and William B. Sinclair, Jr., set off to join the crew of the cruiser *Florida*, an assignment from which he never returned.

In September 1864 the Federal advance along the northside of the James resulted in the battle at Fort Harrison witnessed by Jimmy Morgan and his mates.[66] The proximity of the Federals now made the *Patrick Henry*'s position "not a good one for students," reported Clifton Breckinridge, "so we have moved nearly up to Richmond."[67] For some time thereafter the school ship divided its time between anchorages near the pontoon bridge at Wilton's Farm a short distance upriver from Drewry's and at Rocketts before finally settling in at the latter place.

The excitement of Richmond was now only a stone's throw away and visits to the city were authorized, but by late 1864 the capital was war-weary, "growing rusty, dilapidated," and assuming "a war-torn appearance."[68] Money and craftsmen were scarce and when "a plank fell off or a screw got loose, or a gate fell from its hinges, or a bolt gave way, or a lock was broken, it was most likely to remain for a time unrepaired."[69]

The academic program that had been so frequently interrupted that summer was reintroduced, but another problem cropped up: illness. A sickness of uncertain cause that began in the summer became widespread and continued to affect the school ship as well as the other vessels on the James. "There is but few of my class left on board," a midshipman observed on June 9, "as most of them have been sent down to the hospital."[70] By August, 226 men aboard the James River Squadron's vessels, not including the *Patrick Henry*, were ill and 157 of those were in the hospital. Between July and September, 464 men were admitted to the Richmond Naval Hospital and 13 of them died there.

Captain Mitchell attributed the rampant sickness to a lack of fresh vegetables and unhealthy shipboard conditions, particularly on the notoriously uncomfortable ironclads. The navy's Chief Surgeon Spotswood diagnosed the illness as malaria caused by the river's low water level. Acting Midshipman Morgan, a Louisianan and well acquainted with malaria, disagreed with the doctor's diagnosis. The malady was not, in his opinion, "fashionable 'malaria,' but regular old-time chills and fever, which first made the agonizing tremors pass through the frame and the teeth chatter and rattle, the chill only to be allayed by the heat of a burning fever, which always followed it."[71]

Most of the students, with the exception of some from the "alligator states" of the Deep South, suffered from this illness and many were also "weakened from chronic dysentery brought on by the bad food they had to eat."[72] Surgeon Spotswood suggested that the sailors be given their spirit ration with their morning coffee as a prophylaxis against the "effects of the damp and chilling draughts, so prevalent on all fresh water courses and malarial regions at the dawn of day."[73]

By autumn the interference with learning caused by the levies of midshipmen for Mitchell's squadron had abated, though those attributable to sickness continued. In late October, however, two events occurred that shook Mitchell's confidence. At dawn on October 22 while on patrol the squadron was ambushed by a newly completed Federal battery on Cox Hill. The fort's three thirty-pounder and four twenty-pounder Parrott rifled cannon caught the CSS *Drewry* and hit her sixteen times before she could move out of range. The *Virginia II* and *Fredericksburg* had their smokestacks riddled and the casemate roof of the latter was damaged.

The other October surprise was even more alarming. On October 27, Lieutenant William B. Cushing of the Federal navy led a daring torpedo-boat attack on the CSS *Albemarle* in North Carolina and succeeded in sinking her. The risk posed by these torpedo boats—a technology pioneered by the Confederate navy—unsettled Mitchell and he sought every means to bolster his defenses against these small, deadly craft. Mitchell again turned to the *Patrick*

Henry for resources and asked Parker to turn over the school ship's launch and boat howitzer for use as a torpedo boat destroyer. Parker referred the request to Secretary Mallory, who replied to Mitchell on November 8: "Upon conferring with Lieutenant Commanding Parker, he informs me that the launch is required for teaching the acting midshipmen boat and howitzer exercise. Under the circumstances the Department is constrained to decline to comply with your request, and hopes that you will be able to make other arrangements to accomplish the end in view."[74] Mallory would protect his school even against the combat requirements of his operational commanders.

By December 16 Parker was ready to move the school ship back to Drewry's Bluff and requested that Mitchell furnish him with a pilot. It was now Mitchell's turn to say no: "We are short of pilots, and, as we are liable to be called upon suddenly to make a movement down the river at night, I am unwilling to let them leave the squadron, except during the day."[75] Parker abandoned his plan to relocate the school ship for the time being and the *Patrick Henry* was still tied up at Rocketts for the midshipman's hop on December 28.

December brought bitter cold, snow, and examinations. Approximately twenty-two midshipmen made up this class, which turned out to be the last to graduate from the Confederate States Naval Academy.[76] Ten failed to graduate.[77] One of those who failed was Olly Harrison, who in October had "great hopes of passing & taking a good number in December."[78] Among those "promoted to the dignity of passed midshipman" was Jimmy Morgan.[79] Morgan was first sent to "the perfect inferno" of Battery Semmes and then on to Battery Brooke, where he reported on February 3, 1865.[80]

As 1864 drew to a close, the worth of and need for the Confederate States Naval Academy was unquestioned, at least by Secretary Mallory. Earlier in the year Mallory proposed to President Jefferson Davis increasing the number of acting midshipmen to 150, since the estimated 53 graduates per year, given the current authorized number of midshipmen, were "insufficient to meet the wants of the service present or prospective."[81] He also continued to lament the need for the students to divide their time between active service and the school ship. "A small expenditure will enable us to place the whole number of midshipmen authorized by law under instruction at the school, . . . " Mallory explained to President Davis. "The erection of a few cabins at Drewry's Bluff, in addition to those now in use there will be sufficient to meet this object."[82]

Legislation to grant Mallory's wishes was passed by the Confederate Congress in December, but, inexplicably, was vetoed by President Davis.

Despite the President's lack of support, Mallory was pleased with the school and its students and told Davis so. "The system of instruction conforms, as nearly as practicable, to that of most approved naval schools," and the reefers themselves were due much praise, in Mallory's opinion, particularly after the frequent calls for their services in 1864.[83] "Though but 14 to 18 years of age, they eagerly seek every opportunity presented for engaging in hazardous enterprises," Mallory reported to Davis, "and those who are sent upon them uniformly exhibit good discipline, conduct, and courage."[84]

5

✦✧✦✧✦

Watchword: "Guard the Treasure"

"IT WAS A TERRIBLE DAY ON THE WATER YESTERDAY," Commander John McIntosh Kell, former executive officer of the commerce raider *Alabama* and newly appointed captain of CSS *Richmond*, reported to his wife on January 1, 1865, owing to "a driving snow storm" having swept the river.[1] The cold, wet winter of 1864 had carried through to the new year and Passed Midshipman James Morris Morgan remembered it as "intensely cold" with snow "three to six inches in depth . . . constantly on the ground."[2]

The weather was as miserable as the military situation of the Confederacy was desperate. Atlanta and Savannah were gone; Wilmington, Mobile, and Charleston were soon to follow. The remnant of the Confederate Army of Tennessee was running through South Carolina trying to avoid a pitched battle with Major General William T. Sherman's overwhelming forces. Lee was trapped by Lieutenant General Ulysses S. Grant in Petersburg, a city whose capture would make Richmond untenable as the capital. Morale in the naval forces along the James was understandably deteriorating, but defeat still did not seem possible to the younger officers. "[W]e men in the trenches fought, shivered, and starved outside [Richmond]," recalled Passed Midshipman Morgan, "and danced and made merry whenever we were allowed to come within its limits, little dreaming that the end was so near."[3]

The weather made normally unpleasant duties almost unbearable. Acting Midshipman Hubbard T. Minor, who returned to the school ship in early January to complete his studies when Savannah's capture in December deprived him of his station, stood his first night watch on the *Patrick Henry* soon after his return and afterward had to dry his "feet & socks which I had gotten rather went [wet] on watch & my overcoat."[4] It had been, he concluded, "quite a disagreeable day."[5]

Despite the weather, the academic program of the school ship was in full operation after the distractions of the summer. Boatswain Andrew Blackie lectured the reefers on seamanship; the commandant, Lieutenant Benjamin Loyall, held evening lectures; and small arms, great-gun, broadsword, and small-boat exercises were conducted. Even though suffering from his "bowels being out of order," a malady for which he treated himself with opium, Minor spent most of January laboring over algebra, trigonometry, mathematics, and drawing in preparation for his February examinations.[6]

Notwithstanding the cold that gripped the river, Commander John K. Mitchell was feeling heat, courtesy of Secretary Mallory. The winter snows and rain had caused the James to rise, and on January 15, in a driving rainstorm, Lieutenant Charles W. "Savez" Read, commander of the James River Squadron's torpedo boats, slipped down to Trent's Reach and discovered that the Federal obstructions had been swept away by the river's powerful current, now reinforced by heavy rains and an early snowmelt. Fortuitously, many of the Federal gunboats usually on the river had been withdrawn to support an amphibious assault on Fort Fisher, near Wilmington, North Carolina.

Mallory saw opportunity and was convinced that the time had come for Mitchell to move his squadron downriver and batter its way to City Point, the huge supply depot feeding Grant's army at Petersburg. "I deem the opportunity a favorable one for striking a blow at the enemy," Mallory wrote to Mitchell. "If we can block the river at or below City Point, Grant might be compelled to evacuate his position."[7] Any effort that might loosen Grant's death grip on Petersburg and Lee's army was, Mallory explained, "a movement of the first importance to the country, and one which should be accomplished if possible."[8]

But Mitchell hesitated, and when he had not started downriver by January 20, Mallory scolded him: "You have an opportunity, I am convinced, rarely presented to a naval officer, and one which may lead to the most glorious results to your country. I deplore that you did not start immediately after the freshet, and have deplored the loss of every day since."[9] A chastened Mitchell finally gave orders to his captains to be prepared to move downriver the night of January 23.

William A. Parker, commander of the Federal vessels on the James, was as reluctant as Mitchell to engage in a potentially decisive battle with only the double-turreted monitor *Onondaga* and eight wooden gunboats to oppose Mitchell's three ironclads and their consorts. But the choice was not Commander Parker's to make; on January 21 he received a warning that the Rebels were on the way. Even so, Parker neither increased his vigilance nor monitored the condition of the obstructions at Trent's Reach.

At 6 P.M. the vessels of the James River Squadron got up steam and began to move downriver in what was to be the squadron's final effort to clear the river of the enemy. Mitchell's force consisted of the ironclads *Fredericksburg* (leading the convoy), *Richmond*, and *Virginia II*; the wooden gunboats *Hampton*, *Beaufort*, *Nansemond*, and *Torpedo*; and the torpedo boats *Hornet*, *Wasp*, and *Scorpion*. Two hours after the fleet got under way, alert Yankee gunners in Fort Brady spotted it moving through the gloom of night. The fort's big guns lobbed about twenty-five rounds at the dark and silent ships before they floated out of range, and though no damage was done, the noise alerted the garrisons of Batteries Wilcox, Parsons, Spofford, and Sawyer, farther downstream.

Around 9 P.M. Lieutenant Francis E. Shepperd brought his *Fredericksburg* up to the western edge of the Trent's Reach obstructions. "Savez" Read took *Scorpion* on a reconnaissance trip up to the obstructions through a steady stream of musket and mortar fire from shore. Read determined that with some minor clearing a passage through the obstructions was possible and so informed Shepperd and Mitchell. Mitchell joined Shepperd aboard *Fredericksburg*, but the impetuous Shepperd butted his way through before Read had a chance to finish clearing the way, damaging his ship in the process. Lieutenant James D. Wilson's *Hampton* followed the ironclad through.

The way to City Point and its fat warehouses, busy wharves, and vulnerable supply ships was open. At quarter till two in the morning, Mitchell returned to his flagship, *Virginia II*, to lead the remainder of his command through the obstructions, but to his "inexpressible mortification" he found her aground.[10] For three hours *Nansemond* and *Beaufort* labored to free her, but things went from bad to worse when Captain John M. Kell reported his *Richmond* also aground.

The whole operation quickly deteriorated into a black comedy as the *Drewry* grounded herself while assisting the *Richmond*, the torpedo boat

Scorpion ran aground while aiding the flagship, and the torpedo boat *Hornet* suffered the same fate while coming to the assistance of the *Scorpion*.

Once daylight broke Mitchell's grounded vessels would be sitting ducks for Federal gunners, and since he could not support them he reluctantly recalled the *Fredericksburg* and *Hampton* and sent them to an anchorage beneath the guns of Battery Dantzler.

Dawn presented the Federal artillerists with a choice of targets. The grounded *Drewry* was blasted first, and at 7:10 A.M. she blew up, the explosion killing two men aboard the nearby *Scorpion* and sending the little torpedo boat careening downstream toward the Federal obstructions, where she was captured. The *Richmond* and *Virginia II* were "pelted . . . for over six hours," Kell reported to his wife afterward; the Yankee gunners did "little or no damage to this ship, but succeeded in cutting up the Virginia considerably."[11]

As the two battered ironclads, *Richmond* and *Virginia II*, finally floated free, Federal Commander Parker belatedly appeared with the monitor *Onondaga*, the gunboats *Hunchback* and *Massasoit*, and the torpedo boat *Spuyten Duyvil*. The monitor's fifteen-inch guns opened fire at a distance of a half a mile, slightly damaging *Virginia II* and *Richmond*.

Mitchell and his captains were up for another try, but night revealed a powerful Drummond searchlight ashore, which would rob the Confederates of the cover of darkness and blind the vessels' pilots. At a council of war convened by Mitchell at around 10:30 P.M., he and his captains voted to return upstream.

With that, the "series of misfortunes" that was the last advance of the James River Squadron came to a merciful end.[12] Passed Midshipman Jimmy Morgan at Battery Semmes had watched the squadron go downriver and sadly observed them return: "[O]ur ironclads, on which we had based such high hopes, fired their last shot. The end was near."[13]

The midshipmen aboard the school ship were undoubtedly aware of this major effort made by the squadron. In fact, several acting midshipmen were still in service aboard the squadron's ironclads.[14] Curiously, Midshipman Minor did not mention the battle in his diary, but then he was ill with dysentery at the time and was focusing on an event of greater importance to him than the fate of the squadron—his examinations.

Minor was examined on February 2, 1865, and afterward felt confident that he would be made a passed midshipman in June. He resigned himself to remaining at the school ship until then, despite having earlier contemplated paying a visit to Secretary of War James A. Seddon and requesting "a commission as Capt of light Artillery & orders to join the Trans Mississippi dept & get my Company."[15] At the time a return to the army also recommended itself to young Minor because of the effect such a promotion might have on a certain Miss Stendod: "how much she would think of me if I were the Capt in Artillery."[16]

Later that month, a new commandant reported for duty on the school ship. Lieutenant James H. Rochelle, a veteran of the Mexican War and an 1848 graduate of Annapolis, formerly commander of the Charleston ironclad *Palmetto State*, was ordered to the *Patrick Henry* after the fall of Wilmington, North Carolina, where he had commanded a 300-man detachment of Charleston sailors in defense of the city.

Not long after the failure at Trent's Reach, the James River Squadron received a new commander, Captain Raphael Semmes, the daring former commander of the very successful commerce raider CSS *Alabama*, now promoted to rear admiral. But the initiative had been surrendered to the reinforced Federal James River Flotilla, and not even the legendary Semmes was going to be able to get it back. The naval officers on the river knew it was only a matter of time before the Federals brought overwhelming force against them.

It was probably with regret and some apprehension that Superintendent William Parker sat in his cabin on the *Patrick Henry* on February 28 writing to Secretary Mallory. "I respectfully desire to know," he wrote, "whether in the event of the evacuation of the city of Richmond by our Forces it is the intention of the Department to remove the Naval School to some other locality."[17]

The end seemed near and Superintendent Parker needed to make some plans for the future of his command. Relocating the school, he pointed out to Secretary Mallory, would not be too difficult, since "most of the material belonging to it can be taken away in one Canal boat and six freight cars—this includes provisions for two months and some of the rigging of the ship."[18] Finding suitable facilities away from the advancing Yankees would be the primary challenge, but Parker thought that "by sending an officer in the direction in which it is proposed to move I think it very probable that a convenient building or buildings can be secured."[19] Parker believed that a move toward Lynchburg, Virginia, or Charlotte, North Carolina, would be advisable, but the direction taken ultimately "would be for the Military authorities to decide."[20]

Mallory forwarded the superintendent's letter to the chairman of the Senate Naval Affairs Committee, Senator Albert Gallatin Brown of Mississippi, on

March 2, 1865, and invited the committee's "attention to the expediency of providing for the removal of the School in the event of our evacuation of Richmond."[21] The secretary explained that the chief cost of the move would be that for the housing and subsistence of the midshipmen and faculty, but the money so invested would enable the academy to "give to the country a class of educated officers, not only essential to naval service, but whose ability . . . will be felt by the country generally."[22]

Mallory was determined to save his school and was unrealistically optimistic concerning its continuation in the event that Richmond fell. Even Parker later noted, "It was strange how Mr. Mallory clung to the idea of keeping up the Naval School, even if Richmond had to be abandoned."[23]

With Mallory's approval and Congress's authorization, Parker sent Lieutenant Charles Graves on a quick reconnaissance through North and South Carolina and Georgia in search of a suitable location. His report was discouraging, but not surprising, since after his initial optimism, Parker had conceded that Sherman's army advancing through the Carolinas and Federal cavalry raiders elsewhere would "make it difficult to find a quiet spot."[24] Lieutenant Graves's report confirmed for Parker the hopelessness of the situation and further convinced him that the loss of Richmond would mean the fall of the Confederacy and the destruction of his academy.

The fighting around Petersburg was not going well for the Confederates and after the pounding taken by the James River Squadron at Trent's Reach it was expected that the Federal flotilla would soon attempt to force its way past Drewry's Bluff. To help counter this threat, on March 28 Parker was ordered to prepare the *Patrick Henry* for scuttling in the James River obstructions. Parker rented a tobacco warehouse in Richmond at the corner of Twenty-fourth and Franklin streets to house the midshipmen and the school's supplies and equipment, should the destruction of the school ship become necessary.[25]

Despite the widespread belief that Richmond was soon to fall, the naval forces on the river were inexplicably taken by surprise when the end did come. On April 1, 1865, Superintendent Parker left the school ship, now anchored at Rocketts, for a long-delayed visit to Richmond. He headed first for Stephen Mallory's home, where he found the secretary "walking to and fro on the pavement in front of his house, with a revolver in his hand."[26] Parker assumed for some reason that the gentleman had been target shooting and did not ask why he was armed. Parker did ask for permission to spend the night in the city, and

School ship USS *Somers* with the bodies of two of the alleged mutineers hanging from her yardarm. *U.S. Naval Historical Center*

294   HARPER'S WEEKLY.   [MAY 11, 1861.

References.—1. Catholic College.—2. City Hotel.—3. Battery.—4. Capitol.—5. Midshipmen's Quarters.—6. *Constitution.*—7. Recitation Hall.—8. Chapel.—9. Observatory.—10. Officers' Quarters.—11. St. John's (Episcopal) College.— 12. Hospital.—13. Monument—the same that was in front of the Capitol at Washington.—14. Naval Monument.

USS *Constitution* anchored off of the United States Naval Academy, Annapolis, Maryland. "Old Ironsides" was used as a school ship and evacuated the academy to its wartime home at Newport, Rhode Island. *U.S. Naval Academy*

CSS *Patrick Henry* prior to her conversion to a school ship. *U.S. Naval Historical Center*

Sketch of school ship *Patrick Henry* by Midshipman John Thomas Scharf. *U.S. Naval Historical Center*

Confederate Secretary of the Navy Stephen R. Mallory, chief proponent of the Confederate States Naval Academy. *Library of Congress*

Students reef sails and attend lectures aboard Charleston, South Carolina's school ship *Lodebar*. *Stern*, The Confederate Navy, A Pictorial History

An 1867 photo of Commander John Mercer Brooke, whose Office of Ordnance and Hydrography oversaw the operation of the naval academy and its school ship. *Virginia Military Institute*

LIEUTENANT COMMANDER WILLIAM HARWAR PARKER,
CONFEDERATE STATES NAVY.

Lieutenant William Harwar Parker, superintendent of the Confederate States Naval Academy and commanding officer of the school ship *Patrick Henry. U.S. Naval Historical Center*

Lieutenant James H. Rochelle, last commandant of the school ship *Patrick Henry*. *Scharf,* History of the Confederate States Navy

Belgian Gustave Adolphus "Gus" Peple taught French and Spanish to midshipmen on the *Patrick Henry*. This is a previously unpublished photograph. *Chuck Peple*

Captain John Taylor Wood led an expedition including ten midshipmen from the *Patrick Henry* in the capture of the USS *Underwriter*. *U.S. Naval Historical Center*

Navy Surgeon Daniel B. Conrad served as surgeon to the *Underwriter* expedition and attended to the fatally wounded Midshipman Palmer Saunders. *U.S. Naval Historical Center*

Appointment of Arthur H. Beall, son of Confederate Marine Corps Commandant Lloyd Beall, as a midshipman in the Confederate States Navy with instructions to report to the school ship *Patrick Henry*. *National Archives*

Rockett's Navy Yard, Richmond, Virginia, after its capture by Federal forces. Graves's Yard is on the far bank, and one of the wrecks visible along the river bank in the left background is that of the school ship *Patrick Henry. Library of Congress*

Mallory, citing good news from Lee at Petersburg, gave his consent, this despite the fact that Admiral Semmes, who had visited Mallory earlier that day, saw clear evidence of government departments "packing for a move!"[27]

Parker passed a restful night in the city and returned to his ship on Sunday morning, April 2. Soon after the usual Sunday muster and inspection of all hands, Parker received a communication from Mallory: "Have the corps of midshipmen, with the proper officers, at the Danville depot today at 6 P.M., the commanding officer to report to the Quartermaster General of the Army."

Parker directed Commandant Rochelle to have the ship's cook prepare three days' cooked rations for each reefer and march them to the Danville railroad depot at the foot of Fourteenth Street; Parker would remain behind to take care of the ship. Because of his conversation with Mallory just the day before and the fact that he and the midshipmen were expecting orders that they were to be "armed and sent to the front" as infantry at anytime, Parker had no reason to suspect that Mallory's order would result in anything more than a few days' deployment.[28] Nevertheless, the superintendent decided to make his way to the Navy Department offices in Richmond's Mechanic's Institute to receive more details. It was while en route along Main Street that he first heard from an excited government clerk that the capital was being evacuated!

Parker hurried back to the *Patrick Henry* and issued orders for all hands to assemble at the Danville depot at six o'clock. He placed Lieutenant Billups in charge of ten men and gave him orders to destroy the ship and then set out once again for the Navy Department, where he finally saw Mallory, who confirmed that the government had given orders to evacuate. He was also surprised to learn that his students had been selected to guard the gold and silver of the Confederate and Virginia treasuries, which were being taken to a safe haven—a cargo with a total value of $777,000.[29]

In the chaos of Richmond's fall and the abandonment of the school ship, the Confederate States Naval Academy began to dissolve. All thought of relocating the equipment and academic materials was abandoned and some of the midshipmen became separated or drifted away. Several were in the hospital. Hubbard Minor had been sent there that very morning after having "suffered for nearly two weeks with dysentery all of my passages being bloody[.]"[30]

Recent alumni were also caught up in the retreat. Secretary Mallory himself assigned Passed Midshipman Morgan and Midshipman J. A. Carter to the escort of First Lady Varina Davis. The detail had an added bonus for Morgan—

his fiancée, Helen Trenholm, was accompanying Mrs. Davis. Passed Midshipman Jefferson Davis Howell, posted to Charleston until its capture in February, was assigned to Semmes's brigade with a commission as a lieutenant of artillery. Passed Midshipman Willie Wilson, stationed at a shore battery at Chaffin's Bluff, was placed into a hastily organized naval infantry force made up of shore battery personnel and commanded by Captain John R. Tucker.

The specie of the treasury was crated and awaiting the midshipmen when they arrived at the Danville depot. Parker was told that over $500,000 in gold and silver was in the boxes, although he never saw it personally. In addition to Parker, Lieutenants Rochelle, Peek, Armistead, McGuire, Graves, Armstrong, and Huck and Paymaster John Wheless and Mr. Sanxey accompanied the reefers.[31] From now on the midshipmen's watchword would be "Guard the treasure."[32]

At the depot confusion and chaos jointly reigned. Both the President's train and the treasure train were "packed—not only inside, but on top, in the platforms, on the engine,—*everywhere*, in fact, where standing room could be found."[33] To prevent the crowd at the depot from rushing the trains, Parker placed midshipmen at the doors of the building with orders to bar unauthorized entry. Undeterred, many tried to talk their way into the depot and onto the trains and Mallory noted with some amusement those "artful dodgers" who tried to pass the guards "upon the ground of their vast importance to some great public interest."[34]

Even a slave dealer with fifty shackled slaves tried to board a train with his "inventory." A midshipman's bayonet turned him back and, without transport, he was forced to liquidate his assets by unchaining the slaves, who promptly disappeared into the city's crowded streets.

Word had spread that gold was on the train, and greed outweighed panic in the minds of some. Although no overt assault on the treasure was made, the grim-faced midshipmen were credited with deterring a mob from attempting to seize it.[35]

At eleven o'clock a dejected Jefferson Davis, accompanied by his recently appointed secretary of war, John C. Breckinridge, who had come to see him off, took his seat, and the first train pulled out of the station heading south toward Danville, Virginia.

The treasure train's departure was delayed for several hours. Secretary Breckinridge and Superintendent Parker spent some very apprehensive hours waiting in the depot for the train to depart, as "large numbers of ruffians" sucked up the government whiskey dumped in the gutters and the "screams and yells of the drunken demons . . . and the fires which were now breaking out in every direction, made it seem as though hell itself had broken loose."[36]

Finally the train pulled out, only to stop across the river at Manchester. From here the midshipmen could see "the smoke of the burning city . . . rising up in dense columns."[37] After a short delay the train slowly steamed on, leaving the blazing city behind.

On the river the destruction continued. Despite having noticed the preparations for an evacuation while in Richmond, Rear Admiral Semmes on his flagship anchored at Chaffin's Bluff was nonetheless surprised to receive orders on April 2 to destroy the ships of the squadron and join Lee's army with his crews armed and equipped as infantry. Preparing the fleet for destruction and turning sailors into soldiers took some time, since "arms had to be served out, provisions gotten out of the hold, and broken into such packages, as the sailor's could carry. Hammocks had to be unlashed, and the blankets taken out, and rolled up as compactly as possible. Haversacks and canteens had to be improvised."[38]

Semmes decided to move the fleet to the Drewry's Bluff obstructions for destruction. There, between one and two o'clock on the morning of April 3, the "chained and sulky bulldogs" of the James River Squadron were fired.[39] The resulting explosions scattered "fiery fragments to the four winds of heaven," according to a witness, and were plainly heard by Superintendent Parker, waiting at the depot.[40] The effect upon the inhabitants of Richmond was frightening. One resident recalled, "[T]he very foundations of the city were shaken; windows were shattered more than two miles from where the gunboats were exploded, and the frightened inhabitants imagined the place was being furiously bombarded."[41]

The squadron's remaining wooden gunboats carried the ironclads' crews upriver to Manchester. As they passed by Rocketts they noticed the *Patrick Henry* burning furiously in the river opposite C. Y. Morris's sugar refinery at the foot of Louisiana Street.[42]

Among the reefers left behind in the Bellview Block naval hospital were Hubbard Minor and sixteen-year-old John W. Harris.[43] The hospitalized midshipmen received notification of neither Richmond's evacuation nor their comrades' new orders, but on April 2 they nevertheless knew something was up by the anxious looks of the medical officers. Around four that afternoon Harris noticed that "a midshipman, coming into the ward to see a sick comrade . . . was armed and equipped as an infantry soldier instead of the dainty dress of the Confederate 'Middy.'"[44] When questioned about his new uniform, the sailor-turned-soldier explained that the entire corps of midshipmen had been so equipped earlier that afternoon and that a naval brigade had been formed. He said nothing of their orders to report to the Danville depot.

By that evening rumors that the President and his cabinet had fled the city and that the midshipmen had abandoned the school ship spread throughout the wards. At eight o'clock Harris and two friends commandeered the hospital's ambulance and visited the Franklin Street warehouse. They found it empty except for "the mahogany table and the silver table service of the wardroom, watched over by an old boatswain's mate, and, sitting in a solemn state at the bottom of it, drinking and eating crackers, . . . the second lieutenant."[45]

Harris expressed his concern at being left behind to the lieutenant, who laughed and said that there had been no evacuation; the naval school had merely been transferred to Chapel Hill, North Carolina. Come back in the morning, he suggested, and he would take Harris and his companions along with two other middies to Chapel Hill.

That same Sunday evening, Hubbard Minor discovered that the midshipmen had departed for Danville and he decided to make his way to the depot early on Monday. Minor packed what he could carry, sent off a trunk for safekeeping, cashed a draft for $300, and went to bed.

On Monday morning, Minor and Harris and his companions set out separately for the depot, but shared the same frightening experiences as they made their way through the dying city. Minor passed looted stores and burning buildings, including Warrick's huge flour mill, which "from its very bottom to high above its top was one continued sheet of flame."[46]

When Harris stepped out of the hospital onto the street it seemed to him "as if the final day of doom was upon us. . . . Stores were being broken open and rifled; dead men—shot down in the attempt to rob—were lying at intervals, while Negroes fought over barrels of provisions that had been rolled from burning warehouses."[47]

Minor crossed the river to Manchester and departed on a train from there at nine that evening, but Harris and his friends turned back at the sight of the burning Danville Railroad bridge and sought a means of escape on the city's northside. Crossing Main Street the three reefers spotted Federal cavalry coming up the street. The horseman soon overtook the apprehensive sailors, but miraculously "rode by without observing us, although we were in gorgeous full uniform, but without sidearms or accouterments, save small haversacks, in which we stored all the crackers we could get."[48]

With the help of two army officers, Harris and his friends "liberated" a locomotive that they rode until the boiler boiled dry thirty-five miles from Richmond. There, having no steam and no experienced engineer, they abandoned the engine and began to walk. Two days later Harris and his mates reached his birthplace at Mt. Solon in Virginia's Shenandoah Valley.

Minor suffered greatly on his train ride. Still plagued by dysentery, and with no toilet on board, he had to "climb on top of the cars & then down between them & stand on the joints for the connecting link of the two cars to have my passages [which] were all of blood[.]"[49] On Thursday morning, April 6, having eaten nothing except one piece of hardtack the entire trip, Minor arrived at the midshipmen's Danville encampment. He was cordially welcomed by his classmates, who had given him up for lost, and was promptly put on the binnacle list and back in the hospital.

By the time Minor arrived the middies had been camped in a grove of trees near the treasure train and its load of "things," as the boys called the assortment of boxes and kegs full of silver and gold, since the afternoon of April 3.[50] Rear Admiral Semmes and his 500 shipless sailors arrived on a train operated by ship's engineers on the night of April 4 and established a defensive perimeter around the town, relieving the midshipmen of the burden of protecting the new seat of government. More midshipmen resigned at Danville as Raphael Semmes, Jr., left the midshipmen to join his father as a major on staff, and Clifton Breckinridge also, joined the staff of his father, Secretary of War John Breckinridge, as his aide-de-camp when Breckinridge senior arrived on horseback on April 5. In addition to the corps of midshipmen and Semmes's men, a large part of the Confederacy's naval establishment were congregated at Danville, including the inimitable Paymaster James A. Semple, chief of the Office of Provisions and Clothing, who had accumulated sufficient stores to supply not only the naval forces present but the army as well. Secretary Mallory observed of several of his senior naval officers at Danville:

[They often] perched around the store upon the beef and bread barrels, some abstractly shaping strands of cords or marline into fancy
forms. . . . Others were overhauling their trunks and bags . . . at intervals calling attention to some . . . strange relic of distant lands, by
brief allusions to its history, and to 'my first cruise in the China seas,'
or to 'my cruise with old Perry to Japan,' or to 'my last cruise in the
Mediterranean with old Buchanan'.[51]

But, Mallory noted sadly, "they were generally grave and silent, . . . all
adrift upon dry land, they presented a pretty fair illustration of a 'fish out of
water' . . . their occupation as naval men . . . gone."[52] The sailors themselves
made awkward soldiers, but as Semmes—now General Semmes—observed,
"Soldiering was new to Jack; . . . he would do better by-and-by."[53]

While Davis, his cabinet, and the assembled soldiers and sailors awaited
word from Lee, now retreating from Petersburg west toward Appomattox Courthouse, Parker and his young gentlemen kept a watchful eye on the treasure. The
bullion and coins were left on the train, and although Parker believed that some
amount had been taken for the use of the government, "how much was taken, or
for whom it was taken, I never knew—it was not my business to inquire."[54]

On the sixth of April Superintendent Parker received orders to convey
the treasure to the vaults of the mint at Charlotte, North Carolina. In an audi-
ence with Mallory before his departure, the superintendent expressed his dis-
pleasure with the conduct of Treasury Secretary George Trenholm and his
senior staff. The senior treasury official traveling with Parker was only a teller,
and Parker believed that Secretary Trenholm or his assistant secretary ought
to be with the treasure. "It was their duty . . . ," he argued. "It was not a time to
be falling sick by the wayside, as some high officials were beginning to do."[55]
Trenholm had indeed been ill since leaving Richmond, and his sickness did
seem to worsen as the flight south continued; nevertheless, Parker's insinua-
tion was probably unfair.

Rebuffed, Parker, the treasure, and the teller arrived in Greensboro, North
Carolina, "a pretty little town of about 4,000 inhabitants," sometime on April 9.[56]
While in Greensboro, a nineteen-year-old midshipman, Robert Fleming, managed to lose his knapsack and continued on to Charlotte with just the clothes
"what are on my back."[57] Also at Greensboro $39,000 in silver was withdrawn
from the rolling treasury to pay General Joseph E. Johnston's soldiers.[58]

The middies left Greensboro and passed through the "beautiful town" of Salisbury, arriving at Charlotte, "another very pretty place," the evening of April 10.[59] Here Parker unloaded the "things" into the mint. Afterward the midshipmen "feasted at the leading hotels."[60]

In the city Parker's command was strengthened by Captain Tabb's company from the Charlotte navy yard, men from the "game little town of Portsmouth, Va.," lauded by the superintendent as being "true as steel."[61]

Also staying in Charlotte were First Lady Varina Davis and her escort, which included Passed Midshipman Morgan. Leaving Richmond on the Friday before the evacuation of the government, Mrs. Davis, her children, and her escort endured a slow train ride to Charlotte in cars that Morgan described as being outfitted with "lumpy seats . . . covered with dingy threadbare brownish red plush, very suggestive of the vermin [with] which it afterwards proved to be infested."[62] The journey to Charlotte took four days, and the city's welcome of the first lady was less than respectful. As news of her arrival at the train station spread, "stragglers and deserters—conscripts—the very scum of the army . . . gathered round the car in which she sat . . . [and] reviled her in the most shocking language."[63] Morgan and Colonel Burton Harrison, the President's private secretary, confronted and turned away several of the bolder hooligans on the very steps of Mrs. Davis's railroad car.

Into the midst of this confusion strode Superintendent Parker offering the services of his command for Mrs. Davis's protection. After some persuasion by Parker, she accepted his offer and the immediate threat to her safety was eliminated.

While at Charlotte, Parker attempted to make contact with Secretary Mallory, but telegraphic communications from the north had been severed by the Federal occupation of Salisbury. Parker realized that movement was the key to avoiding capture, and lacking further instructions, he decided to head south for Macon, Georgia, with the treasure and the President's family. In preparation for the journey Parker sought to draw provisions from the well-stocked naval storehouse in the city. But when he appeared at the storehouse to requisition the supplies, the bureaucratic storekeeper objected and demanded Secretary Mallory's authorization. Parker explained that this was not the time for red tape and vowed to take what he needed by force if necessary. Having made the obligatory objections for duty's sake, the storekeeper saw no need for further resistance and unlocked the gates. Details of midshipmen quickly collected large amounts of bacon, coffee, sugar, and flour. On the thirteenth, the treasure train and Mrs. Davis's party set out for Chester, South Carolina, en route to Macon.

Hubbard Minor left the hospital when his classmates departed Danville and despite his worsening sickness managed to stay with them until reaching Charlotte. By the morning of the thirteenth, however, he recognized that he could go no farther and asked a naval surgeon to issue him a certificate allowing him to remain in Charlotte. His request granted, he was admitted to Dr. John Ashby's Way Hospital Number 6. While waiting for dinner at a hotel that evening, Minor was surprised to see his brother Henry, a soldier, enter the dining room. Henry had come to Charlotte searching for his brother and arm-in-arm they walked to the hospital. Hubbard's stay was short, for by the next morning his capture by the Yankees seemingly imminent, Minor checked himself out. He could not follow his shipmates, since he "could not walk any distance whatever without fainting," so his brother led him on his own horse to his regimental encampment five miles from town to await the end.

In Danville the President and his cabinet still awaited word from Lee. Finally news arrived on the afternoon of April 9—General Robert E. Lee had surrendered the Army of Northern Virginia to Grant at Appomattox Courthouse. Captain Tucker's naval brigade had not been surrendered at Appomattox—it had been captured along with a large part of Lee's army at Saylor's Creek, Virginia, on April 6, after winning the respect of its enemies by its stout resistance.

At eleven that night, after much delay and confusion, the government train departed Danville for Greensboro, North Carolina. General Semmes's brigade was not with them, having been ordered to Greensboro earlier to reinforce Johnston. But the curtain was ringing down on the drama that was the final days of the Confederacy and no one wanted to die in the last act, so Semmes's sailors began to drift away as they marched south. "Commissioned officers," Semmes bitterly observed, "slunk away from me one by one, and became deserters! I was ashamed of my countrymen."[64] The admiral-turned-general finally surrendered what remained of the James River Squadron at Greensboro on May 1. Parker's command arrived at Chester on the evening of April 13 but found that the railroad south of Chester had been cut by the Federals. They loaded the treasure and the President's family on wagons and headed for Newberry, South Carolina. "What a distressing spectacle this train of three or four wagons, including an ambulance for the first family, hauled by broken-down and leg-weary mules, must have presented," Midshipman Morgan wondered as they rattled along, "and what must have been the apprehensions of that stately and serene woman, the wife of a President of a nation [of] Anglo-Saxons, as she sat, surrounded by her helpless children, on one of these primitive vehicles while the half-starved animals slowly dragged her over the weary miles."[65]

Midshipmen led the column as advance guard. Others followed as rearguard. The rest of the young gentlemen marched along on either side as flank guards. Parker had a total of 150 men and boys at his command and if attacked, expected to "give a good account of ourselves."[66]

Woodward Baptist Church, eight miles from Chester, served as a shelter that night. Mrs. Davis, her children, and the rest of her party slept on the floor, Parker slept in the pulpit, and those midshipmen not on guard "lay down under the trees outside, in company with the mules."[67] Before departing the next morning, Parker published orders "regulating the march, declared martial law, and made every man carry a musket."[68]

The party passed through "hilly country" and Parker overheard some of his students speculate whether "Old Parker" would break down on the march, having no horse to carry him.[69] But Parker smiled at their concern: "I had walked too many midwatches to have any fears of it."[70] The Broad River was crossed by ferry and Parker set up camp two miles on the other side, thirty miles from Newberry. The Davis family spent the night at the nearby home of Lieutenant Edward C. Means, an antebellum shipmate of the superintendent's.

Very early the next morning they were on the road again and reached Newberry around 4 P.M. "We rejoiced at the sight of a railroad again," recalled a footsore Midshipman Fleming, and Parker quickly had the army quartermaster prepare a train to take them to Abbeville, forty-five miles away.[71] The treasure and passengers were loaded aboard the cars and they reached Abbeville by midnight.

Davis and his cabinet finally reached Greensboro, after narrowly avoiding capture by Federal cavalry. No prior arrangements had been made for lodgings, and although there were many fine homes in the vicinity, Mallory observed that, fearing Federal reprisals, their "doors were closed and their 'latch-strings' pulled in against members of the retreating government."[72] President Davis was ill, as was Treasury Secretary Trenholm, and all but these two slept on the train. Food was not a problem since the navy storehouse in the city provided bread and bacon and the resourceful Paymaster Semple located luxuries such as biscuits, eggs, and coffee. Cups, plates, knives, forks, and spoons had to be borrowed and shared. Mallory complained that he had to down his coffee "scalding hot that he might not keep the venerable Adjutant-General [Samuel Cooper] waiting too long for the coveted tin cup!"[73]

The government attended to business even in flight, and in Greensboro President Davis and his cabinet met at the home of Captain John Taylor Wood with General Johnston and General Pierre G. T. Beauregard concerning the military situation. Both generals advised Davis that further resistance by their troops was futile and that good terms might be had from General Sherman for their surrender. Davis reluctantly gave his consent to the opening of negotiations with General Sherman, even though he was not optimistic of the outcome. But General Ulysses Grant had established the precedent of magnanimity in his terms for Lee, and Sherman followed suit. On April 16 the government departed Greensboro on its continuing exodus south. That night, as one American President fled, the other was assassinated while watching a play at Washington's Ford's Theater. Ten days later, on April 26, Johnston surrendered his army to Sherman at Bennett's Farm, near Durham, North Carolina.

Since news of the treasure somehow preceded them despite Parker's best efforts at secrecy, he considered it safe to remain in Abbeville only until the morning of April 19. The wagon train was re-formed with the midshipmen and Captain Tabb's men as guards and started for Washington, Georgia, en route to Macon. Mrs. Davis and her escort, however, decided to remain in Abbeville to await word of the President.

The forty-mile march to Washington took two days, and the rumors heard on the way concerning the military situation were uniformly bad. To stay ahead of the tidal wave of disaster, Parker "'lightened ship' . . . —throwing away books, stationery, and . . . Confederate money," observing, "One could have traced us by these marks, and have formed an idea of the character of the news we were receiving."[74]

The column camped just across the Savannah River on the night of the first day of their journey. The following day they marched into Washington and learned there that Macon had fallen to Major General James H. Wilson's Federal cavalry. Parker decided to change course and head for Augusta, Georgia. The treasure was once again loaded aboard railroad cars.

The treasure train departed for Augusta around the twenty-first. On the train Parker heard news of Lee's surrender, but for some reason refused to believe it and ordered Lieutenant Rochelle to find and arrest the man who was spreading this "rumor." Arriving in Augusta, Parker reported to the district commander, Brigadier General Birkett D. Fry, and Captain William Hunter, the senior naval officer.

Fry confirmed the rumors of Lee's surrender and informed Parker that Wilson's cavalry was expected in Augusta very soon and that when he arrived Fry intended to surrender the city to him without a fight. Consequently Parker did not unload the gold and silver and had the midshipmen and Tabb's men billeted in the railroad depot near the train.

In Augusta Parker found a Treasury Department official and with Fry's and Hunter's assistance, persuaded the reluctant gentleman to take charge of the treasure on behalf of his department. He finally agreed to do so, with the proviso that Parker's men continue to guard it. Parker readily agreed; he had no intention of entrusting the treasury's safety to any other command, but he was relieved to be shed of the responsibility of accounting for it.

Parker established his headquarters at a hotel near the depot and waited for instructions. Some soon arrived in the form of a telegram from Mallory advising him to disband the midshipmen. This he declined to do, since they and the treasure were in a precarious situation. A concerned Paymaster Wheless confided to Parker his belief that if Johnston surrendered "a complete collapse of the Confederacy would immediately follow" and the "thousands of people of Augusta, and the large force of soldiers employed in the arsenal and other government shops there, having no other means with which to purchase supplies, would attempt the capture of the Confederate treasure."[75] In that event, Wheless feared, the reefers and Tabb's men would be overwhelmed.

Others advised Parker that since the war was lost he ought to pay out the gold and silver to the ragged soldiers and poor townspeople before the Federals inevitably captured it. Parker ignored the fears and advice of all, reminding them that the treasure had been put in his hands for safekeeping and he would keep it safe until President Davis relieved him of that duty. Should any doubt his resolve to protect the treasure, he made it known that "if necessary, the command would be killed in the defense of it," and, further, that "his officers and men stood firmly by me" in this determination.[76]

The Confederate military situation in Georgia continued to worsen, and General Fry informed Parker that since the armistice between Johnston and Sherman, which had afforded some respite against further Federal advances, was at an end and since Wilson's men were still advancing on Augusta, it would be best for the superintendent to take his "things" and "move on."[77] Unsure where to move on to, Parker decided that since Mrs. Davis's presence at Abbeville was sure to attract the President and the rest of the government's officials to that place, they would return there.

On April 24, the treasure train departed Augusta for Washington, Georgia, and arrived there later that day. A wagon train was again formed and Mrs. Parker and Mrs. McGuire, who had most likely accompanied the party from Richmond but who had chosen to remain behind in Washington, were retrieved. As the wagons plodded along, they met Mrs. Davis and her party heading south in a "comfortable ambulance" escorted by Burton Harrison.[78] They had, however, no news of the president's whereabouts. Parker bid the first lady godspeed and continued north.

As they retraced their route to Abbeville, the responsibility for the treasure and the stress of carting it to and fro through country teeming with parolees, deserters, renegades, and Yankee raiders began to wear on Parker. While recrossing the Savannah River, he remarked to Commandant Rochelle that if he had his way he would "throw it overboard rather than be burdened with it."[79] Parker was also distressed by the ragtag condition of his young charges and the effect upon them of almost thirty days on the march. The reefers were "suffering for shoes, hats and clothing" and the responsibility for their welfare under these conditions weighed heavily upon their commander.[80]

Arriving at Abbeville around the twenty-eighth of April, Parker deposited the "things" in a warehouse on the public square. A guard was placed on the building, a strong patrol was kept in the town, and a locomotive with a full head of steam stood waiting round the clock, should escape become necessary.[81]

Paroled soldiers from Lee's army, renegades, and deserters all passed through Abbeville and many idle threats were made to seize the treasure. On May 1, however, a paroled officer warned Parker that a genuine attack on the warehouse was planned for that night. Parker considered this information reliable, so he doubled both the guard and the patrol before going to sleep on the floor of the parlor of a nearby house. Around 3 A.M. Lieutenant Peek, the officer of the guard, tapped on the parlor window. Awakened, Parker raised the sash expecting to be told that the anticipated attack had begun, but instead heard Peek say in a low voice, "Captain, the Yankees are coming."[82] A civilian from a town thirty miles away had escaped from Federal cavalry the evening before and made his way to Abbeville. The Yankees would be upon them by morning, the frightened gentleman had warned.

Buckling on his sword, Parker gathered the command and began loading the heavy boxes and barrels of treasure aboard the waiting train. By dawn it was all loaded, but Parker paced the platform grappling with the decision whether to run or not. He had just determined to leave when he noticed horsemen descending the hills in the distance. Two scouts were dispatched and returned with word that the horsemen were part of President Davis's advance guard. By ten Davis was in the city and was, according to Parker, "well received by the population."[83]

Parker quickly sought out Mallory, who ordered the treasure transferred to Postmaster General and Acting Treasury Secretary John H. Reagan (the ailing Trenholm had left the party in Abbeville). Reagan in turn directed the superintendent to place the "things" in the custody of Brigadier General Basil H. Duke, commander of the President's escort. Mallory also ordered Parker to disband his command.

Parker was glad to be shed of the treasure, but less pleased with the order to disband his students. But orders were orders. Captain Tabb's men, loaded down with bacon, sugar, and coffee for the trip home, set out as soon as Parker relieved them of duty, Tabb having first refused a keg of pennies for distribution among his men.

Parker then bid his young gentlemen farewell, supplying each with a letter in which he contemplated a reunion that never came:

Abbeville, S.C., May 2, 1865

Sir: You are hereby detached from the naval school, and leave is granted you to visit your home. You will report by letter to the Hon. Secretary of the Navy as soon as practicable. Paymaster Wheliss [*sic*] will issue you ten days rations, and all quartermasters are requested to furnish you with transportation.

Respectfully your obedient servant,
Wm. H. Parker, commanding

Parker had bacon, coffee, and sugar issued to each midshipman and Secretary Reagan authorized the payment of two $20 gold pieces to each, and so supplied "the midshipmen left in detached parties, and an hour after President Davis' arrival the organization was one of the things of the past."[84] The middies had guarded the treasure for over thirty days and turned it over at Abbeville not a penny short.

Parker's admiration for his midshipmen remained strong almost thirty years later as he paid

> . . . tribute to these young men—many of them mere lads—who stood by me for so many anxious days. Their training and discipline showed itself conspicuously during that time. During the march across South Carolina, footsore and ragged as they had become by that time, no murmur escaped them, and they never faltered. I am sure that Mr. Davis and Mr. Mallory, if they were alive, would testify to the fact that when they saw the corps in Abbeville, way-worn and weary after its long march, it presented the same undaunted front as when it left Richmond. They were staunch to the last.[85]

Davis had certainly heard of the midshipmen's courage and discipline in guarding the treasure and inquired after them when Parker came to see him after the disbanding of the corps. When Parker informed him that the corps of midshipmen was disbanded, a surprised Davis said several times, "Captain, I am very sorry to hear that."[86] Parker described the broken-down condition of the boys and stated that in any event he was only following Mallory's order. Davis answered sadly, "Captain, I have no fault to find with you, but I am very sorry Mr. Mallory gave you the order."[87] "After seeing [his] escort," Parker admitted, "I understood Mr. Davis' regret."[88]

That afternoon the treasure was loaded onto wagons and taken away by Duke's men. Parker and his officers obtained $1,500, about twenty days' pay for each man when the amount was divided among them. The government departed that evening; Mallory invited Parker to accompany them, but he declined since he had no horse and the President's party was all mounted. The President finally caught up with his family, and on May 10, near Irwinville, Georgia, they and those few remaining with them were captured by Wilson's cavalry.[89]

Parker and his wife, Lieutenant and Mrs. McGuire, and Lieutenant Rochelle remained at Abbeville until the Federals reached Washington. Having by then received word of Johnston's surrender, Parker sent to the Federal commander at Washington for paroles for himself and his officers. The proper papers were obligingly sent and the party boarded a train for Newberry. By wagon and train they made their way from Newberry across South and North Carolina to Richmond and thence to Norfolk, where William Harwar Parker, late lieutenant commanding in the Confederate States Navy and former superintendent of the Confederate States Naval Academy, entered his home for the first time in three long years.

6

"A Most Realistic War College"

O N APRIL 5, 1865, L. L. CROUNSE, A CORRESPONDENT with the *New York Times*, was aboard the steamship *Mattine* in the company of the United States' Assistant Secretary of War C. Henry Dana and Congressman Roscoe Conkling of New York as it picked its way through the wreckage of the James River defenses, en route to the conquered Confederate capital. From City Point to Richmond, Crounse described for his readers the images of defeat along the way.

The battery at Howlett's stood "silent and gloomy, with its twelve large guns still in the embrasures."[1] Just past Howlett's, the *Mattine* exchanged salutes with the steamer carrying President Abraham Lincoln on his way back to City Point after his triumphant tour of Richmond.

Passing Drewry's Bluff the reporter described Fort Darling and the Rebel river obstructions for his readers, noting that together they formed an "impossible barrier to the naval advance on Richmond."[2] Farther upstream the wreck of the mighty ironclad *Virginia II* lay "in deep water, . . . careened on her side, . . . a portion of her overhang visible above the water-line."[3]

The remains of the bridge at Wilton were passed, and soon, "The City of Richmond is in view. The spires pointing heavenward; the smoke still rising from the conflagrations awful ruin, and the Stars and Stripes from a hundred house-tops and mastheads."[4] The *Mattine* tied up at Rocketts, most likely at the dock often used by the school ship *Patrick Henry*, and certainly, although Crounse did not mention it, within sight of its charred wreck.

The school ship did not remain in her watery grave for long. On April 25, Commander William Radford of the James River Flotilla surveyed the wrecks of the *Shrapnel*, *Nansemond*, and *Patrick Henry* and reported to John Lenthall, chief of the U.S. Bureau of Construction, that they were "scarcely worth raising."[5]

Once the wrecks had been rejected for salvage, the Union navy wasted little time removing them as hazards to navigation, and hired the submarine engineer B. Maillefert for the job. By May 10, Maillefert reported he had cleared a "channel 200 feet wide from Trent's Reach to Richmond . . . [and] at Richmond, demolished and removed a large portion of the wrecked steamer *Patrick Henry*."[6]

The few remaining tangible reminders of the Confederate Naval Academy school ship are limited to a piece of recitation-room furniture, some wardroom china, her compass, and Midshipman William D. Good's yellowed copy of Superintendent Parker's *Elements of Seamanship*.[7]

With the benefit of over 130 years of hindsight it's fair to ask why the Confederacy even bothered to establish a naval academy after the disasters at Gettysburg and Vicksburg had all but sealed the country's fate. The most obvious answer is that they didn't know they were dying as a nation. And in truth, Secretary of the Navy Stephen Mallory's plans for his academy remained grander than just the school ship—which was never intended by him to be more than a temporary arrangement—long after it should have been obvious to all that the war was lost. As he explained to President Davis, the school ship was a "nucleus" for a more permanent institution for which Secretary Mallory had "a well considered plan and organization," one that he was prepared to submit to the President "whenever the condition of the country may seem to call for legislation upon the subject."[8]

But Davis never called. The Confederate President's philosophical support for, but practical neglect of, military education in the Confederacy was not limited to the naval school; he also failed to materially support the state-owned military academies such as the Virginia Military Institute and South Carolina Military Academy, his army's primary sources of trained and educated junior officers. And although he missed his reefers after they disbanded at Abbeville, Davis failed to properly support them, neither spending the money appropriated to expand the naval school nor advocating legislation to increase the number of acting midshipmen.

A possible explanation for Davis's attitude may come from how he viewed the role of president. Davis, a graduate of West Point, always seemed to focus more energy on his role as commander-in-chief than as chief executive. This was altogether understandable, for he was the President of a nation that was at war almost since its birth and one that did not outlive that initial phase. So even though expanding the academy would have promised more and better-trained junior officers for the navy in the future, it could not meet the new nation's current needs: it would neither put more regiments in the field nor ships to sea, and therefore the issue did not command the full attention of Commander-In-Chief Davis. Nor was his view necessarily unjustified—a naval academy was not essential for winning the war, but winning the war was critical for the continued existence of a naval academy. Thus, the President's policy, or lack thereof, concerning formal military education and training, while shortsighted if there had in fact been a long run, in the short run was perhaps not unjustified.

Even conceding that the establishment of the Confederate Naval Academy midwar at a time when the tide was turning against the Confederacy "seems the plan of a madman," and that Davis's neglect stunted its growth, the institution nevertheless provided two distinct benefits, one to the navy, the other to the nation as a whole.[9]

First, the academy did provide the professional and academic training necessary to a successful naval officer. Navy Secretary Mallory rightly declared that "naval education and training lie at the foundation of naval success."[10] Civilian institutions could, Mallory noted, supply "a liberal education" preparing "men for useful service not only in the Army, but in most branches of public affairs, [but] special education and training, and such as these institutions can not afford, are essential to form a naval officer."[11]

The education and training provided on the school ship or, under the auspices of the academy, at sea, served its purpose. In Secretary Mallory's opinion the graduates compared "favorably with those of like grades in any naval service."[12] Superintendent William Parker believed that the midshipmen "showed extraordinary aptitude for the naval service"; furthermore, where former officers of the bluewater U.S. Navy felt cramped in the brownwater Confederate navy, the young officers produced by the Naval Academy "had none of this feeling. They knew of nothing better, and were ready to risk everything."[13] The Confederacy had in 1863 created the Provisional Navy of the Confederate States to promote deserving junior officers free of the regular navy's glacial seniority system inherited from the U.S. Navy, but Parker nevertheless felt that the navy missed an opportunity by not taking better advantage of the drive and determination of "the young lieutenants, passed midshipmen, and midshipmen" by elevating them "to more important commands."[14]

Although Confederate navy records are notoriously incomplete, it is safe to say that the Naval Academy during its brief existence was responsible for the education and training of approximately 180 midshipmen. Twenty-eight of them were former U.S. Naval Academy midshipmen assigned to the Confederate Naval Academy to complete their studies. A total of forty acting midshipmen graduated and were promoted to the grade of passed midshipman or higher. One who did not graduate, Joseph M. Gardner, was promoted to second lieutenant on January 7, 1864, for gallantry in action. Thirteen of the graduates ended the war as masters and one rose to the rank of lieutenant.

That less than one quarter of its students graduated says much about the obvious shortcomings of running a school in a war zone. In fact, the academic curriculum of the school ship was both diminished and enhanced by its location in a combat zone. Diminished by the frequent calls to duty that interrupted the orderly progress of the academic program, yet enhanced in that even newly appointed midshipmen without prior naval or army service received at least a taste of actual military operations.

But the midshipmen lived a schizophrenic existence characterized by one of them as "school-boys one hour and fighting men the next, dropping their books to take their carbines and cutlasses, exchanging in a moment their studies for places in the trenches a few hundred yards distant from those of the enemy."[15] When called upon for active duty, they were, said Parker, "bold, daring and enterprising."[16] With a young man's sense of invincibility, in danger they invariably exhibited "the happy, hearty, healthy spirit of brave boys" coupled with "the courage and understanding of men."[17] The Confederate States Naval Academy was, as Jimmy Morgan said, "a most realistic war college."[18]

The academy's second contribution was to higher education in the South in general. With the coming of the war, most of the Confederacy's antebellum colleges and universities closed as faculty and students flocked to the colors. The effect on higher education was such that Colonel Landon C. Garland, superintendent of the University of Alabama, which had transformed into a military academy, feared in 1861 that the postwar South would be left "destitute of cultivated intellect."[19]

Federal advances threatened the few Southern educational institutions that remained open after the outbreak of war, and attending a school that was subject to Federal domination did not suit many patriotic youths. Clifton R. Breckinridge attended Oakland College in Kentucky until the Yankees threatened the area in the spring of 1863. After that, young Breckinridge wrote his father that he would not return to the college, explaining, "[R]ather than have an education by submiting [*sic*] to a tiranical [*sic*] rule I would grow up in ignorance & debauchery."[20]

The Naval Academy and the few remaining state military schools gave young men an opportunity to serve while obtaining an education for their benefit and that of the South. In later years, when Superintendent Parker reviewed the accomplishments of his former students in law, medicine, politics, and government service or at sea, he took pride "that in all the losses of the war, here at least, was something saved in the education . . . of the Confederate midshipmen."[21] His pride was justified by the postwar careers of many of his students, who succeeded in a variety of professions, though they were denied the privilege of ever wearing the blue of the U.S. Navy.

James Morris Morgan, after taking his leave of Mrs. Davis, remained in Abbeville at the home of Secretary of the Treasury George Trenholm and received his parole from the Federal commander at Washington, Georgia. He married Helen Trenholm and entered the law school of the University of Louisiana (now Tulane University). When Helen died after less than a year of marriage, leaving him with a small daughter, Morgan left law school and tried his hand at cotton planting. Unsuccessful as a planter, he joined the army of the khedive of Egypt (the viceroy of Egypt within the Ottoman empire) as a captain in 1866. Many other expatriate Southerners found work with the khedive, including Beverly Kennon, who, much to Morgan's renewed mortification, often regaled the officer's mess with the story of that day on the *Patrick Henry* when young Mister Morgan told him to "pass forward." Returning to the States as a lieutenant colonel in 1872, Morgan tried farming in South Carolina and engineering in Mexico. President Grover Cleveland appointed him as consul to Australia, a post he held until 1893. Returning from "Down Under," Colonel Morgan settled in Maryland, where he farmed and ranched until 1903, when he went to Panama as the representative of a New York bank. Morgan remarried after Helen's death, and his second wife, Frances, gave him two more daughters. As World War I began, his children prevailed upon him to write his memoirs. He did, and the lively, entertaining *Recollections of a Rebel Reefer*, published in 1917, has become a Civil War classic. Jimmy Morgan died much lamented by family and friends in 1928.

Hubbard Taylor Minor remained near Charlotte recovering from his illness and managed to escape capture, although Federal soldiers did "capture" his sword from him. He made his way back to Virginia and enrolled in the 1865 session of the University of Virginia to finish his education. He married Miss Annie Lamar of Savannah in 1867, but she died three years later, leaving him with two small children. Four years after Annie, Hubbard died at age twenty-nine.

William Francis Wilson was captured at Sayler's Creek and imprisoned in the prison camp at Johnson's Island, Ohio, until June 20, 1865, when he was released after "swallowing," as he put it, the Oath of Allegiance to the U.S. of America.[22] He married Sarah Burnside in December 1868 and settled in Texas, where he took up farming and practiced medicine until his death on February 3, 1919.

John W. Harris attended the University of Virginia and, following in his father's footsteps, became a physician. While tending to patients during an epidemic in Staunton, Virginia, he caught pneumonia, which precipitated a heart attack that killed him on January 24, 1890.

William Force Clayton served on various ships of the Savannah River Squadron after graduating from the academy. He surrendered on May 4, 1865, and after the war became a lawyer in Florence, South Carolina. In 1910 his *Narrative of the Confederate States Navy* was published.

John Thomas Scharf resigned from the academy in January 1865 and was arrested and imprisoned by Federal authorities in March. After his release, he returned to his native Baltimore, eventually to become land commissioner of Maryland and a commissioner of the National Exposition in New Orleans. His classic work, *History of the Confederate States Navy*, was published in 1887.

Clifton R. Breckinridge was sent off toward home by his father and was captured, along with his brother Cabell, near Macon, Georgia, on May 10, 1865, carrying his father's favorite sword. After the war he entered politics like his father before him and was elected to two terms in the United States House of Representatives from Arkansas. Thereafter he served as U.S minister to

Russia from 1894 to 1897. He died December 3, 1932, and was buried in Lexington, Kentucky.

Robert H. Fleming received his parole at Charlotte, North Carolina, on May 11, 1865. Returning to Virginia, he graduated from Washington College, in Lexington, Virginia, and became a prominent Presbyterian minister. He died in 1922.

James Oliver Harrison's father was not successful in obtaining a commission in the army for him and practically nothing is known of his life after the Naval Academy.

Although also barred from ever serving in the U.S. Navy, the founders and faculty of the Confederate Naval Academy also reconstructed their lives.

Stephen R. Mallory left President Davis at Washington, Georgia, and joined his family at La Grange, Georgia, where he remained until May 20, 1865, when he was arrested by Federal troops and imprisoned in Fort Lafayette in New York Harbor. He was paroled in March 1866 and settled in Pensacola, Florida, where he practiced law until his death on November 9, 1873.

John Mercer Brooke was paroled at Greensboro on May 1, 1865. In July 1868, Brooke joined the faculty of the Virginia Military Institute at Lexington as professor of physics and astronomy. He retired from this post in 1899 and died on December 14, 1906.

Wilburn B. Hall was paroled at Augusta, Georgia, on May 26, 1865. After the war he served in Egypt in the khedive's army as a major of engineers, having been recommended for the position by his former enemy, General William T. Sherman. He returned to the United States and by 1887 was a prominent teacher in Baltimore.

James H. Rochelle returned to his home in Southampton County, Virginia. In June 1871 he accepted a position with the Peruvian Hydrological Commission of the Amazon and along with John Randolph Tucker was involved in surveying 3,393 miles of the Amazon River and its tributaries. When the commission was dissolved he returned to Southampton County and served as honorary commander of the Southampton Camp of Confederate Veterans.

Benjamin P. Loyall was paroled at Greensboro on April 28, 1865, and returned home to Norfolk. He died there on January 24, 1923.

Superintendent William Harwar Parker had probably the most varied, most productive, and in some ways the most turbulent postwar career of any of the Naval Academy's faculty or founders. By the end of 1865 he was back at sea captaining vessels of the Pacific Mail Steamship Company between San Francisco and Panama City, Panama. The knowledge he gained of the waters between these two ports he set out in a book, *Remarks on the Navigation of the Coasts Between San Francisco and Panama*, published in 1871.

In 1873, Parker accepted an appointment as professor of engineering at the Maryland Agricultural College (now the University of Maryland). By 1875 the trustees had voted him president of the college and Parker proceeded to totally revamp the curriculum and "militarize" the school along the lines of West Point and Annapolis. He even obtained a ship to teach the "cadets" seamanship. But the changes were too much for some of the faculty and trustees and they pressured him to resign in September 1882. It was while serving as college president that he wrote his memoirs, *Recollections of a Naval Officer*.

With the 1884 election of the Democrat Grover Cleveland of New York as U.S. President, Southerners once again began receiving appointments to government positions. Cleveland named Parker U.S. minister to Korea, and in June 1886 he arrived in Korea to take up the post. However, George C. Foulk, the man Parker was to replace, reported to the secretary of state that Parker was a hopeless drunkard completely addicted to the bottle. Although anxious to return home, Foulk was reluctant to entrust Korean-American relations to a man he described as a "contemptible old drunkard" until he received Parker's promise that he would stay away from the bottle.[23] On the way home, however, Foulk was turned back by a message waiting for him in Japan directing him to return and relieve Parker. Parker challenged neither his recall nor Foulk's reports concerning him, and one is left to conclude that he had indeed become an alcoholic.

Parker retired to Washington, D.C., never again to hold public office. He lived quietly, writing accounts of his wartime experiences and another book, *Familiar Talks on Astronomy*, published in 1889.

Of all his various occupations and achievements, Parker seemed proudest of his time as superintendent of the Confederate Naval Academy. More than thirty years after the midshipmen were disbanded, Parker noted the postwar accomplishments of his reefers and commented that amidst the destruction, something had been saved from the ruins of the Old South by their education. "I had a share in saving it," he reflected.[24]

William H. Parker died suddenly on December 30, 1896, and was buried in the U.S. Naval Academy cemetery at Annapolis. He was seventy years old.

Appendix A

⚜

List of Midshipmen
of the Confederate States Naval Academy,
July 1863 to April 1865

T HERE ARE SEVERAL PARTIAL LISTS OF NAVAL ACADEMY MIDSHIPMEN, including an 1863 list in the Library of Virginia; the July 1864 order in the National Archives in Washington supplied by the former midshipman George A. Joiner; a list for the years 1864 and 1865, also in the National Archives, compiled shortly after the end of the war by another former midshipman, Robert H. Fleming; a roster of the crew of the *Patrick Henry* in the *Official Records;* and William Clayton's biographical sketches of his classmates in *Narrative of the Confederate States Navy.* The only listings that seek to be comprehensive are those compiled by G. Melvin Herndon in his article "The Confederate States Naval Academy" and more recently a list by R. Thomas Campbell in his book *Academy on the James: The Confederate Naval School.* Herndon's list incorporates Clayton's, and Campbell's relies upon them both as well as upon the *Register of Officers of the Confederate States Navy 1861–1865* (abbreviated *Register*). None, however, is complete.

The list below takes the Herndon-Clayton-Campbell list as its starting point, but also includes the names of acting midshipmen who served in that grade after the opening of the school ship in July 1863 (after this date all acting midshipmen became part of the Confederate Naval Academy, regardless of whether they were assigned to the school ship). These names are in boldface. Also given is the source of each added name and the source relied upon when the lists and other sources do not agree. "Not in *Register*" indicates names that appear on a list but do not appear in the *Register of*

Officers. "NFI" means "No first initial." "State from . . . " (for instance, "State from Fleming") means that source lists the state of origin given.

Names of midshipmen who resigned from the United States Naval Academy are in italics. Names of graduates of the Confederate Naval Academy are underlined.

Name	State	Source
Anderson (NFI)	Missouri	Fleming
C. C. Anderson	Alabama?	—
Edwin M. Anderson	Georgia	—
J. A. Anderson	Maryland	—
Richard H. Bacot	—	Letter, Brooke to Barron, 19 Nov. 1863
James G. Baldwin	Mississippi	—
Ball (NFI)	Texas	1863 Virginia List; not in *Register*
Bassel (NFI)	Virginia	Fleming list; not in *Register*
Arthur H. Beall	Texas	—
<u>*Andrew P. Beirne*</u>	?	Letter, Brooke to Barron, 19 Nov. 1863
Louis Bennett	Virginia	—
Thomas M. Berrien	Georgia	—
Samuel P. Blanc	Louisiana	—
F. L. Blume	Tennessee	In *Register* as Blum; Fleming lists state as North Carolina
T. M. Bowen	?	Not in *Register*
Clifton R. Breckinridge	Kentucky	—
Bridges (NFI)	Virginia	Fleming list; not in *Register*
Thomas R. Brooks	Missouri	—
Brown (NFI)	Mississippi	Fleming
Orris A. Browne	Virginia	—
George D. Bryan	South Carolina	—
Buffington (NFI)	Virginia	Fleming list; not in *Register*
James D. Bulloch, Jr.	Georgia	—
J. H. Busby	?	1863 Virginia list; not in *Register*
William Butler	?	1863 Virginia list; not in *Register*

Richard E. Butt	Georgia	—
W. Allen Carrington	Virginia	Fleming
William T. Carroll	Arkansas	—
Barron Carter	Georgia	—
J. A. Carter	Virginia	State from Fleming, who lists as "Alex" Carter
Clarence Cary	Virginia	—
Edward Chapman, Jr.	Louisiana	—
W. J. Claiborne	Tennessee	State from Fleming
F. T. Clarke	North Carolina	Fleming
William F. Clayton	Georgia	—
George B. Cloud	Texas	—
Daniel D. Colcock	South Carolina	—
W. H. Collins	Alabama	Not in *Register*
William A. Collier	Virginia	—
Henry S. Cooke	Virginia	—
William J. Craig	Kentucky	—
Robert J. Crawford	Kentucky	—
Crutchfield (NFI)	Kentucky	Fleming list; not in *Register*
Charles G. Dandridge	Virginia	State from Fleming
Wilbur S. Davidson	North Carolina	State from Fleming
William L. Davis	District of Columbia	State from Fleming
Ralph J. Deas	South Carolina	—
Duncan A. Dixon	Mississippi	—
Algernon S. Doak	Tennessee	—
Franklin B. Dornin	Maryland	—
James H. Dyke	Florida	—
Henry T. Ellett, Jr.	Mississippi	—
Ellington (NFI)	Virginia	Fleming
Robert H. Fleming	Virginia	—
Robert Flournoy	Georgia	—
Richard S. Floyd	Tennessee	On Herndon list but probably promoted to acting master prior to July 1863
Joseph M. Gardner	Virginia	—
Paul H. Gibbs	South Carolina	—
Beverly Tucker Gibson	Virginia	Fleming

William D. Good	South Carolina	—
Louis Gounart	?	*Register*; *Official Records, Navies*, series 2, vol. 1, 300
W. D. Haldeman	Kentucky	State from Fleming
William K. Hale	Alabama	—
John H. Hamilton	Texas	—
William P. Hamilton	South Carolina	—
Lorenzo D. Hamner	Mississippi	—
John W. Harris	Virginia	—
A. M. Harrison	Kentucky	State from 1863 Virginia list
James O. Harrison	Virginia?	Harrison Papers; not in *Register*
Hudson (NFI)	—	—
William S. Houge	Florida	—
W. D. Holdman	?	Not in *Register*
Jefferson D. Howell	Louisiana	Fleming shows state as Mississippi
Alexander T. Hunt	Kentucky	—
Ferdinand S. Hunter	Virginia	—
John H. Inglis	Tennessee	—
Irvin (NFI)	Georgia	Fleming; not in *Register*
Bartlett S. Johnson	?	Not in *Register*
Edward B. Johnson	Missouri	—
B. Johnston	North Carolina	Fleming; could be Bartlett Johnson, above
John Johnston	North Carolina	Herndon lists as Johnson
George A. Joiner	Alabama	—
E. M. Jones	Missouri	—
E. A. Keeble	Tennessee	State from Fleming
Ferdinand B. Kennett	Missouri	State from Fleming
John Krause	?	1863 Virginia list; not in *Register*
J. C. Kerr	Virginia	State from Fleming
Daniel M. Lee	Virginia	—
John A. Lee	Kentucky	—
William A. Lee	Missouri	—

Lindsay (NFI)	North Carolina	Fleming list; not in *Register*
Lewis P. Levy	Missouri	—
John T. Lomax	Alabama	—
James C. Long	Tennessee	—
Lott (NFI)	Texas	Fleming list; not in *Register*
William C. Love	North Carolina	—
Patrick Henry McCarrick	North Carolina	—
Edward J. McDermett	Texas	Letter, Brooke to Barron, 19 Nov. 1863
Malcom J. McRae	Mississippi	State from Fleming
McWhorter (NFI)	Georgia	Fleming list; not in *Register*
E. C. Machen	Kentucky	State from Fleming
Eugene A. Maffitt	Georgia	—
Buddy Mallory	Florida	Not in *Register*
O. S. Manson	North Carolina	State from Fleming
John S. Mason	Virginia	—
Robert W. Maupin	Virginia	State from Fleming
W. R. Mayhew	?	Not in *Register*
Wyndam R. Mayo	Virginia	—
Cassius Meyer	Mississippi	—
James G. Minnigerode	Virginia	—
Hubbard T. Minor, Jr.	Missouri	Fleming lists state as Virginia
Preston B. Moore	Arkansas	—
Frank C. Morehead	Kentucky	—
James M. Morgan	Louisiana	—
Raphael J. Moses, Jr.	Georgia	—
T. Munroe	South Carolina	—
C. Myer	Mississippi	Not in *Register*
W. F. Nelson	?	Not in *Register*
Virginius Newton	North Carolina	—
J. D. Nicholson	Mississippi	State from Fleming
James R. Norris	Georgia	—
John B. Northrop	Arkansas	—
William H. Payne	Alabama	State from Fleming
James M. Pearson	Tennessee	—

Henry L. Peeples	Georgia	State from Fleming
James W. Pegram	Virginia	—
James A. Peters	Arkansas	—
Jefferson Phelps	Virginia	—
Eugene Phillips	Louisiana	—
R. H. Pinckney	Texas	—
Roger Pinckney	South Carolina	—
Thomas C. Pinckney	South Carolina	—
H. Pinkney	?	*Register*
W. W. Pipkins	?	Letter, Brooke to Barron, 19 Nov. 1863
Francis L. Place	Louisiana	—
Robert S. Quarles	Virginia	State from Fleming
Rapier (NFI)	Louisiana	Fleming list; not in *Register*
James B. Ratcliffe	Virginia	—
F. C. Reneau	Mississippi	—
William R. Ricks	North Carolina	—
Robinson (NFI)	Georgia	Fleming list; not in *Register*
John F. Rodman, Jr.	?	*Register*; letter, Brooke to Barron, 19 Nov. 1863
Lawrence M. Rootes	Virginia	—
Palmer Saunders	Virginia	—
John T. Scharf	Maryland	—
Henry H. Scott	North Carolina	Herndon shows Virginia
Raphael Semmes, Jr.	Alabama	—
Charles F. Sevier	Tennessee	—
William N. Shaw	Texas	—
Shawhan (NFI)	Kentucky	Fleming list; not in *Register*
James S. Shearman	Virginia	—
Herman C. Shewmake	Georgia	Fleming lists as Shewmaker
George T. Sinclair, Jr.	Virginia	—
William B. Sinclair, Jr.	Virginia	—
William H. Sinclair	Virginia	—
Sion P. Skinner	Alabama	—
Richard C. Slaughter	Arkansas	Fleming shows state as Virginia

William M. Snead	Georgia	State from Fleming
Gale W. Sparks	Louisiana	—
Neil H. Sterling	North Carolina	—
Thomas D. Stone	Alabama	State from Fleming
Daniel B. Talbott	Kentucky	—
Francis M. Thomas	South Carolina	Herndon shows North Carolina
E. B. Trescott	South Carolina	—
Conally Trigg	Virginia	1863 Virginia list; not in *Register*
John D. Trimble	Maryland	—
Clarance W. Tyler	North Carolina	—
Henry H. Tyson	Maryland	—
Henry L. Vaughan	Louisiana	—
Henry J. Warren	North Carolina	—
George S. Waterman	Louisiana	—
R. J. Watkins	?	Letter, Brooke to Barron, 19 Nov. 1863; not in *Register*
Wescott (NFI)	South Carolina	Fleming list; not in *Register*
Thomas Wherritt	Kentucky	—
Wilkes (NFI)	South Carolina	Fleming; possibly G. G. Wilkes in *Register*
Gilbert A. Wilkins	Georgia	—
William W. Wilkinson	South Carolina	—
Henry S. H. Williams	North Carolina	—
John A. G. Williamson	Virginia	Letter, Brooke to Barron, 19 Nov. 1863
John A. Wilson	Maryland	May have been promoted to passed midshipman prior to July 1863
William F. Wilson	Alabama	—
Augustus O. Wright	Alabama	Fleming lists state as Mississippi
Joshua C. Wright	Virginia	State from Fleming

Appendix B

REGULATIONS

FOR THE

CONFEDERATE STATES SCHOOL-SHIP

PATRICK HENRY.

REGULATIONS

OF THE

CONFEDERATE STATES SCHOOL-SHIP

PATRICK HENRY.

C. S. NAVY DEPARTMENT,
OFFICE OF ORDNANCE AND HYDROGRAPHY,
Richmond, July 23d, 1863.

SIR—The accompanying "Regulations of the C. S. School-Ship Patrick Henry," prepared by Lieut. Wm. H. Parker, commanding, are approved and recommended for adoption.

I have the honor to be,

Very respectfully,

Your obedient servant,

JOHN M. BROOKE,
Commander in Charge.

Hon. S. R. MALLORY,
Secretary of the Navy.

REGULATIONS

OF THE

C. S. SCHOOL-SHIP, PATRICK HENRY.

CHAPTER I.

ORGANIZATION.

1. The C. S. School-Ship, Patrick Henry, shall be under the supervision of the officer in charge of the office of Ordnance and Hydrography, and he shall personally inspect the vessel at least once a year.

2. A commandant, of rank not lower than that of a lieutenant, will have the immediate government and command of the school-ship, and will be held responsible for its discipline and good management. All communications to the Navy Department on subjects connected with, or relating to the ship, are to be made, or forwarded by the commandant to the officer in charge of the office of Ordnance and Hydrography.

3. An executive officer shall also be attached to the ship, whose rank shall not be below that of 2d lieutenant. He shall be the executive officer of the school-ship, and also in charge of either the department of seamanship, gunnery, or navigation.

4. There shall be attached to the ship two officers, of rank not lower than that of master, who, in addition to the duties of the ship, shall have charge, each, of one of the departments of seamanship, gunnery, or navigation.

5. No officer of the navy shall exercise military command on board the school-ship unless subordinate to the commandant, excepting the officer of the navy who may at the time be in charge of the office of Ordnance and Hydrography.

6. There shall be attached to the school-ship, a surgeon or assistant surgeon, paymaster or assistant paymaster, master, secretary, and such warrant and petty officers, and other persons of inferior ratings, as may be authorized by the Secretary of the Navy.

7. There shall also be attached to the ship the following professors, viz:
   One Professor of Mathematics.
   One Professor of English Studies.
   One Professor of Modern Languages.

8. The relative rank and precedence of the members of the academic staff to be determined by the date of commission or appointment.

6

CHAPTER II.

ACADEMIC BOARD.

1. The Academic Board shall be composed of the following officers and professors, viz:

The Commandant.
The Executive Officer.
The Second Lieutenant.
The Third Lieutenant.
The Professor of Mathematics.
The Professor of English Studies.
The Professor of Modern Languages.

2. The commandant, or, in his absence, the executive officer, shall preside at the meetings of the Academic Board. In the event, however, of the absence of both, from illness or otherwise, then the senior officer present shall preside; but all reports, returns, &c., of the board, under such circumstances, shall be made to or through the commanding officer. as usage or the nature of the case may seem to require.

3. The Academic Board shall be convened for the transaction of business as often as the commandant may judge necessary.

4. A majority of the board shall constitute a quorum for the transaction of business; but a less number may constitute a quorum for the examination of candidates for admission, provided at least three members be present.

5. Unless called on by the Navy Department to act upon other matters, or by the commandant to do so upon other affairs concerning the school, the Academic Board shall confine its duties to the examination of candidates for admission, and of students, at the times prescribed by regulations; the preparation of necessary papers, reports, or returns, connected with examinations; the arrangement, for the approval of the Navy Department, of the order of instruction in the several branches of each course of study, and the time to be employed in each branch; the arrangement of the order in which the several classes and their sections composed of midshipmen are to present themselves at a December or June examination; the recommendation of students, found deficient, for further trial; also of individuals for restoration to the service; the recommendation, for the approval of the Navy Department, of the text-books best suited for each department of instruction; the recommendation for purchase of all such books, maps, models, instruments, and apparatus as may be necessary in the different departments of instruction for the purposes of tuition; to reporting, from time to time, on the system of studies and instruction pursued and proposing any improvements therein that experience may suggest; and to granting certificates of graduation.

6. In questions of order at the Academic Board, relating either to the propriety of deportment of a member, observance of decorum, or routine of business, the presiding officer is to decide upon his own motion; but

7

in cases which involve a consideration of the course and order of proceedings, a vote of the board is to be taken.

7. The adjournments of the Academic Board will be directed by the presiding officer.

8. The commandant will designate a member of the Academic Board to act as its secretary, and keep a correct record of its proceedings, which record shall be carefully kept in the office of the commandant, and transmitted by him to his successor. In case, however, of the illness or absence of the member so designated, at a time a meeting of the board is held, the presiding officer will then appoint another member to act in such secretary's stead for the time being.

9. Any officer connected with the school-ship, or any member of the academic staff not a member of the Academic Board, may be required by the commandant, in the name of the Academic Board, to attend its meetings for the purpose of giving information, or expressing opinions: but such individual is not to vote in any decision of the board.

CHAPTER III.

RULES OF ADMISSION.

1. Application for admission to the school-ship, addressed to the Secretary of the Navy, can be made at any time, by the candidate himself, or by his parent, guardian, or any of his friends, and his name will be at once placed on the list of applicants; but the registry of a name does not give any assurance of an appointment. No preference will be given on account of priority of application. No application for an appointment as an acting midshipman will be considered where the candidate is under or over the prescribed age; where the precise age and actual fixed residence are not stated, or where the applicant is not a resident of the congressional district of the State from which he applies.

2. The law limits the number of midshipmen, and requires that they shall be divided among the several States and Territories with reference and in proportion, as near as may be, to their number of representatives and delegates to Congress; that appointments shall be made from those States and Territories which have not their relative proportion on the navy list; that appointments from each State shall be apportioned, as nearly as practicable, equally among the several congressional districts therein; and that the person so appointed shall be an actual resident of the congressional district of the State from which appointed, and be recommended by the member of Congress representing the district in which he resides.

3. The selection of candidates is made semi-annually, and candidates who receive permission will present themselves to the commandant of the school in January and July, when they will be examined by a board of medical officers, and by the Academic Board of the school, as to their qualifications for admission.

8

4. No candidate will be admitted on board the school-ship unless he is found, in the opinion of a medical board, to be composed of the surgeon of the school-ship, and two other medical officers to be designated by the Secretary of the Navy, qualified to discharge the arduous duties of an officer of the navy, both at the time of his examination, and probably, during the rest of his life, until age shall disable him; and shall have passed a satisfactory examination before the Academic Board.

5. Any one of the following conditions will be sufficient to reject a candidate, viz:

First. Feeble constitution and muscular tenuity; unsound health, from whatever cause; indications of former disease; glandular swellings, or symptoms of scrofula.

Second. Chronic cutaneous affections, especially of the scalp, or any disorder of an infectious or immoral character.

Third. Severe injuries of the bones of the head; convulsions.

Fourth. Impaired vision, from whatever cause; inflammatory affection of the eye-lids; immobility, or irregularity of the iris, or fistula lachrymalis.

Fifth. Deafness; copious discharge from the ears.

Sixth. Loss of many teeth, or teeth generally unsound.

Seventh. Impediment of speech.

Eighth. Want of due capacity of the chest, or any other indication of a liability to a pulmonic disease.

Ninth. Impaired or inadequate efficiency of one or both of the superior extremities on account of fractures, especially of the clavicle, contractions of a joint, extinuation, or deformity.

Tenth. An unnatural excurvature or incurvature of the spine.

Eleventh. Hernia.

Twelfth. A varicose state of the veins, of the scrotum, and spomatic cord (when large) sarcocele, hydrocele, hemorrhoids, fistulas.

Thirteenth. Impaired or inadequate efficiency of one or both of the inferior extremities on account of varicose veins, fractures, malformation, flat feet, lameness, contraction, unequal length, bunyons, overlying or supernumerary toes.

Fourteenth. Ulcers, or unsound cicatrices of ulcers likely to break out afresh.

6. Candidates must be over fourteen and under eighteen years of age at the time of examination for admission; must be of good moral character; able to read and write well—write from dictation and spell with correctness; and to perform the following elementary operations of arithmetic, viz: numeration, and the addition, subtraction, multiplication, and division of whole numbers; all of which must be established to the satisfaction of the Academic Board.

7. A candidate who has passed the required examinations will receive the appointment of an acting midshipman, become an inmate of the ship, and be allowed his travelling expenses from his residence to Richmond. If, on the contrary, he shall not pass both examinations, he will receive neither an acting midshipman's appointment nor his travelling expenses.

8. A candidate who has once presented himself for examination, under

| 9

the authority of the Navy Department, and been rejected, cannot be allowed to present himself for examination a second time.

9. No one who may be admitted on board the school ship under these regulations shall receive a warrant as a midshipman in the navy, unless he graduate thereat.

10. When candidates shall have passed the required examinations, and have been admitted as members of the school, they must, if not already supplied, immediately furnish themselves, and at all times keep themselves supplied with the following articles, viz :

> One complete suit of steel gray uniform.
> Two pairs white pantaloons.
> Six white shirts.
> Six pairs of socks.
> Four pairs of drawers.
> Six pocket handkerchiefs.
> One black silk handkerchief or stock.
> One mattress.
> One pillow.
> One pair of blankets.
> One bed cover or spread.
> Two pairs of sheets.
> Two pillow cases.
> Six towels.
> Two pairs of boots or shoes.
> One hair brush.
> One tooth brush.
> One coarse comb for the hair.
> One fine comb for the hair, and
> One thread and needle case.

Messmates will jointly procure for their common use and will keep their room at all times supplied with one looking-glass, one wash-basin, one water-pail and one slop-bucket.

11. On admission, each acting midshipman will be credited with his actual and necessary travelling expenses, and if they do not amount to the sum of fifty dollars, he will be expected to make up the deficiency by a deposit of money current in Richmond. This sum will be expended, under the direction of the commandant, for his further equipment.

CHAPTER IV.

UNIFORM.

1. All officers attached to the school-ship, shall wear their service-dress uniforms at all times while on duty, unless the commandant should, on any occasion, direct the officers to appear in some other particular kind of uniform prescribed for their respective grades.

2

10

2. The uniform of an acting midshipman to be the same as that now authorized for midshipmen.

3. A service or fatigue dress of the same color and form, but of coarser and stronger fabric; jumpers of gray flannel, pantaloons of gray flannel, and straw hats and white jackets, may be worn when authorized by the commandant.

4. Changes of clothing from gray to white, or the reverse, suggested by different seasons of the year, are not to be made by students until directed by the commandant.

5. Students appointed to act as officers of crews, companies, &c., shall wear such badges of designation on the sleeves of the jacket as the commandant may prescribe.

6. No student shall be allowed to wear on board the ship, or in the city of Richmond, or its immediate vicinity, any article of clothing, or wearing apparel, not permitted to be worn with, or as a part of, his uniform.

CHAPTER V.

COURSE OF INSTRUCTION.

1. The studies which shall be pursued, and the instruction which shall be given on board the school-ship, are comprised under the following departments and branches:

FIRST DEPARTMENT—SEAMANSHIP, NAVAL TACTICS, AND STEAM.

First Branch—Seamanship.
Second Branch—Naval Tactics.
Third Branch—Steam.

SECOND DEPARTMENT—GUNNERY, FIELD ARTILLERY, AND INFANTRY TACTICS.

First Branch—Theory and Practice of Gunnery.
Second Branch—Field Artillery.
Third Branch—Infantry Tactics.
Fourth Branch—The Art of Defence.

THIRD DEPARTMENT—ASTRONOMY, NAVIGATION, AND SURVEYING.

First Branch—Astronomy.
Second Branch—Navigation.
Third Branch—Surveying.

11

Fourth Department—Mathematics.

First Branch—Arithmetic.
Second Branch—Algebra.
Third Branch—Geometry.
Fourth Branch—Trigonometry.
Fifth Branch—Application of Algebra and Trigonometry to the mensuration of planes and solids.

Fifth Department—English Studies.

First Branch—English Grammar.
Second Branch—Descriptive Geography.
Third Branch—Physical Geography.
Fourth Branch—History.
Fifth Branch—Political Science.   -

Sixth Department—Modern Languages.

First Branch—French.
Second Branch—Spanish.

2. The foregoing studies shall be distributed into four annual courses, and the acting midshipmen shall be arranged in four classes, each class pursuing one of these courses; and each class may be subdivided into convenient sections, according to the relative standing of the members in the several branches of study.

3. The studies for the fourth class shall be: Practical Seamanship, Gunnery and Artillery and Infantry Tactics, Arithmetic and Algebra to Equations of the first degree, English Grammar and Descriptive Geography. For the third class: Practical Seamanship, Gunnery and Artillery and Infantry Tactics, Algebra, Geometry, Plane and Spherical Trigonometry, Physical Geography and History—French. For the second class: Seamanship and Steam, Gunnery and Field Artillery, Astronomy and Navigation, Application of Algebra and Trigonometry to the mensuration of planes and solids, Political Science, French. For the first class: Seamanship and Naval Tactics, Gunnery and Infantry Tactics, Navigation and Surveying, French and Spanish.

4. The professors and heads of departments of instruction, in order to ascertain the proficiency of the sections intrusted immediately to their assistants, the relative merits and qualifications of the students of the whole class, and the manner in which the assistants have performed their duty, shall, occasionally, instruct each of the sections intrusted to the assistants.

5. Professors and instructors will be held responsible for the regular and orderly conduct of their respective classes and sections whilst under their immediate instruction. They will not allow any student to absent

12

himself from the recitation room, unless for satisfactory reasons; no will they fail to report the wants of preparation, the absence or misconr duct of any student at recitation.

6. Each professor, instructor, or assistant, shall keep daily notes of the progress and relative merit of those in the classes or sections under his charge. The assistants shall make weekly reports of such notes to the heads of departments to which the classes or sections respectively belong. These reports shall be rendered weekly to the commandant by the head of each department, accompanied by a similar report of his own section or sections, with such explanatory remarks as may be necessary to show the relative progress in the sections; and he shall, at the same time, recommend the transfers which should, in his judgment, be made from one section to another. (See Forms.)

7. Monthly reports shall be made up according to Form C, for every academic month in the academic year, and be signed and forwarded to the Secretary of the Navy by the commandant. These reports shall show the relative standing of the members of each class in the different studies in which they have been instructed, and their conduct or demerits. For the months in which there has been an examination, these reports shall be based on the weekly reports and the results of those examina tions, and for other months upon the weekly reports only.

8. The academic month shall be understood to terminate on the Satur day which may happen to fall nearest the last day of the month, whether such Saturday precede or follow that day. Monthly academic returns will be made to the commandant by the professors and heads of depart ments accordingly.

9. The academic year shall begin on the 15th of January, and end on the completion of the following December examination. The academic year shall be divided into two terms; the first to commence with the ac ademic year, and to terminate at the close of the June examination; and the second to commence on the 15th July, and to terminate with the close of the December examination, or the end of the academic year.

CHAPTER VI.

ACADEMIC EXAMINATIONS.

1. An annual examination of all the classes shall be held by the Aca demic Board, commencing on the first day of December; (the second when the first falls on Sunday.) This examination shall be sufficiently thorough to enable the board to decide upon the proficiency and the rel ative merits of the members of the several classes; and it shall embrace all the studies, theoretical and practical, pursued by the several classes during the year, except such as may have been completed before the pre vious June.

2. A semi-annual examination of the same kind, of all the classes, shall also be held by the board, commencing on the first day of June;

18.

(the second when the first falls on Sunday.) This examination shall be sufficiently thorough to enable the board to decide upon the proficiency and relative merits of the members of the several classes; but the board may, at its discretion, omit the examination of the first class in any department of study not completed before the period assigned for their semi-annual examination to commence.

3. Those who may be found by the board, at either an annual or semi-annual examination, deficient in any department of study, shall be so reported to the Secretary of the Navy, for his decision, whether they shall be dropped from the Navy List and returned to their friends, or be allowed to continue on board the school-ship for further trial. If there should be circumstances attending the case of any student thus found deficient, entitling him, in the judgment of the board, to a longer continuance on board the school-ship, they shall be duly stated in the report of the board to the Secretary of the Navy, upon the report by Form D.

4. Any acting midshipman may be advanced to any class which he may be qualified to join, either upon his admission or at any subsequent examination; and he may be graduated at any December examination at which he shall be found fully qualified to pass a graduating academic examination.

5. Every acting midshipman who succeeds in passing a graduating examination in December, will receive from the Academic Board a certificate of graduation which will entitle him to a warrant as a midshipman in the navy; bearing the same date as that certificate.

6. When the exigencies of the service so require, acting midshipmen who succeed in passing a graduating examination, may be promoted to the grade of passed midshipman, master, or lieutenant.

7. No acting midshipman who shall have been dismissed from the school ship, or dropped from the navy list in consequence of being found deficient in studies at an academic examination, or deficient in conduct at any time, will be restored to the school-ship, except upon the recommendation of the Academic Board. In the event of such restoration, the Secretary of the Navy, after considering the report and recommendation of the board, will prescribe the class the individual is to join, and the other conditions under which he is to be received.

8. The examination in each department will be made or directed by the professor or head of that department; and during the time any class or section is under examination in any branch, not only the professor, but also the immediate instructor of the class or section, shall be present with the Academic Board, and he may, under the direction of the head of the department to which he belongs, make the examination of his class or section.

9. The Secretary of the Navy will, when expedient, annually invite not less than five persons, such as he may judge well qualified, to attend on board the school-ship during the December examination, as a board of visitors, for the purpose of witnessing the examination of the several classes, and of examining into the state of the police, discipline, and general management of the institution, the result of which examination they will report to the Secretary of the Navy.

APPENDIX B

14

CHAPTER VII.

MERIT ROLLS.

1. The relative weight, or the maximum numbers, which are to be assigned to each of the, "principal branches of study, and to conduct, in each of the several classes, in forming the merit rolls, will be as follows, viz:

DEPARTMENT.	BRANCHES.	First Year, or 4th Class.	Second Year, or 3rd Class.	Third Year, or 2nd Class.	Fourth Year, or 1st Class.	Graduating Maxima.	Maxima of the several departments
Seamanship, Naval Tactics, and Steam,	Seamanship,	......	......	50	100	150	} 215
	Naval Tactics,	......	......	......	30	30	
	Steam,	......	......	35	......	35	
Gunnery, Artillery and Infantry Tactics,	Gunnery,	......	......	50	100	150	} 215
	Field Artillery,	......	......	30	......	30	
	Infantry Tactics,	......	......	......	35	35	
Astronomy, Navigation and Surveying,	Astronomy,	......	......	50	......	50	} 160
	Navigation and Surveying,	......	......	......	110	110	
Mathematics,	Mathematics,	40	60	80	......	180	180
English Studies,	Grammar,	10	......	......	......	10	} 90
	Geography,	15	15	......	......	30	
	History,	20	......	......	......	20	
	Political Science,	......	......	30	......	30	
Modern Languages,	French,	......	30	30	......	60	} 90
	Spanish,	......	......	......	30	30	
Conduct,		5	10	15	20	50	50
Aggregate.		......	......	......	......	1000	1000

2. If any students shall, at any June or December examination, fail to pass satisfactory examinations, in any of the principal branches of study in which they have been instructed, or shall have recorded against them respectively more than two hundred demerits since the commencement of the academic year, the Academic Board shall prepare a report of the same, to be transmitted to the Secretary of the Navy, according to Form D, showing the habits of study, aptitude for study, &c. If the Academic Board should consider any of them thus reported deserving of being allowed to remain on board the ship for further trial, they shall designate the individuals, and assign upon the report their reasons for recommending their continuance.

3. At every December examination, the Academic Board shall form a "general merit-roll" (See Form E,) for each class, in the following

15

manner, viz: Of those members of each class who shall have passed a satisfactory examination, the individual having the highest standing in any principal branch for that year, shall receive the maximum number assigned to it for that class and year in the table of weights of this chapter, and the one having the lowest standing shall receive the minimum number, which, in every case, shall be one-third of the maximum for the same branch and class. The members of the class having intermediate standings, shall receive numbers proceeding by equal differences from the maximum to the minimum, in the order of their relative merit, as fixed by their "class merit-rolls." Of those who have not two hundred demerits recorded against them, such as have no demerits shall receive the maximum number allowed for that class and year, and the others shall have that maximum diminished by one three-hundredth part of it for every demerit recorded against them. All the numbers which shall be thus assigned to the several members for the several branches of study, and for conduct, shall then be added together, and the names of the members shall be arranged in each class according to the aggregates thus obtained, the highest number being placed first on the list, and the others in their order. Only those who shall have passed in all the principal branches of their classes, and have not exceeding two hundred demerits recorded against them, are to be included in the "general merit-roll."

4. At the December examination, the Academic Board shall also form the "graduating merit-rolls," (See Form F,) for the graduating class, by adding the aggregate numbers which each member of the class shall have received on the several "general merit-rolls" for December during the four years, and arranging the order of the members according to the aggregates, placing the highest first.

CHAPTER VIII.

FINAL EXAMINATION OF MIDSHIPMEN.

1. A Board to consist of five Captains and Commanders, of whom at least three shall be Captains, will convene, annually, on the first day of December, (the second, if the first should fall on Sunday,) at such place as the Secretary of the Navy may direct, for the purpose of making the "final examination" of Midshipmen, to ascertain and decide upon their qualifications for promotion.

2. Candidates must produce certificates from their respective commanding officers of their good conduct and attention to duty, together with journals of all their cruises; and, besides, watch, quarter and station bills of at least one of the vessels in which they have served, in their own hand writing.

8. The examination by the Board will embrace Seamanship, Naval Tactics, Steam, the theory and practice of Naval Gunnery, Field Artillery, Infantry Tactics, Navigation, and French; but the relative standing

16

of the candidates will be decided by their standing in Seamanship, Gunnery and Navigation, unless their relative standing in these branches shall be equal; in which case, superior proficiency in the other branches shall be entitled to precedence.

4. In assigning numbers to candidates on their final examination, the number 402 is to be considered as expressing the maximum, and 134 as the minimum, to be allowed; and the Board will assign to such candidates as shall, in its opinion, be duly qualified for promotion, the number within those limits which, in the judgment of the Board, will fairly express their relative qualifications.

5. In the case where the candidates have not graduated from the school-ship, the numbers so assigned will determine their standing as passed midshipmen; otherwise, the numbers thus assigned, when added to the numbers which have already been assigned to them respectively on the "graduating merit-roll" of the school-ship, will determine their standing as passed midshipmen; the highest number, in both cases, to take precedence.

6. The Secretary of the Navy will cause the Board of Examiners to be furnished with the numbers which had been assigned by the Academic Board to each of the midshipmen, to enable the Board of Examiners to determine the relative standing of those whom they may examine, as required in the next preceding article.

7. As many of the same graduating class as can be conveniently assembled, will be ordered before the same Board for their "final examination;" but should it be necessary to examine members of the same graduating class by different Boards, then a majority of the members of each of those Boards will, when practicable, be composed of the same officers.

CHAPTER IX.

CONDUCT ROLL.

1. For offences not considered deserving severe punishment, the following classification of delinquencies shows the numbers which are to be marked as *demerits* against the students on board the School-ship, in making up the conduct rolls:

First class of delinquencies counting ten demerits.—Repeated neglect of orders; overstaying verbal leave; absent from room at night after "taps;" and violation of articles 5, 7, 11, 12, and 15, of Chapter X.

Second class of delinquencies counting eight demerits.—Light in room after "taps" at night; and violation of articles 10 and 14 of Chapter X.

Third class of delinquencies counting six demerits.—Absence without authority from parade; roll-call; drill; quarters; inspection; exercise; muster; recitation; or other prescribed duty. Also, improper noise in rooms or steerage; unnecessary or unauthorized absence from room during study hours; out of prescribed uniform when on duty, &c.

Fourth class of delinquencies counting four demerits.—Slovenly dress

17

at parade, inspection, or recitation; talking at recitation or in ranks; loud talking or rude conducting mess; being superintendent of the steerage and failing to keep it in proper order, or allowing it to be in disorder; or to report visits to it in study or other prohibited hours; or to report a breach of regulations occurring therein.

Fifth class of delinquencies counting two demerits.—Late at any exercise, recitation, or other duty; inattention on drill, or at recitation; out of uniform when not on duty.

Miscellaneous class of delinquencies, to count from one to ten demerits according to the circumstances of each particular case.—Disrespectful, ungentlemanly, disorderly, insubordinate, or unmilitary conduct; wilful neglect of studies or other duties; and violation of such regulations of the school-ship as are not specifically mentioned in the course of this chapter, and which carry with them no positive penalty.

2. In all cases of delinquencies where demerits positively attach, the Commandant will, after due inquiry, determine whether those reported to him for record shall be placed thereon; and in cases of a "miscellaneous" character, he is to decide upon the number of demerits, between one and ten, to be assigned to each of such cases.

3. The *total* demerits of each student will be expressed by the sum of all the demerits standing against him upon record.

4. Whenever a student shall have a number of demerits recorded against him greater than two hundred during any one academic year, he shall be declared deficient in conduct, and be immediately reported to the Secretary of the Navy for his decision, whether he shall be dropped forthwith from the Navy or otherwise.

5. The Commandant may reduce or remit recorded demerits upon satisfactory explanation in writing being made in reference to a particular case, or upon satisfactory assurance in writing, or well-grounded hopes of future good conduct; but all such reductions or remissions must be stated in the first monthly report to the department of delinquencies after they are made.

———

CHAPTER X.

DISCIPLINE.

1. The laws for the government of the Navy of the Confederate States are to be strictly observed by every person attached to the school-ship.

2. The commandant being charged with, and held responsible for, the good order and discipline of the school-ship, all persons attached thereto, for any purpose, are to give implicit obedience to his commands.

3. Any student who shall be intoxicated, or shall use, or bring into the school-ship, or have in his quarters, or elsewhere within the limits of the ship, any spirituous, vinous, fermented, or other intoxicating drinks, may be dismissed from the navy.

3

18

4. Any student who shall leave the ship without permission first duly obtained, shall be dismissed from the naval service.

5. Profane, obscene, or vulgar language, is strictly prohibited.

6. Any person attached to the school-ship who shall publish, prepare, or submit for publication, in any manner or form, any matter relating to transactions or occurrences, official or private, which have taken place within the ship, or are in any wise connected with it, without permission previously obtained from the Secretary of the Navy or the commandant, shall be dismissed.

7. No fire-arms or fire-works of any description, or gunpowder in any form, shall be introduced by any student on board the ship; nor shall the same be used *by any person* on board, without the sanction of the commandant.

8. Students are strictly forbidden to contract debts while connected with the school-ship, unless with the sanction of the commandant.

9. All combinations, under any pretext whatever, are strictly prohibited.

10. Students must never present themselves to the commandant or to any other superior officer set over them, or at their offices or quarters, to make known a complaint, or for any other purpose, except by invitation, in greater numbers than three at a time.

11. Students are not only required to abstain from all vicious, immoral, and irregular conduct, but are enjoined to conduct themselves upon every occasion with the propriety and decorum which characterize the society of gentlemen. Those guilty of conduct unbecoming an officer and a gentleman, may be punished by dismission from the service.

12. No student is to visit the room of another, or to absent himself unnecessarily from his own room, during the hours of recitation or study.

13. No student shall remove from the mess assigned him without the authority of the commandant.

14. No student shall introduce any improper character on board the ship; nor shall he introduce any person into the students quarters at any other time than during the hours of recitation, prior to the time prescribed to commence evening studies.

15. No student shall answer for another at any roll-call, or muster of any kind.

16. The customary salute of officers in addressing or passing each other, is to be strictly observed on board. The junior or inferior will be the first to extend the salute, and the senior or superior will be scrupulously careful in returning it.

17. No person shall be excused from the performance of his duties on the plea of sickness, unless so excused by the surgeon; and no person whose name is on the sick-list, will be permitted to leave the ship, unless it be recommended by the surgeon and approved by the commandant.

18. Any student who shall, when absent from the ship, commit any immoral or disgraceful act, may, on satisfactory proof, be punished as though the offence had been committed on board, even to dismissal, if necessary, from the naval service.

19. Officers and others having cause of complaint against any person

connected with the ship, or employed in any capacity on board, will make the same known to the commandant; and they are not, to undertake to address a complaint to a higher authority, unless the commandant should fail promptly to notice the same, or the decision given by him should be unsatisfactory.

20. It shall be the duty of every officer, professor, and instructor attached to the ship, having knowledge of any violation of a law or regulation, or of any crime, irregularity, neglect, or other improper conduct of which a student or any other person has been guilty, to report the same without delay to the commandant.

21. No student shall use any reproachful or provoking speech or gesture towards another, or shall by any means traduce or defame another, or strike, or in any manner offer violence to another, without subjecting himself to the severest punishment which the offence may require.

22. The punishments to which students shall be liable for offences they may commit whilst borne on the rolls of the school-ship exclusive of those resulting from demerits, or such as may proceed from judicial investigations by courts-martial, or courts of inquiry, will be distributed among the following three classes:

First Class.—Confinement to the limits of the ship; private reprimands; deprivation of recreation within the ship; confinement to room or apartment; reprimand to be read on parade; suspension from recitations and from all drills and exercises.

Second Class.—Confinement in guard-room.

Third Class.—Dismissal, unless the offender avail himself of a privilege that may be granted to him of resigning; public dismission.

23. Punishments of the first or second class, just mentioned, may be directed by the commandant, or the commanding officer of the ship for the time being; but, unless in an extreme case, the circumstances of which are to be communicated to the department with all proper dispatch, "deprivation of recreation within the ship" shall not be prolonged beyond *twenty days;* "suspension from recitations and all drills and exercises" beyond *fourteen days,* or "confinement in the guard-room" beyond *one week,* without the direct sanction of the Secretary of the Navy.

24. "Confinement in guard-room" shall only be ordered upon those who, in the judgment of the commandant or commanding officer, shall be guilty of highly insubordinate, riotous, or mutinous conduct, or who shall not conform to the conditions imposed when ordered to confine themselves to their rooms, apartments, or to other limits which may be prescribed to them.

25. Any student who shall leave the guard-room without express permission, when placed there for punishment, may be regarded as guilty of the very serious military offence of *breach of arrest.*

26. Removal from the service, either with or without permission to resign, will only be authorized or ordered by the Secretary of the Navy, with the sanction of the President of the Confederate States.

27. While a student is under the punishment of "confinement to the limits of the ship," he is, on no account, to go out of the ship, either in a boat or otherwise, unless *ordered* so to do by a superior officer.

20

28. When a student is under the punishment of "deprivation of recreation within the vessel," he is, on no account, to absent himself from his room or apartment, except during the times absolutely necessary to enable him to attend the recitations of his studies, meals, parades, drills, exercises of small arms, swords, or great guns, and to answer the calls of nature.

29. While a student is under the punishment of "confinement to room or apartment," he is, on no account, to absent himself from his room or apartment, except during the times absolutely necessary to enable him to attend meals, and to answer the calls of nature.

30. While a student is under the punishment of "suspension from recitations and all drills and exercises," he is, on no account, to absent himself from his room or apartment, except during the times absolutely necessary to enable him to answer the calls of nature.

31. Any student who shall hesitate or refuse to submit to any of the foregoing punishments of the first or second class, when ordered so to do by the commandant, or the commanding officer for the time being, may be dismissed forthwith from the naval service; and if any student or students shall, individually or collectively, decline or refuse to convey into confinement, either to a guard-room or other designated place, any other student or students, when ordered so to do by competent authority, or shall not obey the order promptly and literally, he or they may likewise be so dismissed.

CHAPTER XI.

LEAVES OF ABSENCE.

1. No person connected with the School-ship shall go beyond the limits of the ship without a general or special permission of the Commandant.

2. As a general rule, no student will be allowed to leave the ship for the purpose of visiting Richmond or its vicinity, except on Saturday; and then for a period not to exceed twenty-four hours.

3. Not more than one-half of the students attached to the ship shall be absent on leave at the same time, and those only who have merited it by general good behavior shall receive this indulgence.

4. On very particular occasions, the Commandant may grant leave during the week to those who shall have deserved such indulgence by exemplary conduct.

5. The Commandant, during the academic year, may grant to students leave of absence, upon an application in writing, for not exceeding forty-eight hours. He may also grant, upon similar application, leave of absence to professors and instructors for forty-eight hours, or for a period of time which shall not at all interfere with the regular recitations. All applications for longer time must be submitted for the decision of the Navy Department.

21

6. At the close of each term, the Commandant, when authorized by the Secretary of the Navy, may grant leave of absence to such of the students as can be spared from the duties of the ship; provided their conduct has been satisfactory, and they have not received more than one hundred and fifty demerits during the academic year. No extension of this indulgence beyond the 10th of the following July or January, will be granted.

7. Leave of absence may be granted by the Secretary of the Navy to the professors, assistant professors, instructors, and other officers attached to the ship, from the close of one academic term to the commencement of another; provided their services are not required for duties pertaining to their respective positions or departments.

8. Any person connected with the ship who shall overstay his leave of absence, verbal or written, must be reported to the Navy Department; and unless he produce satisfactory evidence of his having been detained away by sickness, or other unavoidable cause, he will be subject to punishment according to the circumstances of the case.

9. When a student of the ship applies for leave of absence on account of ill health, his application must be accompanied by a certificate of the senior medical officer present after the following form:

——— ———, midshipman (or acting midshipman) of the C. S. School-ship, having applied for a certificate on which to ground an application for leave of absence, I do hereby certify that I have carefully examined his case, and find that [here the nature of the disease, wound, or disability, is to be fully stated, and the period during which the individual has suffered under its effects.] And, in consequence thereof, he is, in my opinion, unfit for duty. I further declare my belief that he will not be able to resume his duties in a less period than [here state explicitly an opinion as to the period which will probably elapse before the individual will be able to resume his duties. When there is no reason to expect a recovery, or when the prospect of recovery is distant and uncertain, it must be stated.]

Dated at ———, this ——— day of ———, 18—.

[Signature of the medical officer.]

Which certificate is to be forwarded to the Navy Department, through the Commandant, for its orders in the case.

10. When a student, absent on leave, is prevented by ill health from re-joining the ship, he must, on the first day of each month, transmit a certificate of the state of his health, in the foregoing form, to the Commandant, which shall be signed by a medical officer of the navy when practicable; but, should there be none in the vicinity, a resident physician of the place must sign the same, whose standing must be attested by a magistrate, or some person known to the authorities at the School.

11. Students, on obtaining leave of absence, will report to the Commandant their intended place of residence, and, during their leave, any change of such residence.

23

CHAPTER XII.

HOSPITAL.

1. The surgeon, will, if he discovers in any student diseases or defects, which are enumerated as causes to prevent the admission of a candidate for the service, or any bodily or mental defect disqualifying in its consequences, report the case to the Commandant, who will forward the report to the Secretary of the Navy, that he may order an examination and a report to be made by a medical board, for his decision whether such student shall be retained in the service or dropped from the navy.

2 The surgeon will have the immediate control of the hospital, hospital steward, and hospital attendants, as well as of all who are sick in the hospital, or in their own quarters.

3. He will be responsible for all expenditures of medicines and stores belonging to the hospital department of the ship. No article of medicine, of diet, or of drink, shall be issued from the dispensary or hospital department without his order.

4. The police regulations of the hospital shall be established by the surgeon, subject to the approval of the Commandant.

5. The surgeon shall report to the Commandant, daily, by 10 o'clock. A. M., the names of those whose condition of health unfits them for any academic duty, or renders it desirable that they should be excused from employment as a means of recovering their health. He shall also furnish to the Commandant a daily "sick list, and an "excused list," of those to be excused from military drills and exercises only.

6. When a student is ill enough to be excused from attendance at mess-formations, morning and evening roll calls, or recitations, his name must appear on the regular sick-list, and not on the list of those excused only from military drills and exercises.

7. No person whose name is not on the sick or excused list will be excused from duty in consequence of alleged indisposition.

8. No person will be permitted to visit any patient in the hospital without the sanction of the surgeon.

9. No student shall visit any patient in the hospital without a written permission, signed by the surgeon and approved by the Commandant. Every such permission must be left with the hospital steward.

10. The hospital steward shall obey all orders he may receive from the surgeon, and observe such police regulations as may be established for the hospital.

11. No patient in the hospital will be permitted to exercise any authority over the hospital steward, or over any nurse or other attendant. Every instance of neglect or inattention towards any patient may be reported to the surgeon.

12. No person shall be employed in the hospital without the approbation of the Commandant. All persons employed in the hospital as nurses, cooks, and servants, shall obey the orders of the hospital steward.

13. No student who is on the sick-list, and directed to remain in

23

quarters, shall leave there except at such times as the surgeon may have
prescribed; but no student whose name is on either the sick or excused
lists shall, for any purpose, be absent from his room or sick-apartment,
when one is assigned him, during any drill; parade, roll-call, exercise, or
other duty of a military cast, from which he shall have been excused by
the surgeon's list.

14. When more than one medical officer shall be attached to the ship,
both shall not be absent at the same time.

15. The sick in the hospital shall conform to the directions of the
surgeon, and to all the police regulations of the hospital.

16. Any person feigning disease may be dismissed from the service by
order of the Secretary of the Navy.

17. There shall be a sick-call, every morning throughout the academic
year, half an hour after the breakfast call, when all the sick, not in the
hospital, who are able to attend, shall report to the surgeon until dis-
charged by him.

CHAPTER XIII.

SECRETARY.

1. The Secretary, under the direction of the Commandant, will keep
all the records of the school, viz: rolls of the school, which shall contain
a list of the students, with the date of each admission, place of birth,
age, whence appointed, residence, and name of parents or guardians;
results of class reports, conduct and general merit rolls; an inventory
of public property of every description, and records of requisitions. He
shall also make out all consolidated reports of conduct, and of merit,
for the Navy Department, and file and preserve the public correspondence, and other papers of the school-ship.

CHAPTER XIV.

PAY MASTER.

1. The Commandant may, from time to time, authorize the pay master
to pay fo or to the students such small sums of money due them as he
may deem proper.

2. The remainder of the pay of the students will be kept to their
credit by the pay-master, on the pay-rolls of the school, and paid to
them when they shall be detached, or shall graduate.

3. The pay master shall present to the Commandant, at the end of
each month, a statement of the account of each student, showing the
amount paid and the balance due.

24

CHAPTER XV.

MISCELLANEOUS.

1. All communications to the Navy Department, from persons connected with the school, must be made through the commandant, whose duty it shall be to forward them, accompanied with such remarks as he may deem proper.

2. The Executive Officer will carefully inspect, at least once a day, the mess and recitation rooms, quarters, and the ship; and his principal assistant will also visit the students' quarters daily, and more frequently, if necessary, to preserve good order and strict obedience to regulations. In event of discovering anything damaged, or out of place, the Executive Officer will have it repaired or adjusted, unless it be a matter of serious moment, or involving expense of importance, in which case he will report the same to the commandant, and receive his orders upon the subject.

3. After "taps" at night, no lights are to be allowed in any part of the students' quarters, except by the authority of the commandant.

4. Students shall, when passing up and down the ladders, always do so in an orderly manner. Loud talking, scuffling, or unnecessary noise of any kind, is never to take place in their rooms. Boisterous behaviour is prohibited everywhere within the limits of the ship, and in the boats when beyond those limits.

5. Each professor and instructor at the head of a separate department shall have charge of, and be accountable for, the instruments and aparatus supplied for the use of his department.

6. No student shall address his instructor upon the subject of his recitation marks without the permission of the commandant.

7. One of the students of each mess will perform the duties of superintendant of that mess for one week at a time, and be held responsible for the cleanliness and general neat arrangement of the room; the preservation of the public property in it; and for the strict observance there of all the regulations of the ship.

8. Officers to whom special duties are not assigned by these regulations, are to perform such as may be directed by the commandant; and when special duties are herein assigned the commandant may require the officer to perform other duties when circumstances shall, in his opinion, render it advisable.

9. All regulations necessary for the interior police and discipline of the school-ship, not inconsistent with the foregoing, will be established by the commandant, and shall be duly observed and obeyed.

The foregoing regulations are approved and are to be observed by all persons to whom they are applicable.

                    S. R. MALLORY.
                              Secretary of the Navy.

NAVY DEPARTMENT.

25

FORM A.

Employment of time during the day on board the C. S. School-Ship Patrick Henry.

Class	Reveille to 8 A. M.	8 A. M. to 9 A. M.	9 A. M. to 11.30 A. M.	11.30 A. M. to 1.30 P. M.	1.30 P. M. to 3.30 P. M.	3.30 P. M. to 4.30 P. M.	4.30 P. M. to sunset.	Sunset to call to evening studies.	Call to evening studies to 9.30 P. M.	9.30 P. M. to 10 P. M.
First Class.			Recitation in Gunnery, &c. Study.	Recitation in Seamanship, &c., or in Spanish. Study.		Recitation in Navigation. Study.			Study.	
Second Class.	Drum beats at 7 A. M. Roll call at 7.50 A. M. Inspection of Rooms.	Breakfast at 8. Sick call at 8.45. Recreation.	Recitation in Seamanship, &c., or in Navigation or in French. Study.	Recitation in Gunnery, &c., or in Political Science. Study.	Dinner at 2 P. M. Recreation—Class parade at 3.30 P. M.	Recitation in Mathematics or in Astronomy. Study.	Military Exercises. Art of defence—Drill. Recreation—Parade and roll call at sunset.	Supper immediately after parade. Recreation. Call to studies at 8 P. M.	Study.	Tattoo at 9.30 P. M. Taps at 10. Inspection of Rooms.
Third Class.			Recitation in Mathematics. Study.	Recitation in Geography and History. Study.		Recitation in French. Study.			Study.	
Fourth Class.			Recitation in Grammar. Study.	Recitation in Mathematics. Study.		Recitation in Geography. Study.			Study.	

NOTE.—The recitations within the above-named hours vary with the day of the week and with the academic term.

4

FORM B.

C. S. SCHOOL-SHIP PATRICK HENRY.

Class Report for the Week ending   18 .

Dept. of Study...... ....
Branch of Study................ ....
....Class. ....;.....Section.

Scale of daily merit.	Thorough.	Very good.	Good.	Tolerable.	Indifferent.	Bad.	Failure.
	4.0	3.5	3.0	2.5	2.0	1.0	0

No.	Names.	M.	T.	W.	Th.	F.	S.	Average.	Remarks.
1	A. B.		3.5	3.0	2.5	1.0	1.0	2.2	
2	C. D.	3.0	2.8	2.8	1.5	0.0	3.0	2.2	
3	T. B. W.	4.0	3.0	2.0	3.0	4.0	3.0	3.2	
9									
10									
11	T. B. W.	3.0	4.0	3.0	2.0	3.0	4.0	3.2	

(Signed.)   A. B.. *Professor.*

The average for any individual who has recited any number of days, will be determined by adding together his daily marks, and then dividing their sum by the number of days.

27

FORM C.

C. S. SCHOOL-SHIP PATRICK HENRY.

Monthly report of the relative standing in the different branches of study, and of the conduct of the members of the —— class, for the month of ——, 18   .

DEPARTMENTS OF STUDY.	Seamanship, Nav'l Tactic. and Steam.	Gunnery, Artillery and Inf. Tactics.	Astronomy, Navigation & Surveying.	Mathematics	Eng'lsh Studies.	Modern Languages.	Conduct.	
BRANCHES OF STUDY.							Demerits	
							Month.	Year.
NAMES.								

NOTE.—A number expressive of the standing of each member of the class, in each head of study to which he has attended, is inserted opposite to his name, and under the respective heads.

ꝛ6

FORM D.

C. S. SCHOOL-SHIP PATRICK HENRY.

Report of the aptitude, habits, &c., of the acting midshipmen found "deficient" at the examination in.——, 18 , and subject to be dropped from the navy list

No.	Name.	State.	Class.	Age.		Time on board.		In what deficient.	Aptitude for Study.	Habits with regard to—		Aptitude for the Naval Service.
				Years.	Months.	Years.	Months.			Study.	General conduct.	
	A.........	Ala.	1	18	5.	2	3	Gunnery and Tactics.	Fair. Little.	Idle.	Inattention to Regulations	Little.
5	C.........	S. C.	3	15	6	1	7	History.	Fair.	Idle.	Regardless of Regulations.	Fair

Note.—In all cases reported "deficient," as above, whenever, in the judgment of the Academic Board, there is sufficient reasons for recommending that the acting mid shipman shall not be dropped from navy list, such a recommendation and reasons are to be annexed to this report.

FORM E.

C. S. SCHOOL-SHIP PATRICK HENRY.—ANNUAL EXAMINATION IN DECEMBER, 18 .

General Merit-Roll for the . . . . Class, consisting of . . . . Members.

DEPARTMENTS.	Branches.	Maxima for this class and year.	Names.
Seamanship, Naval Tactics, and Steam.	Seamanship		
	Naval Tactics.		
	Steam.		
	Sum.		
Gunnery, Artillery and Infantry Tactics.	Gunnery.		
	Artillery Tactics.		
	Infantry Tactics.		
	Sum.		
Astronomy, Navigation and Surveying.	Astronomy.		
	Navigation.		
	Surveying.		
	Sum.		
Mathemat.	Mathematics		
English Studies.	Grammar.		
	Dec. Geography.		
	Phys. Geog.		
	History.		
	Int. Law.		
	Sum.		
French Language.	French.		
Spanish Language.	Spanish.		
Conduct.	Demerits.		
Aggregate.	Aggregate annual number entitled to for the year.		

FORM F,—

C. S. SCHOOL-SHIP PATRICK HENRY—ANNUAL EXAMINATION IN DECEMBER, 18 .

Graduating Merit-Roll of the ——— Class.

Names.	Years.	Departments.	Maxima for this class and year.

Appendix C

REGULATIONS

FOR THE

INTERIOR POLICE

OF THE

CONFEDERATE STATES SCHOOL-SHIP

PATRICK HENRY.

REGULATIONS

FOR THE

INTERIOR POLICE

OF THE

·C. S. SCHOOL-SHIP, PATRICK HENRY.

ORGANIZATION OF CREWS.

"1. For the purpose of instruction in the use of arms, in Infantry Tactics, great gun exercise, &c., the students will be organized into guns-crews; each to consist of an odd number of persons, which is not to exceed twenty-one, and will be, generally, about seventeen.

2. Each gun's-crew is to have two Captains, one to be designated and respected as the First, and the other as the Second. All of these Captains are to be made from members of the first or second classes; and, as far as practicable, the First Captains are to be selected from the first class, and the Second Captains from either the first or second classes. Members of the second class are not to be appointed either as First or Second classes. Members of the second class are not to be appointed either as First or Second Captains of crews to which members of the first class belong.

3. In arranging the classes into crews, students of the same class are to be associated together—to the extent circumstances will permit. Numerical deficiencies of crews to which members of the first and second classes belong, are to be made up by resorting to members of the third; and such deficiences of crews to which the latter belong, are to be made good by resorting to members of the fourth. This is to be regarded as the general rule, subject to such exceptions as expediency may suggest.

4. Each crew is to be numbered, in regular succession, from one to ten (or last) inclusive, beginning with a crew composed, (exclusively of Captains) in whole or in part of members of the first class; and so on, in order of classes, to crews composed of the fourth.

. 5. The Executive officer is to carry out the above directions concerning the organization of guns'crews, and he is to nominate to the Com-

4

mandant for the appointment of Captains of crews, such students as he may judge best qualified to discharge the duties.

6. An Adjutant will be appointed by the Commandant, should one be required.

DAILY ROUTINE—AFFECTING ROLL-CALLS—MEALS—STUDIES—RECITATIONS, &c.

7. *Reveilie* at 7 A. M ; *Morning Roll-call* at 7.50 A. M ; *Breakfast* at 8 A. M ; *Sick-call* at 8.45 A. M ; *Morning call to studies* (which are to continue until 4.30 P. M., except during the hours prescribed for dinner), and also call to *First Forenoon Recitations* at 8.55 A. M. ; call to *Second Forenoon Recitations* at 9.55 A. M.; call to *Third Forenoon Recitations* at 11.25 A. M ; call to *Fourth Forenoon Recitations* at 12.25 P. M. ; *Dinner* at 2 P. M.; call to *Afternoon Recitations* at 3.25 P. M. *Exercise at great guns, small arms* to commence at 4.35 P. M. ; *Evening Roll-call and Parade* at sunset—*Supper* immediately after ; call to *Evening Studies* at 7.55 P. M.; *Tattoo* at 9·30 P. M.; and *Taps* at 10 P. M.

8. The above Routine will be modified by the Commandant to suit the change of seasons, if necessary.

9. Students are to turn out promptly at *Reveille*; dress themselves properly without delay, and arrange their effects; then those who may be Superintendents of the Steerages are to see them swept out, and otherwise prepared for breakfast.

10. An Exercise of Great guns, commencing at 9 A. M. is to take place every Saturday. The remainder of the forenoon is to be occupied in learning to knot, splice, strap blocks, &c.

11. The drum, besides beating for *Reveille* and *Tattoo*, is to beat for the following purposes :—

Morning Roll-call—tune, *Assembly.*

Breakfast,—tune, *Dixie.*

Sick-call—tune, *Surgeon's Call.*

Hoisting and hauling down colors—tune, *Troop.*

Dinner—tune, *Dixie.*

Drills at 4.35 P. M.—tune, *Drill Call.*

Evening Roll-call—tunes, *Call and Retreat.*

Supper, *Dixie.*

Inspection on Sunday—tunes, *Call and Retreat*

12. The bugle shall sound the calls for Morning and Evening Studies and for all Recitations.

13. Every Sunday morning, at a quarter before 10 o'clock, an Inspection-parade of Students shall take place, at which each is to appear dressed in his best uniform suit, and clean and tidy in every respect.

14. When the drum beats for *General Quarters*, the students are to repair to their stations, as per quarter-bill. Only those belonging to Divisions will be required to attend at Morning and Evening Inspections.

15. At each evening parade, the daily report of delinquences, involving demerits, is to be read out; and a detail of Students, to serve

5 ·

the following day, as Officer of the Deck, and Superintendents of Steerages, is to be made.

16. No Student shall be absent from any duty whatever, without permission from the Commandant, unless excused by the Surgeon.

POLICE OF STUDENTS' QUARTERS, &C.

17. The Executive Officer is to inspect the Steerage and Recitation rooms at least once a day, and see that they are kept in good order.

18. No Student shall play upon any musical instrument on Sunday, nor in study hours on any other day.

19. Smoking will only be allowed on the Hurricane Deck and in the Gangways.

20. No Student shall post any placard or notice anywhere about the ship, or affix to the bulkheads any map, picture, or piece of writing, without the permission of the Executive Officer.

21. No person is ever to be allowed to set or lounge upon the Quarter Deck during the day. Officers upon reaching the Quarter Deck must not omit to pay the customary salute of raising the cap.

22. Officers are to wear their uniform at all times when on duty; and no officer is ever to appear on the *Quarter Deck* without it.

28. All orders coming through the *Officer of the Deck, Superintendents of Steerages, Adjutant, Captains of Crews*, as well as through an *Instructor*, or a *commissioned* or *warrant officer* of the ship, must be considered by the Students as official, and obeyed and respected accordingly

24. Students are not to wear their hands in their pockets, and all officers of the ship are expected to exhibit a good example in this particular.

SUPERINTENDENT OF STEERAGE.

25. One Student shall be detailed by the Executive Officer to serve for one day as Superintendent of Steerage.

26. He shall be responsible for the cleanliness and general police of the room; and for the strict observance of regulations and orders therein.

27. He shall be responsible for the preservation of all public property, attached to the steerages, for the common use of its occupants.

28. Although punishable for violations of regulations and orders. occurring in the steerage, which can not be traced to others, yet he may relieve himself from this dilemma by a satisfactory excuse, or by reporting the offender. '

29. The Superintendent is to see the Steerage and Study-rooms properly lighted every evening. He will also see that they are extinguished at the proper time.

80. He is at all times to be in readiness to perform boat service. He will also attend to the opening of the Spirit-Room, and serving of grog.

81. He will report the Steerage "ready for inspection," daily, at 10 A. M.

6

32. He will be excused from attending all recitations, drills and exercises during his tour of duty.

33.

34.

35.

36.

37.

38.

39.

OFFICER OF THE DECK.

40. The Midshipman detailed to serve as *officer of the deck* is to keep his watch on the starboard side of the quarter deck—he is, however, to attend forward when any particular work is going on, and will occasionally visit the hurricane deck.

41. He is not to sit down or lounge while on deck, but will *walk his watch.*

42. He is not to engage in conversation while on watch, and will exert himself to see the orders of the ship carried out.

43. He will receive all the boats coming alongside, and will see that they "haul out to the booms" after the officers have left them.

44. He is to be particularly careful to carry out the *routine* of both the school and the ship.

45. He is never to leave the deck before being regularly relieved.

46. He will receive with courtesy all strangers who may visit the ship and apply to him for information concerning it, or any one on board.

7 .

47. He is not to visit the recitation-rooms except on duty.

48. He shall see that all regulations concerning the quarter deck are observed by all officers.

49. He shall attend at all parades, roll-calls and formations, and assist in maintaining order, and perform any other service he may be called upon to do by the Officer in Charge.

50. On receiving the reports of absentees from Section formations, he shall seek them, and order all, except those excused, to join their respective sections.

51. He is to report the 8 o'clock, 9½ o'clock and 10 o'clock lights to the Commandant. During the night he will send the Quarter Master around every hour to inspect the lights authorized.

52. He is to visit the Steerage at *Taps*, and will report the Midshipmen "in their hammocks" to the Officer in Charge.

52. He shall cause all the Academic and other signals to be sounded as prescribed by the bugle or drum as the case may be.

54. The Officer of the Deck shall have charge of the " Liberty Book," in which he shall enter the names of all Students going on, or returning from, leave. To this end all Students are required to report to him whenever they leave or return to the ship.

55. He shall always keep the "Log" of the ship, in which he shall record the date of his remarks; the state of the weather; the force and direction of the wind; the degrees of temperature at 8 A. M., Meridian, and 8 P. M.; the occupation' of the crew; all drills and exercises; receipt of stores and provisions; movements of vessels on the river; the enlistment, discharge or desertion of men; confinement of men; men going on, or returning from liberty; signals; surveys; the visits of public functionaries of high rank or position, and the ceremonies attending their reception; the commencement, continuance and end of semi-annual and annual examinations; the departure of officers on leave and their return from it; the dismissal of Students, or their resignation: the suspension of Students from duty, and their subsequent restoration to it; and, in short, all matters pertaining to the school or ship.

56. No person is to scribble on the Log-slate; and the Officer of the Deck will be held responsible for the observance of this order.

57.

58.

59.

60.

8

61.

62.

63.

64.

65.

66.

67.

68.

SECTION FORMATIONS.

69. The class-sections shall assemble at their respective calls of the bugle or otherwise, to recitation, on the port side of the quarter deck.

70. Silence and orderly deportment will be required of all Students while on section-parade, and while marching to and from the recitation-rooms:

71. Every Student, unless properly excused, shall assemble and march with his section.

72. No Student shall leave the recitation-room without the permission of the Instructor, unless ordered so to do.

73. The Student whose name stands at the head of his section shall be its leader, unless otherwise ordered.

74. At the given signal the Leader shall form his section at the place appointed, in two ranks, call the roll, note and report the absentees, and march it to the recitation-room in a military and orderly manner.

9

75. When dismissed, he shall form his section as before, and march it in like manner to the Steerage or Study room.

76. He shall promptly report to the Officer of the Deck every violation of the regulations or orders committed by any member of his section.

77. Whenever a Section-leader is absent, the Student standing next to him on the section list shall perform his duties and be obeyed accordingly.

78. Besides reporting absentees to the Officer of the Deck, the Section-leader is to report them to each Instructor before whom ho goes to recite, upon reaching the recitation room.

79.

INSTRUCTORS.

80. Every instructor shall note on his weekly class-report the names of all Students of the section under his charge who may have neglected their studies.

81. He will also state in his report the progress made during the week by his section, and the particular subject in which it has been engaged.

82. He is to arrange the names of the members of his section, on his weekly class-report, according to the order or relative standing in study; and a transcript of this is to be kept by the Section-leader for the purpose of mustering his section, &c.

83. Heads of departments will hand in their weekly class-reports to the Commandants, on Saturday, by half-past one o'clock, P. M.

84. Transfers from one section to another of a class, may be made at the close of any week; subject to the approval of the Commandant.

85. At the close of a recitation of a section,, the Instructor who conducted it is to report to the Executive Officer any Student who may have violated any regulation of the School thereat, or absented himself therefrom improperly.

INDULGENCE OF LEAVE.

86. With a view of enabling as many as one-half the whole number of Students to visit the city every Saturday, they are to be divided into two liberty parties, to alternate with each other—one to consist of the odd numbered crews, and the other of the even numbered.

87. Only Students, however, who may merit it by their good behavior, shall be allowed this indulgence. Gross violation of regulations; previous abuse of liberty; general neglect of studies, or duties of any sort; disrespectful or insubordinate conduct; or having over twenty demerits recorded during the current month, or the one immediately preceding it; shall be regarded as sufficient reasons for withholding it.

88. A list of Students' names to go on leave is to be prepared under

10

the direction of the Executive Officer, and read at the Evening Parade on Friday.

89. The Officer of the Deck is to be furnished with a copy of this list.

90.

91.

92.

93.

DRESS.

94. Officers attached to the ship are to wear their *prescribed uniforms* at all musters and inspections. Blue flannel or cloth may be worn for Service-dress, *provided the proper buttons and badges of distinction are adhered to*. As a general rule, officers will be required to dress with the crew; either in blue or white.

95. Straw hats may be worn in Summer instead of caps, but no slouched hats will be allowed.

96.

97.

98. The Executive Officer is to see that the Students at all times present themselves dressed as they should be, and that they keep themselves tidy in their persons and attire.

REPORTS AND EXCUSES.

99. Delinquencies on the part of Students, which may occur either at recitations or drill, are to be promptly reported by the Instructors to the Executive Officer, or Officer in Charge.

100. A summary of these delinquencies will be read out at Evening Parade, and the following day, between the hours of 1.30 and 2.30, P. M., excuses concerning them, (made verbally,) will be received by the Executive Officer at his office.

101.

12

OFFICER IN CHARGE.

115. The lieutenants and master shall in turn discharge the duties of *officer in charge.*

116. His tour of duty is to commence at 8 A. M. and last 24 hours, and during its continuance he is not to leave the ship without special permission and a relief.

117. The officer of the deck and superintendent of steerage are to regard themselves, and he is also to regard them, as placed under his immediate supervision and authority, and he is to see that they perform their prescribed duties properly.

118. He is to command the midshipmen whenever assembled for morning and evening roll-calls and parades, and he is to conduct these services systematically and with all due formality.

119. He shall exert himself to maintain good order among the students, and enforce the regulations and orders which apply to them; and to effect properly these objects, he is to keep himself generally cognisant of all transactions about the ship.

120. He shall observe that the several beats of drum, and the bugle-calls, mentioned under the head of "Daily Routine," are all sounded at the proper time.

121. He shall inspect the recitation rooms and steerages from time to time, during his tour of duty.

122. He shall notice that the attendants about the students quarters do their duty faithfully, and deport themselves properly.

123. He shall render to the executive officer a statement of such delinquencies observed by himself, or reported to him by others, as may require to be noticed by that officer; and shall promptly report to him, in person, any gross violation of discipline that may come to his knowledge.

124. He is to consider himself as in charge of the ship during his tour of duty, and will see that the "Daily Routine" prescribed by the executive officer is properly carried out.

125. He will be particularly attentive to the proper and man-of-warlike carrying on of duty about the ship—all forms and ceremonies usual to the naval service are to be studiously observed.

126.

127.

128.

129.

130.

12

181.

182.

133.

184.

185.

EXECUTIVE OFFICER.

. 136. Besides performing the duties specifically assigned to him by the regulations of the school-ship, issued by the Navy Department, the executive officer is to perform those of executing the regulations and orders concerning police and discipline.

187. He is to be vigilant with regard to the conduct and deportment of students, and see that offences against regulations are not practiced with impunity,

188. In and for the discharge of his duties, he is to regard himself as responsible, directly, to the commandant, whom he will consult in cases of doubt, or unusual occurrence, or before directing changes of moment in existing or established arrangements.

189. The book of record for demerits is to be kept under his particular charge, and no person, except himself and the officer in charge, is to have access to it but by the commandant's orders; nor is any information which it may contain to be communicated to any one except for authorised public purposes.

140. On receiving the excuses for students, and making up the daily report of delinquences, he is to submit that report to the commandant for approval; and its details, as returned to him with such approval, are to be accurately recorded, and then the report itself is to be posted for the consultation of all concerned. All written excuses are to be regularly endorsed and filed, and securely kept.

141. Whenever a student leaves the school-ship in consequence of his resignation or dismissal; and whenever a student is suspended from duty, or restored to duty from suspension; the executive officer will cause an entry of the fact to be be made in the "Log" by the officer of the deck.

14

142.

148.

144.

145. The executive officer is to see that the ship is at all times kept ready for active service. He is strictly to conform to the "Regulations for the Navy of the Confederate States," approved April 29th, 1862, and to the Ordnance Manual—in a word, he is to make the vessel a *model man-of-war*, and all officers attached to the ship are enjoined to assist him to this end.

146. He will cause a "Daily Routine" to be prepared for the guidance of the officer of the deck—exhibiting the hours of drill, inspections at quarters, wash-days, cleaning decks, boats for the shore, sweepers, meal hours, &c., &c.

147.

148.

149.

150.

151.

MESS ARRANGEMENTS.

152. Until further orders the messes will be divided into numbers of twelve or fifteen each; who will appoint their own caterer.

153. The hours appointed for meals must be strictly adhered to. No student will be excused from study or drill upon the excuse of not having had his meals.

15

154. The caterers are to preside and preserve order at their respective tables; a non-compliance with this order will compel the executive officer to direct the officer in charge to preside during meal hours.

155.

156.

157.

158.

159.

160.

161.

162.

163.

EXAMINATION OF CANDIDATES FOR ADMISSION.

164.

165.

16

166.

167.

168.

169.

170.

171. The attention of all officers and men attached to the school-ship is called to the "Regulations for the Navy of the Confederate States," approved April 29th, 1868. *A strict compliance with those Regulations will be required.*

WM. H. PARKER,
Commandant.

C. S. SCHOOL-SHIP PATRICK HENRY,
James River, July, 1863.

Notes

The following shortened references are used in the notes:

Campbell, *Midshipman in Gray*. Campbell, R. Thomas, ed. *Midshipman in Gray: Selections from Recollections of a Rebel Reefer by James Morris Morgan.* Shippensburg, Pa.: Burd Street Press, 1997.

***Civil War Naval Chronology*.** *Civil War Naval Chronology 1861–1865.* United States Navy Department. Washington, D.C.: Government Printing Office, 1971.

Clayton, *Narrative*. William F. Clayton. *A Narrative of the Confederate States Navy.* Weldon, N.C.: Harrell's Printing House, 1910.

Conrad, "Capture and Burning of 'Underwriter.'" Conrad, Daniel B. "Capture and Burning of the Federal Gunboat 'Underwriter', In the Neuse, Off New Bern, N.C., in February, 1864." *Southern Historical Society Papers* 19, no. 93 (1891).

Dudley, *Going South*. Dudley, William S. *Going South: U. S. Navy Officer Resignations & Dismissals on the Eve of the Civil War.* Washington, D.C.: Naval Historical Foundation, 1981.

Harrison Papers. James O. Harrison Papers. Manuscripts Division, Library of Congress, Washington, D.C.

Herndon, "Fleming's Diary." Herndon, G. Melvin. "The Confederate Naval Cadets and the Confederate Treasure: The Diary of Midshipman Robert H. Fleming." *Georgia Historical Society Quarterly* (June 1960).

Herndon, "Naval Academy." Herndon, G. Melvin. "The Confederate States Naval Academy." *Virginia Magazine of History and Biography* 69 (July 1961).

***Interior Police Regulations*.** *Regulations for the Interior Police of the Confederate States School-Ship Patrick Henry.* N.p.: n.d.

Letter Book. "Miscellaneous Letters Sent, Office of Ordnance and Hydrography, Navy Dept. Nov 1864 – Mar 1865." Record Group 109, chapter 7, vol. 292, National Archives.

Minor, part 1. Minor, Hubbard T. "I Am Getting a Good Education . . . : An Unpublished Diary by a Cadet at the Confederate Naval Academy." Part 1. *Civil War Times Illustrated* 13, no. 7 (November 1974).

Minor, part 2. Minor, Hubbard T. "Diary of a Confederate Naval Cadet." Part 2. *Civil War Times Illustrated* 13, no. 8 (December 1974).

Moebs, *Research Guide*. Moebs, Thomas Truxton, ed. *Confederate States Navy Research Guide*. Williamsburg, Va.: Moebs Publishing, 1991.

Morgan, "Most Realistic War College." Morgan, James M. "A Most Realistic War College." *Naval Institute Proceedings* (March-April 1916).

***Navy Regulations*.** *Regulations for the Navy of the Confederate States*. Richmond: Macfarlane & Fergusson, 1862.

***Official Records, Armies*.** *Official Records of the Union and Confederate Armies in the War of the Rebellion*. Washington, D.C.: Government Printing Office, 1880–1901.

***Official Records, Navies*.** *Official Records of the Union and Confederate Navies in the War of the Rebellion* (Washington, D.C.: Government Printing Office, 1894–1927.

***Ordnance Instructions*.** *Ordnance Instructions for the Confederate States Navy*. London: Saunders, Otley & Co., 1864.

Parker, *Confederate Military History*. Parker, William H. "The Confederate States Navy," in vol. 12. *Confederate Military History*. 12 vols. ed. Clement A. Evans. Atlanta: Confederate Publishing Co., 1895.

Parker, *Questions on Seamanship*. Parker, William H. *Questions on Practical Seamanship; Together With Harbor Routine and Evolutions*. Richmond: Macfarlane & Fergusson, 1863.

Parker, *Recollections*. Parker, William H. *Recollections of a Naval Officer 1841–1865*. New York: Scribners, 1883; reprint, Annapolis: Naval Institute Press, 1985.

Scharf, *History*. Scharf, John T. *History of the Confederate States Navy*. New York: Fairfax Press, 1977.

***School-Ship Regulations*.** *Regulations for the Confederate States School-Ship Patrick Henry*. N.p.: 1863.

Still, *Confederate Navy*. Still, William N. Jr., ed. *The Confederate Navy: Its Ships, Men and Organization, 1861–1865*. Annapolis: Naval Institute Press, 1997.

Wilson, "Wilson's War." Wilson, Beverly E., ed. "Willie Wilson's War, 1861–1865: An Account of Some of the Experiences of Midshipman W F Wilson, C S Navy." Unpublished manuscript, 1969. Nimitz Library, United States Naval Academy.

Chapter 1

1. Edward L. Beach, *The United States Navy: A 200 Year History* (Boston: Houghton Mifflin, 1986), 177.

2. The term "midshipman" originated in the Royal Navy and referred to junior officers stationed amidships to relay orders along the length of the ship. A "reefer" generally is any sailor who reefs a sail, which means to roll it up at the foot and make this fast in order to decrease the area exposed to the wind. Since it was midshipmen who were usually responsible for reefing the topsails, "reefer" soon came to refer specifically to midshipmen.

3. Beach, *United States Navy*, 177.

4. Ibid., 178.

5. U.S. Naval Academy, www.nadn.navy.mil/VirtualTour/150years/history 1.html (October 1997).

6. Ibid.

7. For example, in Patrick O'Brian's historically detailed novels of life in the Napoleonic-era Royal Navy, Captain Jack Aubrey often laments his lack of knowledge of non-nautical subjects to his learned friend, Dr. Stephen Maturin. Despite the need for broader education, however, the Royal Naval College was not readily accepted in British naval circles as a substitute for shipboard training. N. A. M. Rodger's *The Wooden World: An Anatomy of the Georgian Navy* (New York: Norton, 1996) contains a good discussion of the college and its teething problems, as does Brian Lavery's *Nelson's Navy: The Ships, Men and Organisation 1793–1815* (Annapolis: Naval Institute Press, 1989).

8. U.S. Naval Academy, "A Brief History of the United States Naval Academy." U.S. Naval Academy website, www.nadn.navy.mil/VirtualTour/150years.

9. Parker, *Recollections*. The quarterdeck was traditionally the domain of officers; common sailors were allowed upon its planks only if summoned or if there in performance of their duties. As officers, midshipmen were allowed on the quarterdeck and berthed separately from the sailors, who slung their hammocks in the forecastle, or fo'c'sle.

10. The surgeon of the *Somers*, a reluctant participant in this death sentence, killed himself in the ship's wardroom after the vessel returned to New York. No official explanation was given for the suicide, but many at the time believed it was due to the guilt he felt for his part in what transpired on the brig.

11. Phillip Spencer's father and Elisha Small's widow had Mackenzie charged with murder in a civilian court. Navy Secretary Upshur convinced Spencer and Mrs. Small to withdraw the civilian complaint and allow Mackenzie to be tried in a navy court-martial. Upshur appointed Mackenzie's brother-in-law, Oliver Hazard Perry, as president of the court, and, not surprisingly, the captain was acquitted. Spencer became so enraged at Upshur's actions that the two men had to be physically separated at a cabinet meeting soon after the court-martial verdict. Beach, *United States Navy* contains a good account of the *Somers* affair and its aftermath.

12. U.S. Naval Academy, "A Brief History of the United States Naval Academy." U.S. Naval Academy website, www.nadn.navy.mil/VirtualTour/150years.

13. The original curriculum included mathematics and navigation, gunnery, chemistry, English, natural philosophy (physics), and French. The course of study took five years with the first and last spent at the school and the other three at sea. In 1850 the name of the institution was changed to the United States Naval Academy and the course of study was shortened to four years with summers spent at sea; this is still the basis of the U.S. Naval Academy curriculum. Franklin Buchanan resigned his commission at the start of the Civil War and served as commander of the CSS *Virginia* and of the Confederate Mobile Squadron. He became one of the Confederacy's only two admirals. For three of the academy's first six years, Captain Sidney Smith Lee, Robert E. Lee's brother and the father of two future Confederate officers, Major General Fitzhugh Lee and Midshipman Daniel M. Lee, served as commandant of midshipmen.

14. Moebs, *Research Guide*, 90; Scharf, *History*, 773.

15. *Official Records, Armies*, series IV, vol. 1: 267.

16. *Journal of the Congress of the Confederate States of America, 1861–1865* (Washington, D.C.: Government Printing Office), 1 (1904): 547.

17. Joseph T. Durkin, *Stephen R. Mallory: Confederate Navy Chief* (Columbia: University of South Carolina Press, 1987), 44.

18. Parker, *Recollections*, 346.

19. Ibid., 345.

20. *Official Records, Navies*, series II, vol. 2: 533.

21. Ibid.

22. St. George Tucker Brooke, "Autobiography" (Library of Virginia, Richmond, Va.). A naval recruit's first contact with the navy was usually a receiving ship. These ships, considered unsuitable for more active service, were manned by a small compliment of experienced officers and petty officers and served as a sort of boot camp for new recruits and replacement depots for ship's crews. At different times during the war receiving ships were docked at Mobile, Alabama (CSS *Dalman*); Wilmington, North Carolina (CSS *Arctic*); Charleston, South Carolina (CSS *Indian Chief*); Savannah, Georgia (CSS *Sampson*); New Orleans, Louisiana (CSS *St. Phillip*, formerly the Fort Sumter resupply ship *Star of the West*); and Norfolk, Virginia (CSS *Confederate States*, ex-USS *United States*).

23. Clayton, *Narrative*, 113.

24. Of 671 Southern naval officers, 321 resigned or were dismissed from the United States Navy (Scharf, *History*, 32–33). "Tar" or "Jack-tar," slang terms for a sailor, had been in use in the Royal Navy since at least 1676. Early sailors wore overalls and broad-brimmed hats made of tar-impregnated fabric called tarpaulin cloth. The hats, and the sailors who wore them, were called tarpaulins, which may have been shortened to tars (Naval Historical Center, www.history.navy.mil/trivia/trivia03.htm [October 1997]).

25. Dudley, *Going South*, 19.

26. One hundred-eleven acting midshipmen, a total of 42 percent of those serving in that grade, resigned from the U.S. Navy between December 1860 and November 1861. Not all of them sought appointments in the Confederate navy (Ibid., 16–18). A complete list is available at www.wisc.edu/wendt/frus/753s.html.

27. Scharf, *History*, 773; Moebs, *Research Guide*, 107. A passed midshipman was a midshipman who had passed his final examining board examination. A passed midshipman was generally equivalent to an army second lieutenant and an acting midshipman was generally equivalent to an army cadet. In 1862, the United States Navy established the rank of ensign to replace that of passed midshipman; the Confederate States Navy did not follow suit. In June 1864 all acting midshipmen in the Regular Confederate States Navy were appointed midshipmen in the Provisional Navy of the Confederate States (PNCS) that had been created in 1863.

28. James David Altman, "The Charleston Marine School," *South Carolina Historical Magazine* 88, no. 2 (April 1987): 77, quoting undated newspaper clipping, in the Marine School Schooner *Petrel* Log Book (South Caroliniana Library, Columbia, South Carolina).

29. Ibid., page 77, quoting *Reports and Resolutions of the General Assembly of the State of South Carolina, Passed at the Annual Session of 1860* (Columbia, 1860), 333.

The South Carolina Military Academy (SCMA) consisted of two institutions, the Arsenal Academy in Columbia and the Citadel Academy in Charleston. For a history of the SCMA's Civil War services *see* James Lee Conrad, *The Young Lions: Confederate Cadets at War* (Mechanicsburg, Pa.: Stackpole Books, 1997) and Gary R. Baker, *Cadets in Gray* (Columbia, S.C.: Palmetto Bookworks, 1989).

30. In 1862 the *Lodebar* was sold and the Charleston Marine School transferred to the schooner *Petrel*. The deteriorating military situation at Charleston led to the school's relocation to the inland city of Orangeburg, South Carolina, in August 1863. The school continued its operations until destroyed by the advancing troops of Major General William T. Sherman in February 1865. Approximately sixty students graduated from the Charleston Marine School during its existence.

31. *Official Records, Navies*, series II, vol. 2: 533.

32. *Civil War Naval Chronology* 6 (1971): 280; Moebs, *Research Guide*, 349; Herndon, "Naval Academy," 300. The quotation is from a January 30, 1865, letter by Flag Officer John Randolph Tucker, Reel 3, Folder 29, Raphael Semmes Family Papers, Alabama Department of Archives and History, Montgomery, Alabama.

33. The *Jamestown* was scuttled in the James River in May 1862 in a hurried attempt to obstruct the river near Drewry's Bluff.

34. The Confederate Navy Department was so impressed with the speed and armament of the finished ship that Mallory wanted to send the *Patrick Henry* to sea as a commerce raider.

35. Flag Officer John Randolph Tucker, letter, January 30, 1865 (Reel 3, Folder 29, Raphael Semmes Family Papers, Alabama Department of Archives and History, Montgomery, Alabama).

36. Morgan, "Most Realistic War College," 543.

37. Midshipman Morgan stated after the war that the crew had standing orders to scuttle the *Patrick Henry* in the passage left through the Confederate obstructions in the river should the Federal navy attempt to force a passage (Morgan, "Most Realistic War College," 544). Union sympathizers in Richmond noticed all the work on the ship. One of them, William Harris, relayed information to Federal naval officers on July 3, 1863, that the *Patrick Henry* was at Drewry's Bluff "fitted out as a privateer" and "is ready for sea, and will try and get out" (*Official Records, Navies*, series I, vol. 5: 294). Actually, she was receiving supplies and students and wasn't headed anywhere. It took the Federals some time to realize Harris was mistaken and relax their lookout for the *Patrick Henry*'s "breakout" to sea.

38. It is unclear why the Naval Academy was assigned to Brooke's Office of Ordnance and Hydrography, which concerned itself with weapons and navigational aids, rather than the Office of Orders and Details, which handled personnel matters. Perhaps it was for no other reason than to be able to make use of Brooke's energy and organizational skills.

39. Parker, *Recollections*, 118; *School-Ship Regulations*, chapter 1, paragraph 1, required the bureau chief to inspect the school ship yearly. The regulations as written (chapter 1, paragraph 2) titled the commanding officer of the school ship "commandant" and the second ranking officer "executive officer." In practice, Parker was the superintendent of the Naval Academy, which also supervised the education of acting midshipmen who were not aboard the *Patrick Henry*, while also performing many of the duties prescribed by regulation for the commandant of the school ship, although the title of commandant seems to have been bestowed upon the executive officer.

40. *Official Records, Navies*, series II, vol. 2: 551. Parker's brother, Commander Foxhall Parker, served as a Federal naval officer and was later named superintendent of the United States Naval Academy.

41. Voucher, June 6, 1863, in Record Group 45, Subject File NE, National Archives.

42. Vouchers, September 25 and September 12, 1863, in record group 45, Subject File NE, National Archives.

43. Brooke, letter to Martin, November 9, 1863 (Record Group 45, Subject File NE, National Archives).

Chapter 2

1. Herndon, "Naval Academy," 306. The students of the academy included all acting midshipmen, whether assigned to the school ship or to active service.

2. Parker, *Recollections*, 345. Commanders in the field were also loath to part with their promising young officers so they could attend school. "You are aware," one squadron commander complained to his superior, "that you have detached from this station to Richmond, Charleston, and to the naval school, with scarcely an exception, such officers as I should most confidently rely [upon]."(*Official Records*, *Navies*, series I, vol. 15: 108.

3. Morgan, "Most Realistic War College," 543. Morgan was engaged to marry Helen Trenholm, daughter of Confederate Treasury Secretary George Trenholm.

4. Parker, *Recollections*, 346.

5. Parker wrote several textbooks, including *Harbor Routine and Evolutions, Naval Tactics, Naval Light Artillery Afloat and Ashore*, and *Remarks on the Navigation of the Coasts Between San Francisco and Panama*. Parker's books were used as texts at both the United States and Confederate States naval academies.

6. *Interior Police Regulations*, paragraph 145.

7. When Loyall actually served as commandant of the school ship is unclear. In his memoirs, Parker lists Loyall as the academy's first commandant, whereas other sources clearly do not place him in that position until November 1864. But Parker admitted he did not have a list of the faculty before him as he wrote and he may have been mistaken. In November 1863, Parker praised to Brooke "the exertions of Lieutenants Hall and Comstock, his assistants" with no mention of Loyall (*Official Records, Navies*, series II, vol. 2: 551). Loyall did accompany Commander John Taylor Wood and eight midshipmen on the expedition to capture the USS *Underwriter* in February 1864 and Parker refers to him as serving as commandant at this time (see chapter 4). The *Underwriter* expedition was one of a series of special duty assignments performed by Loyall in 1863 and 1864 and he may have served as commandant for short periods between these assignments. After the *Underwriter* expedition, Loyall was assigned to superintend the construction of the ironclad *Neuse* in North Carolina and was named as her first commander. He was replaced as captain by Commander Joseph H. Price on August 24, 1864. Loyall was reassigned to the *Patrick Henry* as commandant and executive officer sometime after leaving the *Neuse*.

8. Loyall was commissioned in the Provisional Army of the Confederate States and was serving in the grade of major when relieved on February 13, 1862, and ordered to report to Secretary Mallory at Richmond (*Official Records, Navies*, series II, vol. 2: 146).

9. For more on Loyall and the ironclad *Neuse, see* Tyrone G. Martin, "North Carolina's Ironclad" (*Naval History* 10, no. 4 [July–August 1996]); William N. Still, Jr., *Iron Afloat: The Story of the Confederate Armorclads* (Nashville, Tenn.: Vanderbilt University Press, 1971); CSS *Neuse* homepage, www.ah.dcr.state.nc.us/sections/hs/neuse/neuse.htm.

10. Most postwar accounts of the naval academy list a C. J. Graves as the instructor of seamanship; the *Register of Officers of the Confederate States Navy 1861–1865* (Mattituck, N.Y.: J. M. Carroll, 1983) lists him as Charles Iverson Graves. As with some of the other officers assigned to the academy, sources conflict regarding Graves's assignment history. Most postwar accounts, including Parker's,

list him as one of the original 1863 faculty. However, the *Register of Officers* shows him as being on "service abroad" in 1863–64 and reporting aboard the *Patrick Henry* in 1865. Since the majority of sources list him as part of the original faculty, I have done so here.

11. Once again there is some confusion regarding Billups. All postwar accounts refer to J. W. or James W. Billups. The *Register of Former Officers*, while listing a J. W. Billups, credits a G. W. Billups as being assigned to the *Patrick Henry*.

12. George M. Peek is listed in the *Register of Officers of the Confederate States Navy* as first lieutenant and instructor in mathematics. On December 17, 1864, Senate Bill no. 143 was introduced in the Confederate Senate to authorize the hiring of six assistant instructors, two in mathematics and one each for English, ethics, modern languages, drawing and drafting, and sword and bayonet exercise. The instructors were to have the rank and pay of a first lieutenant in the navy. The bill never passed; see T. Michael Parrish and Robert M. Willingham, Jr., *Confederate Imprints: A Bibliography of Southern Publications from Secession to Surrender* (Austin, Texas: Jenkins Publishing Co., 1987), imprint 402.

13. Parker, *Confederate Military History,* vol. 14, p. 96. McGuire's name does not appear in the *Register of Officers.*

14. Listed as Peple in the *Register of Officers*; Peple in Parker, *Recollections*; and Pepley in Scharf, *History.*

15. Sanxey is the only other faculty member not listed in the *Register of Officers*; he may have been a civilian or, given his subject, an army officer. His Christian name is unknown.

16. That Strange had difficulty getting out of the army is evidenced by Commander Brooke's February 17, 1865, letter to him: "Your letter of the 14th inst. to the Secretary of the Navy has been referred to this office. Your appointment as Instructor in the Naval School does not entitle you to report on board the "Patrick Henry" without delay. A regular transfer from the Army will be necessary before you can enter upon the duties of the position to which you have been appointed by the Navy Department." (Letter Book, John Brooke, letter to Strange, February 17, 1865).

17. The *Patrick Henry* had a compliment of 150 men when she previously served with the James River Squadron. A roster of her crew for the period July-August, 1861, and October-December, 1864, appears in the *Official Records, Navies,* series II, vol. 1: 299–301.

18. Minor, a native of Virginia, enlisted in the 42d Tennessee Infantry Regiment at age sixteen and served until his appointment as an acting midshipman in July 1863.

19. *School-Ship Regulations*, chapter 3, paragraph 6. There were exceptions made to the age requirement; Raphael Semmes, Jr., was appointed an acting midshipman at age twelve.

20. J. T. Durkin, *Stephen R. Mallory: Confederate Navy Chief* (Chapel Hill: University of North Carolina Press, 1954), 285.

21. "Form for Examining a Recruit" (no date), author's collection.

22. *School-Ship Regulations*, chapter 3, paragraph 6. The academic board members were the commandant (superintendent), executive officer, second lieutenant, third lieutenant, and the professors of mathematics, English studies, and modern languages. The academic board was responsible for supervising the curriculum of the academy including that of acting midshipmen serving with the fleet.

23. John Brooke, letter to Mallory, February 14, 1865 (Letter Book, 167).

24. J. M. Brooke, diaries, entry for December 20, 1861 (in possession of Colonel George M. Brooke).

25. *School-Ship Regulations*, chapter 4, paragraphs 2 and 3; Morgan, "Most Realistic War College," 546.

26. *Uniform and Dress of the Navy of the Confederate States* (Richmond: Chas. H. Wynne, 1861; reprint, New Hope, Pa.: River House, 1952).

27. Still, *Confederate Navy*, 144.

28. *Uniform and Dress of the Navy of the Confederate States.*

29. *School-Ship Regulations*, chapter 4, paragraph 5. The regulations do not describe these "distinctive insignia," and so far as the author knows no examples or descriptions exist and they may in fact have never been implemented.

30. Ibid., paragraph 1; *Interior Police Regulations*, paragraph 94.

31. *School-Ship Regulations*, chapter 3, paragraph 10.

32. Harrison Papers, letters to "Dear Father," February 9 and 11, 1864.

33. Ibid.

34. Morgan, "Most Realistic War College," 546.

35. Minor, part 1, 26.

36. Morgan, "Most Realistic War College," 546.

37. Ibid.

38. Ibid.

39. Scharf, *History*, 775.

40. Harrison Papers, letter to "Dear Ellen," October 30, 1864.

41. Varina Davis, *Jefferson Davis Ex-President of the Confederate States: A Memoir by His Wife* (New York: Belford Co., 1890), vol. 2, 534.

42. William F. Clayton, "The Confederate Navy," *Richmond Times-Dispatch*, 1908.

43. Ibid.

44. *School-Ship Regulations*, chapter 12, paragraph 5.

45. Morgan, "Most Realistic War College," 550.

46. *Interior Police Regulations*, paragraph 74.

47. Thomas Truxton, "A Short Account of the Several General Duties of Officers of Ships of War; From An Admiral, Down to the Most Inferior Officer," Naval Historical Center http://www.history.navy.mil/faqs/faq59-2.htm#intro. Truxtun, born in 1755 at Jamaica, Long Island, went to sea at age twelve and was impressed into the British Royal Navy in 1771. During the Revolutionary War he commanded the American privateers *Independence*, *Mars*, and *St. James*. In 1778 he was appointed the first captain of the new thirty-six-gun frigate *Constellation*. Truxtun resigned from the navy in 1802 after a disagreement with his superiors. He died in 1822 (Peter Kemp, ed., *The Oxford Companion to Ships and the Sea* [Oxford University Press: Oxford, 1988], 894).

48. Minor, part 1, 29.

49. Ibid.

50. Minor, part 1, 28–29.

51. Harrison Papers, letter to his father, February 9, 1864.

52. Ibid.

53. Breckinridge, letter to "Dear Pa," September 8, 1864 (Record Group 45, M260, Roll 5, Records Relating to Confederate Naval and Marine Personnel, National Archives). Breckinridge was appointed an acting midshipman in February 1864 at which time he withdrew his application to the Honorable J. M. Elliott, Confederate congressman for the 12th District of Kentucky, for an appointment as a Confederate States Army cadet.

54. Minor, part 1, 27.

55. Parker's *Elements of Seamanship. Prepared As A Textbook for the Midshipmen of the C. S. Navy* was published by Macfarlane & Fergusson of Richmond in May 1864. The book contained seventeen chapters: 1, "Rope"; 2, "Blocks and Tackles"; 3, "Docks"; 4, "Construction"; 5–12, "Rigging Ship"; 13, "Stowage"; 14, "Anchors and Chains"; 15, "Sails"; 16, "Boats"; and 17, "Organization." The chapters consisted of discussion or questions and answers or a combination thereof. A much smaller book, *Questions on Practical Seamanship*, was published in Richmond in September 1863. Parker states in the preface that it was prepared from notes he made as an instructor at

Annapolis. The book was in four parts: "Rigging"; "Questions"; "Evolutions"; and "Master's Duties." Many questions posed in its pages were unanswered, for the purpose, Parker wrote, of causing "the student to *think*; and to give the Instructor an opportunity of explaining *the philosophy* of Seamanship and Naval Discipline."

56. A woolding was the rope used to bind curved pieces of wood called fish around a mast or spar to repair it. A stopper is a short length of rope secured at one end with a stopper knot.

57. Minor, part 2, 32–33.

58. Parker, *Questions on Seamanship*, 24.

59. Ibid., 43.

60. Ibid., 62.

61. Ibid., 15, 16, 20, 10, 42, 42, 47, 49, 41. "Holidays" are spots accidentally left unpainted or unvarnished. A "euphroe" is a long cylindrical block with a number of holes for receiving the legs, or lines, of the "crowfoot," which supports a ship's awning. A "timenoguy" is a rope stretched taut between different parts of a sailing ship to prevent fouling of tacks or braces. "Slops" are ready made clothing and sundries sold by the ship's purser. The "Jack of the Dust" is the purser's mate in charge of the bread room; in days past he issued flour for bread making. An individual crewman may complain about the ration in person or in writing. "Goose-winging" was a method of setting partial sail when the wind was too strong to set the entire sail. "Gripe" describes the tendency of a sailing ship to come up into the wind when sailing close-hauled; easing off on the sails lessens the gripe. Whiskey is "started" by opening the keg.

62. *Interior Police Regulations*, paragraph 4.

63. It is not certain that any eight-inch guns remained on board, since the army coveted them. On July 31, 1862, General Robert E. Lee wrote to Secretary Mallory noting that "the land part of the defenses at Drewry's Bluff has as yet no guns upon it. Can any be spared from the Navy for that purpose? I have heard that there are six 8-inch guns on the Patrick Henry. If these can be spared they would serve to add much to the strength of the defenses . . . " (*Official Records, Armies*, series I, vol. 14: 658). In late 1864, a deserter from the ship reported to Federal authorities that the *Patrick Henry* was armed with "four guns, smoothbore, old Navy pattern" (*Official Records, Navies*, series I, vol. 11: 380).

64. The following description is taken from *Ordnance Instructions*, pp. 43–56.

65. Ibid., page 49, paragraph 199. Cartridge bags containing powder charges for distant firing were white, those for ordinary firing were blue, and those for near firing were red. Saluting charges were in red bags marked "saluting."

66. *Interior Police Regulations*, paragraph 4.

67. Harrison Papers, letter to "Dear Ellen," October 30, 1864.

68. *School-Ship Regulations*, chapter 15, paragraph 7.

69. Steerage was the area below deck where the midshipmen slept and studied.

70. *Interior Police Regulations*, paragraph 30.

71. Ibid.

72. Ibid.

73. *Interior Police Regulations*, paragraph 41.

74. Ibid., paragraphs 46, 43.

75. Ibid., paragraph 52.

76. Ibid., paragraph 55.

77. Ibid., paragraph 124, 125.

78. Ibid., paragraph 119.

79. Ibid., paragraph 20.

80. Ibid.

81. *School-Ship Regulations*, chapter 10, paragraph 11.

82. Ibid., paragraphs 3, 4, 11, and 18. Even though Confederate sailors received a daily grog ration and even though there was a spirit room aboard the *Patrick Henry*, it seems that grog was prohibited to midshipmen.

83. *School-Ship Regulations*, chapter 12, paragraph 16.

84. Ibid., chapter 10, paragraphs 5, 7, 9, 10, 15, and 21.

85. Ibid., chapter 11, paragraph 1.

86. Ibid.

87. *School-Ship Regulations*, chapter 9, paragraph 5.

88. Ibid., chapter 10, paragraph 22.

89. Ibid.

90. Ibid., chapter 10, paragraph 24.

91. Ibid., paragraph 23.

92. Ibid., paragraph 25.

93. Ibid., paragraph 27.

94. Ibid., paragraph 28.

95. Ibid., paragraph 23.

96. Ibid., paragraphs 23 and 30.

97. Clayton, "Confederate Navy," 103–4.

98. Minor, part 1, 31.

99. Clayton, "Confederate Navy," 112.

100. Clayton, "Confederate Navy."

101. Harrison Papers, letter to "Dear Ellen," March 31, 1864.

102. Robert Dabney Minor Papers, item c.3233 (roll B29, Virginia Historical Society).

103. Morgan, "Most Realistic War College", 544. Also in residence on the school ship was the son of Colonel Lloyd Beall, Commandant of the Confederate Marine Corps.

104. Clayton, "Confederate Navy," 102.

105. Ibid.

106. Ibid.

107. Clayton, "Confederate Navy," 103.

108. Thomas P. Lowry, *The Story the Soldiers Wouldn't Tell: Sex in the Civil War* (Mechanicsburg, Pa.: Stackpole Books, 1997), 28.

109. Richmond *Daily Dispatch*, February 17, 1864.

110. Harris Levin, letter written from Drewry's Bluff in late 1864, quoted in Lowry, *Story Soldiers Wouldn't Tell*, 28.

111. Minor, part 1, 28.

112. Ibid.

113. Ibid.

114. Caption on reverse of photo of Peple, courtesy of Chuck Peple. Gus and Sarah were married in 1865.

115. Letter to "Dear Pa," September 8, 1864 (Record Group 45, M260, Roll 5, Records Relating to Confederate Naval and Marine Personnel, National Archives).

116. Harrison Papers, letter to "Dear Ellen," October 30, 1864.

117. J. A. Carter was still aboard the school ship at its destruction in April 1865 and accompanied Mrs. Jefferson Davis on her flight from Richmond. William K. Hale was appointed to the Naval Academy from Alabama. Prior to his appointment he served in the army at Drewry's Bluff and aboard the CSS *Baltic* at Mobile. Joshua C. Wright was appointed a midshipman in the Provisional Navy on June 2, 1864, but resigned on December 10, 1864.

118. Morgan, "Most Realistic War College," 549.

119. Ibid.

120. A board of officers appointed by the secretary of the navy examined midshipmen not in residence at the school ship. *See* ibid., chapter 3.

121. *School-Ship Regulations*, chapter 6, paragraph 9.

122. John Brooke, letter to Hon. J. L. M. Curry, November 30, 1863 (Eleanor S. Brockenbrough Library, Museum of the Confederacy, Richmond, Virginia).

123. *School-Ship Regulations*, chapter 6, paragraph 1.

124. Parker, *Recollections*, 346.

125. *School-Ship Regulations*, chapter 6, paragraph 3.

126. Harrison Papers, letter to "My dear wife," December 12, 1864.

127. Ibid.

128. It was possible if required by the exigencies of the service for a successful examination to result in a promotion to master or lieutenant (*School-Ship Regulations*, chapter 6, paragraph 6).

129. *Official Records, Navies*, series II, vol. 2: 550.

130. Ibid., 642.

131. Ibid., 533.

132. Ibid., 757.

133. House Bill no. 276, December 13, 1864, in Parrish and Willingham, imprint 738.

134. *Official Records, Navies*, series II, vol. 2: 634–35.

135. Letter Book, Brooke to Gilmer, December 19, 1864.

136. Harrison Papers, letter, "Dear Ellen," June 9, 1864. The reference to avoiding conscription as a motivation for attending the academy raises the issue of the extent of this practice. While undoubtedly a motivation for some, the need for a congressional appointment and the statutory ceiling of 106 acting midshipmen surely reduced the use of an academy appointment as a means of dodging the draft—but political connections can be used for many ends. Accusations that they were havens for draft dodgers were leveled at the Confederacy's state military colleges (*see* James Lee Conrad *The Young Lions: Confederate Cadets at War* (Mechanicsburg, Pa.: Stackpole Books, 1997), 51–52, 73, and Keith Bohannon, "Cadets, Drillmasters, Draft Dodgers, and Soldiers: The Georgia Military Institute During the Civil War," *The Georgia Historical Quarterly* 79, no. 1 (Spring 1995).

Chapter 3

1. Confederate naval stations were established at Richmond, Virginia; Halifax, Kinston, Charlotte, and Wilmington, North Carolina; Marion Court House and

Charleston, South Carolina; Savannah and Columbus, Georgia; St. Marks, Florida; Mobile, Alabama; New Orleans and Shreveport, Louisiana; and Jackson, Mississippi. The installations at Little Rock, Arkansas; Selma, Alabama; and Yazoo City, Mississippi, are also counted as naval stations by some sources. After 1863, Secretary Mallory separated command of forces afloat from command of the naval stations, thereby facilitating the assignment of younger, more aggressive officers to command of the naval squadrons. A passed midshipman could request an assignment upon graduation from the academy. Olly Harrison noted in a letter that "the majority of the class will be ordered to either this station [Richmond] or to the Wilmington Station. But I have put in my application for Savannah or Mobile" (Harrison Papers, letter to "Dear Ellen," March 31, 1864). The needs of the service, however, always took primacy, regardless of any of the men's assignment preferences. As for the position of "flag midshipman," William F. Clayton described it as "a high-sounding title, but in reality [was] messenger boy for the flag officer" (Clayton, *Narrative*, 69).

2. Estimates of the numbers of Confederate naval vessels vary according to the source consulted and the types of vessels counted. The 130 figure cited here is from Still, *Confederate Navy*, 68. Moebs, *Research Guide* (307–70), in his compilation of vessels lists 123 by name, including privateers, which were not commissioned warships. The *Civil War Naval Chronology* lists over 500 "Confederate Forces Afloat" (vol. 6, pp. 182–354). This list counts all "public vessels" of the Confederate States including privateers, the River Defense Fleet, the Texas Marine Department, and the "Stone Fleet" of ships deliberately sunk to obstruct strategic Southern waterways.

3. *Navy Regulations*, chapter 8, section 3, articles 11 and 13.

4. Robert Watson Diary, quoted in John Kennington, "Clothing, Pay and Provisions for the Savannah River Squadron 1861–1864," at Navy and Marine Living History web site, www.navymarine.org/uniforms.

5. B. A. Botkin, ed., *A Civil War Treasury of Tales, Legends and Folklore* (New York: Random House, 1960), 467.

6. Ibid.

7. *Navy Regulations*, chapter 8, section 1, article 31.

8. The watches were as follows: Noon to 4:00 P.M. — Afternoon watch; 4:00 P.M. to 6:00 P.M. — First dogwatch; 6:00 P.M. to 8:00 P.M. — Second dogwatch; 8:00 P.M. to midnight — First night watch; Midnight to 4:00 A.M. — Middle or mid watch; 4:00 to 8:00 A.M. — Morning watch; 8:00 A.M. to noon — Forenoon watch. The purpose of the dogwatches was to ensure that the same group of men did not constantly stand the same watch. Ship's time was kept with reference to each watch

by strikes on the ship's bell every half hour. For example, one bell was struck at the start of the watch, two bells at, say, 8:30, three bells at 9:00, and four bells at 9:30. Nine-thirty A.M. was referred to as four bells in the forenoon watch and 9:30 P.M. as four bells in the first night watch.

9. Daniel B. Conrad, "The Capture of the CS Ram *Tennessee* in Mobile Bay, August 1864," *Southern Historical Society Papers* 19 (1891): 72–74.

10. Maurice Melton, "The First and Last Cruise of the CSS Atlanta," *Civil War Times Illustrated* 10, no. 7 (November 1971): 6.

11. James C. Long, "The Poorest Ironclad in the Confederacy: An Officer's Opinion of the *Albemarle*," *Civil War Times Illustrated* 13, no. 9 (January 1975): 25.

12. Ibid.

13. Wilson, "Wilson's War," 28.

14. Minor, Part 2, 24.

15. Ibid.

16. Ibid.

17. Minor, Part 2, 28.

18. Ibid.

19. Scharf, *History*, 647.

20. The dead were buried at navy expense. The receipt for Pelot's funeral expenses—$200 for casket, silver name plate, and exterior box—is in the National Archives (Record Group 109, Roll 15, File ME). The navy also paid for the burial of Moses Dallas, but Dallas may not have stayed dead. Dallas was a native of Duval County, Florida, and enlisted as a pilot in the U.S. Navy in 1863. That same year he deserted to the Confederate navy. Three months after his "death" on the *Water Witch*, a Moses Dallas was on the rolls of the 128th U.S. Colored Infantry Regiment. After the war, this Dallas returned to Duval County. It is possible that there were two black men named Moses Dallas from the same county in Florida, but it is unlikely.

21. The *Georgia* was built as the merchant steamer *Japan* and was purchased by Commander Matthew F. Maury from her British owners in March 1863. She was iron-hulled, 212 feet long, and armed, according to Morgan, with two ten-pounder Whitworths, two twenty-four-pounders, and one thirty-two-pounder Blakely cannon. The *Georgia* took nine prizes during a cruise around the South Atlantic. In May 1864 she was sold to a Liverpool merchant and put to sea under her new owner on August 11, 1864. On August 15 she was captured off Portugal by the USS *Niagara* and taken to Boston, where she was condemned (declared converted to public use) and sold as a

prize. After the war she sailed for a time as a merchant vessel out of New Bedford, Massachusetts.

22. Campbell, *Midshipman in Gray*, 93.

23. Ibid.

24. Campbell, *Midshipman in Gray*, 95.

25. Ibid., 143.

26. Ibid., *Midshipman in Gray*, 106.

27. *Naval Regulations*, chapter 13, article 4.

28. *Ordnance Instructions*, chapter 2, paragraph 70.

29. Hester claimed he killed Andrews because the midshipman was about to turn the ship over to the enemy. Mallory and others did not believe Hester's defense and his story was repudiated by other crew members. Confederate authorities asked the British to return Hester to the Confederacy for trial. The British ship carrying Hester was refused entry into a Confederate port by Federal blockaders, so it docked in Bermuda and released him without notifying Confederate authorities. Hester escaped justice. See Scott Rye, "Murder on the *Sumter*," *Civil War Times Illustrated, 36*, no. 5 (October 1997).

30. John M. Coski, *Capital Navy: The Men, Ships and Operations of the James River Squadron* (Campbell, Calif.: Savas Woodbury, 1996), 188.

31. *Navy Regulations*, chapter 13, article 3. Whether these journals were actually kept as contemplated by the regulations is subject to question.

32. Ibid., chapter 14, article 3.

33. Ibid., chapter 8, article 7.

34. Ibid., chapter 10, article 1.

35. Ibid., chapter 11, article 17.

36. Ibid., chapter 15, section 2, article 1.

37. *Instructions for the Guidance of the Medical Officers of the Navy of the Confederate States*, Form A, Allowance Table (Richmond: Macfarlane & Fergusson, 1864).

38. Jones to Flag Officer W. W. Hunter, June 8, 1864 (Record Group 109, Roll 15, File ME, National Archives).

39. Record Group 109, Roll 15, File MM, National Archives.

40. Stanley F. Horn, *Gallant Rebel: The Famous Cruise of the CSS Shenandoah* (New Brunswick, N.J.: 1947), 56.

41. Wilson, "Wilson's War," 26.

42. Clayton, *Narrative, 5.*

43. Still, *Confederate Navy*, 135.

44. Ralph W. Donnelly, "Personnel of the Confederate Navy," *Civil War Times Illustrated* 13, no. 9 (January 1975): 30.

45. *Official Records, Navies,* series I, vol. 15: 108.

46. Campbell, *Midshipman in Gray,* 112.

47. One source states that by February 1865, 1,150 black seamen served in the Confederate navy (Scott K. Williams, "Black Confederates Fact Page," www.geocities.com/BourbonStreet/ Delta/3843/blackconfed.htm). This figure is almost certainly too high, since blacks were limited by navy policy to no more than 5 percent of any ship's crew. Since the total enlisted strength of the Confederate navy was never more than approximately 4,500, these 1,150 blacks would represent over 25 percent of the navy's sailors. The late Ralph Donnelly, in "Blacks in the Confederate Navy" (an unpublished manuscript in the collection of the Richmond National Battlefield Park), identified numerous individual black sailors, and although he was not able to estimate the total number of blacks who served, he did believe that the 5 percent rule kept their overall numbers low. The policy limiting the number of black sailors was a holdover from the U.S. Navy, which did not eliminate the restriction regarding black sailors until after the start of the Civil War.

48. Thomas Truxton, "A Short Account of the Several General Duties of Officers of Ships of War; From An Admiral, Down to the Most Inferior Officer," Naval Historical Center web site, www.history.navy.mil/faqs/faq59-2.htm#intro (October 1997), pp. 5–6.

49. Campbell, *Midshipman in Gray,* 69.

50. Ibid.

51. C. H. Lee, *The Judge Advocate's Vade Mecum: Embracing a General View of Military Law . . .* (Richmond: West & Johnson, 1864), 200.

52. Clayton, *Narrative,* 5.

53. Ibid.

54. Wilson, "Wilson's War," letter of February 14, 1863, 32.

55. Ibid.

56. Ibid.

57. Hunter, letter to Vaughan, December 7, 1864 (Record Group 45, File NJ, National Archives).

58. Ibid.

59. Campbell, *Midshipman in Gray,* 108.

60. *Navy Regulations,* chapter 8, section 3, article 16.

61. Campbell, *Midshipman in Gray,* 131.

62. Campbell, *Midshipman in Gray*, 132.

63. *Navy Regulations*, chapter 4, article 20.

64. Brooke to Barron, November 19, 1863 (Record Group 45, File NE, National Archives). The acting midshipmen listed as abroad were: 1st class—John T. Mason, Orris A. Browne, Richard S. Floyd; 2nd class—William W. Wilkenson (or Wilkinson), Raphael J. Moses, Jr., William B. Sinclair, Jr.; 3rd class—James W. Pegram, Virginius Newton, John M. Morgan, James H. Dyke, George D. Bryan, George T. Sinclair, James D. Bulloch, Jr., Edwin Maffitt Anderson, Eugene A. Maffitt, John H. Hamilton, John A. Wilson. The same letter also directed the examination of midshipmen west of the Mississippi River. Those listed: 1st class—Richard H. Bacot, Edward J. McDermott (or McDermett), Andrew P. Beirne; 2nd class—JHP (or John A. G.) Williamson; 3rd class—James A. Peters, William H. Sinclair, T. S. (perhaps John F., Jr.) Rodman, W. H. (perhaps Neil H.) Sterling, Clarance W. Tyler, James H. Dyke. Midshipmen W. W. Pipkin (not listed in *Register of Officers*), R. J. Watkins (not listed in *Register of Officers*), E. B. Trescott (or Trescot) were listed as "uncertain."

65. *Official Records, Navies*, series II, vol. 2: 673.

66. Ibid., 700.

67. Ibid., 771.

68. *Official Records, Navies*, series I, vol.15, 709.

69. Ibid.

70. *Official Records, Navies*, series I, vol. 15: 710.

71. Wilson, "Wilson's War," 29.

72. "Record for the Board for Examining Midshipmen, 1861–1862" (Record Group 109, Miscellaneous File, National Archives) lists the results of examinations held at Richmond, Savannah, and Mobile. The examiners adopted the following grading system, which was based on that in use at the United States Naval Academy: "Thorough" = 4.0; "Very Good"= 3.5; "Good" = 3.0; "Tolerable"= 2.5; "Indifferent" = 2.0; "Bad" = 1.0; "Complete Failure" = 0.0. Scores were weighted according to the importance of the course to the midshipman's class. The most heavily weighted scores in the upper two classes were those for navigation and seamanship.

73. Ibid., 66. Clayton's classmates examined that day were Charles R. Mallory, Jr., Clarence Cary, Roger Pinckney, Thomas C. Pinckney, Palmer Saunders, Frank Dorn, John T. Mason, Henry St. George Brooke, William B. Sinclair, Jr., Neil H. Sterling, James H. Dyke, James B. Ratcliffe, Virginius Newton, Daniel M. Lee, and Ferdinand S. Hunter.

74. Campbell, *Midshipman in Gray*, 164.

75. "Record for the Board for Examining Midshipmen, 1861–1862," 66.

76. Ibid., 66–67. Ganett is not listed in the *Register of Officers.* The establishment of the school ship and of an academic board for the Naval Academy was an improvement over the roving boards of examiners. At least one observer of the 1863 examinations in Richmond was not impressed, describing them as "very cursory in navigation, firing, making sail and broadsword exercises" (Frank E. Vandiver, ed., *The Civil War Diary of General Josiah Gorgas* [Tuscaloosa: University of Alabama Press, 1947], 130).

77. Captain John N. Mitchell, letter to Crawford, April 16, 1863 (Record Group 109, Roll 19, File NR, National Archives).

78. Forrest, letter to Winder, July 26, 1863 (Correspondence of John H. Winder, Virginia Historical Society, Richmond, Va.). George A. Joiner graduated from the Naval Academy sixth in his class on July 30, 1864. Forrest was either mistaken as to the man's identity or somehow confused concerning Joiner's status.

79. John A. Wilson, "Notes on the War of 1861–62," in "Notes of Midshipman John A. Wilson, CSN, on His Services During the Civil War, 1861–1865" (Record Group 45, National Archives), 42.

80. Wilson, "Wilson's War," 20.

81. General Order, November 17, 1864 (Record Group 109, Roll 15, File ME, National Archives).

Chapter 4

1. Reports on the academy's relocation as well as the training curriculum pursued after arrival at Fort Adams can be found at http://www.wisc.edu/wendt/frus/753s.html.

2. Campbell, *Midshipman in Gray*, 165.

3. Hardin B. Littlepage, "With the Crew of the Virginia," *Civil War Times Illustrated* 13, no. 2 (May 1974): 43.

4. Minor, part 1, 29.

5. Ibid.

6. Parker, *Recollections*, 347.

7. Morgan, "Most Realistic War College," 544.

8. Mason, letter to Robert D. Minor, September 24, 1863 (Minor Papers, Roll B26, Virginia Historical Society, Richmond, Virginia).

9. Morgan, "Most Realistic War College," 546.

10. Clayton, *Narrative*, 113.

11. Clifton Breckinridge, letter to "Dear Pa," 8 September 1864 (Record Group 45, M260, Roll 5, National Archives).

12. Harrison Papers, letter to "Dear Ellen," 5 June 1864. Quarles was Harrison's classmate R. S. Quarles.

13. *Official Records, Navies*, series I, vol. 9: 451.

14. Ibid.

15. Conrad, "Capture and Burning of 'Underwriter,'" 93.

16. Benjamin P. Loyall, "Capture of the Underwriter," *Southern Historical Society Papers* 27: 137.

17. Conrad, "Capture and Burning of 'Underwriter,'" 99.

18. Ibid.

19. Scharf, *History,* 396.

20. Loyall, "Capture of the Underwriter," 138.

21. Conrad, "Capture and Burning of 'Underwriter,'" 94.

22. Ibid., 99.

23. Ibid. Loyall describes Saunders as saying, "Fellows, where will we be this time tomorrow?" earlier in the day (Loyall, "Capture of the Underwriter," 139). Saunders was from Norfolk, Virginia, and had been appointed an acting midshipman on August 14, 1861. He was already a veteran, having seen service with the James River batteries, aboard the *Patrick Henry* in 1862, and in the engagement at Drewry's Bluff in May 1862. His last assignment prior to attending the Naval Academy had been with the Charleston Squadron's ironclad *Chicora*.

24. Scharf, *History,* 397.

25. Loyall, "Capture of the Underwriter," 140.

26. Conrad, "Capture and Burning of 'Underwriter,'" 95.

27. *Official Records, Navies*, series I, vol. 9: 452.

28. Conrad, "Capture and Burning of 'Underwriter,'" 96. Clayton describes Saunders's assailant as a "Swede" who was killed by a bullet to the head (Clayton, *Narrative*, 88). Superintendent Parker, however, noted in his memoirs that after the war a friend of his met the Federal petty officer who felled Midshipman Saunders and was told by him, "[H]e very much regretted having to do so, seeing his youth; but Saunders and another midshipman attacked him with such impetuosity that he was forced to cut him down in self-defence" (Parker, *Recollections*, 347).

29. Morgan, "Most Realistic War College," 547.

30. Scharf, *History*, 399.

31. Loyall, "Capture of the Underwriter," 141.

32. Conrad, "Capture and Burning of Underwriter," 96.

33. Ibid.

34. Ibid. Loyall in his own postwar account of the *Underwriter* expedition wrote that Saunders was "carefully placed in a blanket and lain in the bow of my boat. . . . He was breathing, but entirely unconscious" (Loyall, "Capture of the Underwriter," 141). All accounts describe Saunders's head wound as ghastly and most likely immediately fatal. Surgeon Conrad's recollection as the doctor who examined the youngster is probably more accurate than Loyall's, although not as romantic.

35. Phillip Rutherford, "The New Bern Raid" *Civil War Times Illustrated* 20, no. 9 (January 1982): 14; Scharf, *History*, 400.

36. Scharf, *History*, 400.

37. *Official Records, Armies*, series I, vol. 33: 51.

38. Scharf, *History*, 401.

39. *Official Records, Navies*, series I, vol. 9: 443.

40. Ibid.

41. *Official Records, Navies*, series I, vol. 9: 445.

42. Ibid.

43. Scharf, *History*, 402.

44. *Official Records, Navies*, series I, vol. 9: 452.

45. Ibid.

46. *Official Records, Navies*, series I, vol. 9, 453.

47. Ibid., 806.

48. Ibid., 800.

49. Scharf, *History*, 401.

50. Conrad, "Capture and Burning of Underwriter," 100.

51. Morgan, "Most Realistic War College," 545.

52. Ibid.

53. *Official Records, Navies*, series I, vol. 9: 808–9.

54. Ibid., 809.

55. Tyrone G. Martin, "North Carolina's Ironclad," *Naval History* 10, no. 4 (July–August 1996).

56. *Official Records, Navies*, series I, vol. 9: 811.

57. Milton F. Perry, *Infernal Machines* (Baton Rouge: Louisiana State University Press, 1965), 112.

58. Scharf, *History*, 776; Parker, *Confederate Military History*, vol. 12, p. 96.

59. Scharf, *History*, 776.

60. Harrison Papers, letter to "Dear Ellen," 9 June 1864.

61. Parker, *Recollections*, 338.

62. *Official Records, Navies*, series I, vol. 10: 709.

63. Ibid.

64. Ibid.

65. The names of the graduates and their class standing were as follows: 1. James H. Dykes; 2. Paul H. Gibbes [*sic*]; 3. Ralph J. Deas; 4. William N. Shaw; 5. Charles F. Sevier; 6. George A. Joiner; 7. William B. Sinclair, Jr.; 8. Henry H. Scott; 9. Frank C. Morehead; 10. Clarence Cary; 11. Roger Pinckney; 12. George T. Sinclair, Jr.; 13. Daniel M. Lee; 14. Virginius Newton; 15. Thomas M. Berrien; 16. James B. Ratcliffe; 17. Thomas C. Pinckney; 18. James W. Pegram; 19. John H. Hamilton; 20. William D. Goode ("Good" in *Register of Officers*); 21. Cassius Meyer; 22. Franklin B. Dornin; 23. William F. Clayton; 24. William J. Carroll; 25. Ferdinand S. Hunter; 26. Francis M. Thomas. A typescript of this order is in the National Archives, Record Group 45, File NE, and was provided by George A. Joiner in 1894. However, it may not be complete. William F. Wilson listed himself as graduating with this class and gave the number of fellow graduates as thirty-three (Wilson, "Wilson's War," 31).

66. See chapter 2, p. 31.

67. Clifton Breckinridge, letter to "Dear Pa," September 8, 1864 (Record Group 45, M260, Roll 5, National Archives).

68. Sallie Brock Putnam, *Richmond During the War: Four Years of Personal Observation* (New York: G. W. Carleton, 1867; reprint, Lincoln, Neb.: University of Nebraska Press, 1996), 315.

69. Ibid.

70. Harrison Papers, letter to "Dear Ellen," 9 June 1864.

71. Morgan, "Most Realistic War College," 549.

72. Ibid., 550.

73. *Official Records, Navies*, series II, vol. 2, 759.

74. Ibid., series I, vol. 11: 758.

75. Ibid., 783.

76. Herndon, "Naval Academy," 315.

77. F. E. Lutz, *Chesterfield, an Old Virginia County* (N.p.: 1954), 225.

78. Harrison Papers, letter to "Dear Ellen," October 30, 1864.

79. Morgan, "Most Realistic War College," 550.

80. Ibid.; abstract from the logbook of Battery Brooke (Record Group 45, National Archives).

81. *Official Records, Navies*, series II, vol. 2: 636.

82. Ibid., 635.

83. Ibid.

84. Ibid.

Chapter 5

1. J. M. Kell, letter to "My beloved wife," January 1, 1865 (John Kell Papers, Duke University).

2. Campbell, *Midshipman in Gray*, 215.

3. Ibid., 182.

4. Minor, part 2, 32.

5. Ibid.

6. Minor, part 2, 33.

7. *Official Records, Navies*, series I, vol. 11: 797.

8. Ibid.

9. *Official Records, Navies*, series I, vol. 11: 803.

10. Ibid., 669.

11. John Kell, letter to "My beloved wife," January 26, 1865 (J. M. Kell Papers, Duke University).

12. Ibid.

13. Campbell, *Midshipman in Gray*, 177.

14. Ferdinand Kennett, Bartlett S. Johnson, and Wilbur S. Davidson aboard the *Virginia II*; Francis L. Place on the *Fredericksburg*; and E. C. Machen on *Richmond* (*Official Records, Navies*, series I, vol. 12: 187).

15. Minor, part 2, 32.

16. Ibid.

17. Parker, letter to Mallory, February 28, 1865 (Record Group 45, File NE, National Archives).

18. Ibid.

19. Ibid.

20. Ibid.

21. Mallory, letter to Hon. A. G. Brown, March 2, 1865 (Record Group 45, File NE, National Archives).

22. Ibid.

23. Parker, *Recollections*, 347.

24. Ibid., 348.

25. Midshipman Robert H. Fleming noted in his diary on March 28: "Today we received orders to leave the ship. It is to be sunk in the river to obstruct it and keep off the Yankee monitors. We marched to the corner of 24th and Franklin. The school is broken up indefinitely" (Herndon, "Fleming's Diary," 209). Midshipman John W. Harris recalled after the war that the move was occasioned by the unhealthful conditions aboard the school ship owing to "the foulness of the bilge water" (John W. Harris, "Confederate Naval Cadets," *Confederate Veteran* 12 [April 1904]: 170). Despite these recollections, it appears that with the exception of some in the hospital, many, if not most, of the midshipmen were still on board until April 2.

26. Parker, *Recollections*, 372.

27. William S. Hoole, ed. "Admiral on Horseback: The Diary of Brigadier General Raphael Semmes, February–May 1865," *The Alabama Review*, no. 28 (April 1975): 138.

28. Herndon, "Fleming's Diary," 209.

29. Ibid., 213.

30. Minor, part 2, 35.

31. Parker, *Confederate Military History*, vol. 14, p. 97.

32. Parker, *Recollections*, 375.

33. Ibid., 374.

34. Stephen R. Mallory, "The Flight from Richmond," part 1, *Civil War Times Illustrated* 11, no. 1 (April 1972): 27.

35. F. E. Lutz, *Chesterfield, an Old Virginia County* (N.p: 1954) p. 262.

36. Parker, *Recollections*, 376.

37. Herndon, "Fleming's Diary," 210.

38. Raphael Semmes, *Memoirs of Service Afloat* (Secaucus, N.J.: Blue & Gray Press, 1987), 811. Several academy alumni were pressed into service as infantry officers in Semmes's brigade. In the brigade's 2nd Regiment, Passed Midshipman H. Pinkney served as captain of H Company. Passed Midshipman James B. Ratcliffe and Midshipman E. C. Machen were appointed first lieutenant and second lieutenant, respectively, of K Company. Passed Midshipman James A. Peters was first lieutenant of F Company, and Passed Midshipmen Lawrence M. Rootes and John Pegram held the same positions in Company G and Company I (Muster Roll of Naval Brigade [Reel 4, Folder 7, Raphael Semmes Family Papers, Alabama Department of Archives and History, Montgomery, Alabama]).

39. Mallory, "Flight from Richmond," part 1, 28.

40. Sallie Brock Putnam, *Richmond During the War: Four Years of Personal Observation* (New York: G. W. Carleton, 1867; reprint, Lincoln, Neb.: University of Nebraska Press, 1996), 395.

41. Ibid.

42. Semmes, *Memoirs*, 812; John F. Mayer, letter to Mrs. F. Powell Hardenstern, August 30, 1915 (item M–263, Eleanor S. Brockenbrough Library, Museum of the Confederacy, Richmond, Virginia). Having completed their mission of destruction, Lieutenant Billups and his men, after unsuccessfully attempting to rejoin Parker, attached themselves to Semmes's naval brigade. Thirteen years later, in Baltimore's Barnum Hotel, Parker was approached by a man he initially failed to recognize. "Seeing that I failed to recognize him," Parker later wrote, "he exclaimed: 'I am Lieutenant Billups of the rear guard.' Said I: 'report,' and he did so accordingly" (Parker, *Recollections*, 377).

43. Harris, a Virginian, left Washington College (now Washington and Lee University) in Lexington, Virginia, in 1863 and joined Colonel John H. Mosby's command. He was appointed acting midshipman in January 1865.

44. Harris, "Confederate Naval Cadets," 170.

45. Ibid.

46. Minor, part 2, 35.

47. Harris, "Confederate Naval Cadets," 170.

48. Ibid.

49. Minor, part 2, 35.

50. Harris, "Confederate Naval Cadets," 171.

51. Mallory, "Flight from Richmond," part 1, 30–31.

52. Ibid.

53. Semmes, *Memoirs*, 814.

54. Parker, *Recollections*, 377.

55. Ibid., 378.

56. Herndon, "Fleming's Diary," 210.

57. Ibid.

58. Otis Ashmore, "The Story of the Confederate Treasure," *The Georgia Historical Quarterly* 2, no. 3 (September 1918): 122.

59. Herndon, "Fleming's Diary," 210.

60. Ibid.

61. William H. Parker, "The Gold and Silver in the Confederate States Treasury," *Southern Historical Society Papers* 21 (January–December 1893), 307.

62. Campbell, *Midshipman in Gray*, 185–86.

63. Ibid., 187.

64. Semmes, *Memoirs*, 820.

65. Campbell, *Midshipman in Gray*, 188.

66. Parker, *Recollections*, 379.

67. Campbell, *Midshipman in Gray*, 189.

68. Parker, *Recollections*, 379.

69. Herndon, "Fleming's Diary," 210.

70. Parker, *Recollections*, 380–81.

71. Herndon, "Fleming's Diary," 210.

72. Mallory, "Flight from Richmond," part 1, 31.

73. Ibid., part 2, 28.

74. Parker, "Gold and Silver," 307.

75. "The Confederate Treasure—Statement of Paymaster John H. Wheless," *Southern Historical Society Papers* 10, no. 3 (March 1882): 139.

76. Parker, *Recollections*, 385.

77. Parker, "Gold and Silver," 309.

78. Parker, *Recollections*, 387.

79. Ibid.

80. Ibid.

81. Just how many midshipmen remained with Parker at this time is uncertain. Midshipman Fleming noted on April 27 that at Augusta, "[A]ll the school got furloughs who wished them. All but five of us took them" (Herndon, "Fleming's Diary," 211). Fleming listed the five who remained as himself, R. S. Quarles, Hudson (not listed in the *Register of Officers*), Richard C. Slaughter, and J. A. Carter. Fleming may have made his diary entry after the fact and confused Augusta with the disbanding of the corps at Abbeville five days later. It is certain that more than five midshipmen were with Parker at Abbeville on May 2.

82. Parker, *Recollections*, 388.

83. Ibid., 389. Davis was not as well received by some of his own soldiers, according to Passed Midshipman Morgan, who had remained in Abbeville after Mrs. Davis's departure. According to Morgan, Davis received word that "brigands, learning that a large amount of gold was being taken through the country protected only by a few little boys," were rapidly descending upon Abbeville. Davis rode to the camp of some of his soldiers and asked them to accompany him on an attack on the would-be robbers. One private replied for them all, telling Davis candidly, "Our lives are as pre-

cious to us as yours is to you. The war is over and we are going home!" It was, they were, and none followed their commander-in-chief. See Campbell, *Midshipman in Gray*, 191.

84. Ibid.

85. Parker, "Gold and Silver," 311.

86. Parker, *Recollections*, 391.

87. Ibid.

88. Ibid.

89. After the war, enemies of President Davis, led mainly by General Joseph E. Johnston, implied that the President had stolen the gold and silver and even accused him of this outright. Throughout the late 1800s accusations and counteraccusations raged back and forth in the day's newspapers and magazines. Parker never believed that Davis enriched himself from the treasure and many with direct knowledge gave compelling accounts of every penny. Wherever the treasure went, there is no evidence that it went into the pocket of Jefferson Davis.

Chapter 6

1. *New York Times*, April 9, 1865.

2. Ibid.

3. Ibid.

4. Ibid.

5. *Official Records, Navies*, series I, vol. 12: 124.

6. Ibid., 138. Not all of the wreck was removed, however. In 1872, W. G. Turpin, engineer, James River Improvement, reported, "The wrecks of the 'Patrick Henry' and 'Ben Sheppard,' opposite Orleans street, have been raised and destroyed." ("Report of the Engineer of the James River Improvement for the Year ending December 31st, 1872," in the collection of William S. Craghead, Richmond Civil War Roundtable.)

7. The furniture, china, and compass are in the Museum of the Confederacy in Richmond. Good's textbook, bearing the notation "Captured at Drewry's Bluff at Flag Officer Tucker's headquarters in the evacuation of Richmond, 1865," is in the holdings of the United States Naval Academy, Annapolis.

8. *Official Records, Navies*, series II, vol. 2: 636. The school-ship regulations with their references to "rooms" and "apartments" do seem to have been drafted with a shore-based institution in mind.

9. Winston Folk, "The Confederate States Naval Academy," *U. S. Naval Institute Proceedings* (September 1934): 1235.

10. *Official Records, Navies*, series II, vol. 2: 635.

11. Ibid.

12. Ibid.

13. Parker, *Confederate Military History*, vol. 14, p. 98.

14. Ibid.

15. Scharf, *History*, 776.

16. *Confederate Military History*, vol. 14.

17. Scharf, *History*, 776.

18. Morgan, "Most Realistic War College."

19. "Drummers and Fifers University Need in War of '61, Letter Shows," *Birmingham Age Herald*, November 4, 1934.

20. Clifton Breckinridge, letter to "Dear father," May 3, 1863 (Record Group 45, M260, Roll 5, National Archives).

21. Parker, *Recollections*, 346–47.

22. Wilson, "Wilson's War," 2.

23. Parker, *Recollections*, Introduction, xxi.

24. Ibid., 347.

Glossary of Naval Terms

aft: At or toward the rearmost part of the ship.

azimuth compass: A compass used to observe the amount of magnetic variation between compass north and true north. With an azimuth compass one could take bearings of both terrestrial and heavenly bodies—the sun, the moon, or a star; the difference between that bearing and the ship's calculated bearing would give the amount of variation. Azimuth compasses are no longer in use, having been replaced by azimuth rings on compasses and by the tables of compass variation noted on all navigational charts.

beam: The width of a vessel at its widest point.

berth deck: The deck containing sleeping quarters for the crew.

bilge: The lowest part of the ship, where the hull meets the keel at a near horizontal direction. All water taken aboard accumulates there and is removed by bilge pumps. When a ship is holed in this area she is said to be "bilged," hence the midshipman's slang for flunking out.

billet: Both a place for soldiers and sailors to sleep and a post, assignment, or berth. To fill a billet on a ship meant to be assigned to it as a crewman. To be billeted ashore meant your quarters were located off the ship.

binnacle: The housing containing the gimbeled ship's compass located by the helmsman's station at the ship's wheel. The list of the ship's sick was posted on the binnacle, hence the term "binnacle list."

bow: The part of the ship farthest forward.

bowlines: Ropes attached to and leading forward from the leech (edge) of a square sail, to keep the leech well out when the vessel is sailing close-hauled (close to the wind).

bowsprit: A spar projecting from the bow of a ship to which headsails are fastened and the foremast stayed.

boy: A rating in the Confederate navy for enlistees between 14 and 17 years old.

brig: A two-masted vessel square-rigged on both fore- and mainmast. Also a place of detention on board ship.

bulkheads: Partitions dividing a ship's hull into separate compartments.

bulwarks: The planking along the sides of a ship rising above the level of the deck and forming a solid rail to prevent water from coming aboard and to keep sailors from falling overboard.

buntlines: Ropes that are attached to the foot of a square sail and are used to haul it up to the yards for reefing and furling.

cannon: The "great guns" of a warship. Generally, cannon were classified in pounds or inches. For example, a thirty-two-pounder cannon was one whose projectile weighed thirty-two pounds; inches referred to the diameter of the cannon's bore. Smoothbores were generally typed by the weight of the projectile and rifled cannon were classified by the bore diameter.

cascabel: The portion of a cannon at the base of the breech ending at the knob at the rearmost portion of the gun.

casemate: An armored structure covering the gun deck. Confederate ironclads were noted for casemates that ran one third to two thirds the length of the vessel.

chronometer: A special, highly accurate timepiece with a compensated balance to account for changes in temperature. Chronometers were used to keep Greenwich Mean Time for comparison to local time in order to calculate the longitude of a vessel at sea.

clew-jiggers: The tackle attached to the aftermost corner on a fore-and-aft sail or the two lower corners on a square sail.

companionway: Stairs leading from an upper deck to the deck below.

cutting-out: An operation with the objective of going into enemy waters or an enemy harbor and taking an enemy ship, usually by surprise, usually carried out in ship's boats at night.

displacement: The weight of water displaced by a ship when floating with all stores and equipment aboard. Naval vessels are measured by displacement whereas merchant ships are rated on tonnage calculated on cubic capacity.

fid: A square wooden or iron bar that holds the weight of a topmast. Fiding a topmast is the process where the topmast is raised through a hole in the cap of the lower mast until a hole in the topmast is in line with a similar hole in the lower mast. A fid is then driven through the holes and the two masts firmly lashed together.

fore: Adjective (usually a prefix) meaning at or near the front of the ship, for example, "foremast," "forestay."

forecastle: Pronounced "fo'c'sle," the space beneath the short raised deck or poop just behind the bow. For many years it was where the common sailors berthed. The name derives from the wooden "castles" built over the bow on early wooden warships to house archers for firing on the crews of opponents or for repelling boarders.

frigate: A high-speed, maneuverable man-o'-war in the seventeenth, eighteenth, and nineteenth centuries, with usually three masts and twenty-four to thirty-eight guns on a single gundeck. Because of their superior sailing qualities frigates were often used to operate independently, scouting for less maneuverable line-of-battle ships.

gangway: Originally the platform running along the length of a ship upon which its boats were stored. Also used to describe companionways lowered over the side of the ship while anchored to allow access to the ship from the water.

glim: Any kind of light or lamp.

great gun: A firearm that must be mounted for use; a cannon.

grog: Traditionally a drink of rum diluted with water, but in the Confederate navy made of whiskey. The grog ration survived in the British Royal Navy until 1970.

gunboat: Generally, a small, lightly armed vessel used by most navies for patrolling in rivers and shallow coastal waters.

gun deck: A deck or decks housing the ship's cannon. Most Confederate ships had one gun deck, which was the uppermost deck of the ship. On ironclads this deck was covered by an armored casemate.

hawser: A heavy rope or cable with a circumference of five inches or more.

holystone: A soft sandstone used to scrub wooden decks.

hurricane deck: The upper deck of a passenger ship of inland waterways.

ironclad: The early name for warships built of wood and covered with a protective armor plate of iron. The French *Glorie*, built in 1859, is credited with being the first true ironclad. The first warship built entirely of iron was HMS *Warrior*, launched in 1860.

landsman: A rating for men without any naval experience.

launch: The largest of a ship's boats, it was furnished with a mast and sails and was capable of carrying a small gun. It was the ship's principal lifeboat and also served to carry provisions from shore to ship. Sometimes known as the ship's longboat.

master-at-arms: A warrant officer responsible for police duties aboard ship.

mate: A fellow crewman. As a rating, a sailor appointed to assist a specific petty officer, for example, boatswain's mate, gunner's mate.

mess: Any one of several groups into which a ship's crew was divided for taking meals. Also, a place where meals were served.

ordinary: A ship "in ordinary" is not in commission—fully manned and capable of sailing—and is usually in some sort of storage or disrepair. The modern-day term for being in ordinary is "mothballed."

ordinary seaman: An enlisted rating awarded to those sailors with at least one year of sea service.

petty officer: A naval rank corresponding to that of a noncommissioned officer in the army. Literally, "little officer," from the French *petite*.

pilot: A seaman with special knowledge of and qualification in local waters.

pivot gun: A cannon mounted on a carriage that runs along circular rails in the deck and pivots to expand the gun's field of fire.

port: The left side of the ship. Also, a harbor with facilities for the loading and unloading of cargo and passengers.

quarterdeck: On sailing ships without a bridge, that part of the deck where the helmsman stood and the captain took his walks and made his noon sightings to fix the position of his ship. On modern ships, that part of the deck where the officers take their recreation. On boarding a ship it is traditional to salute the quarterdeck.

quartermaster: The senior helmsman.

ratlines: A series of rope rungs between the shrouds (major side stays) of a mast on a square-rigger, giving the crew access to the yardarms and sails.

"rattle down": The securing of the ratlines to the shrouds.

rigging: The ropes, wires, or chains used for supporting the mast and raising and lowering the sails. Standing rigging supports the masts; running rigging is used to raise, lower, and trim the sails.

royal: In a square-rigged sailing ship, the fourth or fifth sail from the deck.

schooner: A ship with two masts of which the foremast is the shorter.

scuttle: The act of deliberately sinking a ship.

seaman: An enlisted rating awarded to sailors with at least two years' sea service.

shrouds: Standing rigging supporting a mast laterally as the stays support it fore and aft.

spar: Any wooden pole (mast, bowsprit, boom) used in the rigging of a ship.

spar deck: The upper deck of a flush-decked ship, a ship with a continuous fore-to-aft deck without any break and no smaller decks forward or aft.

starboard: The right side of a ship looking forward.

stays: A part of the standing rigging supporting the masts of a ship. Those that lead forward are forestays; those that lead aft to the vessel's sides or, sometimes, the stern are called backstays.

steerage: A large space below deck used for crew accommodation or for passengers who could not pay for a private cabin.

stem: The foremost timber at the bow joined to the keel.

stern: The after end of the ship.

tack: The direction a vessel takes in relation to the wind; a starboard tack means the wind comes over the starboard side and the main boom is on the port side.

tattoo: A signal on bugle or drum calling soldiers or sailors to their quarters at night.

tompion: A plug or cover to keep out dust or moisture from the barrels of the great guns.

tricing lines: Ropes used to "trice up" or make something more secure or move it to a different position.

walking-beam engine: A type of engine used only in the United States, in side-wheeler vessels. A lever situated on top of a vertical piston converted the reciprocal motion from the engine to rotary motion and transmitted power to the side paddle-wheels through long crankshafts connected on either end of the beam to the paddle-wheel shaft. The beam was high above the deck and in full view and its up-and-down motion gave the engine its name, "walking" beam.

yardarm: On a square-rigged vessel, the outer ends of a yard, extending out over the sides of the ship, beyond the lifts, or ropes, by means of which the yard was hoisted into position on the mast. Signal flags were hoisted from the yardarms and capital punishment was traditionally carried out by hanging the condemned from a yardarm.

yard: On a square-rigged vessel, a wooden or metal spar crossing a mast horizontally or diagonally from which a sail is set.

Bibliography

Published Sources

Primary Sources

Ashmore, Otis. "The Story of the Confederate Treasure." *The Georgia Historical Quarterly* 2, no. 3 (September 1918).

____. "The Story of the Virginia Bank Funds." *Georgia Historical Quarterly* 2, no. 4 (December 1918).

Blake, T. B. "Retreat from Richmond." *Richmond Dispatch*, May 2, 1897.

Botkin, B. A., ed. *A Civil War Treasury of Tales, Legends and Folklore*. New York: Random House, 1960.

Campbell, R. Thomas. *Academy on the James: The Confederate Naval School*. Shippensburg, Pa.: Burd Street Press, 1998.

Campbell, R. Thomas, ed. *Midshipman in Gray: Selections from "Recollections of a Rebel Reefer" by James Morris Morgan*. Shippensburg, Pa.: Burd Street Press, 1997.

Clark, Micajah H. "Twighlight of a Treasury." *Civil War Times Illustrated* 9, no. 10 (December 1972).

Clayton, William F. *A Narrative of the Confederate States Navy*. Weldon, N.C.: Harrell's Printing House, 1910.

____. "The Confederate Navy." *Richmond Times-Dispatch*, 1908.

Conrad, Daniel B. "Capture and Burning of the Federal Gunboat 'Underwriter,' in the Neuse, Off New Bern, N.C., in February, 1864." *Southern Historical Society Papers* 19 (1891).

Coski, John M. *Capital Navy: The Men, Ships and Operations of the James River Squadron*. Campbell, Calif.: Savas Woodbury, 1996.

Dukeshire, T. S. "Confederate Midshipmen and the Treasure Train." *Naval Institute Proceedings* (June 1957).

Edwards, John W. "CSS *Patrick Henry*—Famed Training Ship." *Richmond Times-Dispatch Magazine*, April 16, 1939.

Folk, Winston. "The Confederate States Naval Academy." *Naval Institute Proceedings*, September 1934.

Harris, John W. "Confederate Naval Cadets." *Confederate Veteran* 12 (April 1904).

Herndon, G. Melvin. "The Confederate Naval Cadets and the Confederate Treasure: The Diary of Midshipman Robert H. Fleming." *Georgia Historical Society Quarterly*, June 1960.

____. "The Confederate States Naval Academy." *Virginia Magazine of History and Biography* 69 (July 1961).

Hoole, William S., ed. "Admiral on Horseback: The Diary of Brigadier General Raphael Semmes, February–May 1865." *The Alabama Review*, no. 28 (April 1975).

Journal of the Congress of the Confederate States of America, 1861–1865. Washington, D.C.: Government Printing Office, 1904.

Loyall, Benjamin P. "Capture of the Underwriter." *Southern Historical Society Papers* 27 (1989).

Lutz, F. E. *Chesterfield, an Old Virginia County*. N.p: 1954.

Mallory, Stephen R. "The Flight from Richmond." Part 1. *Civil War Times Illustrated* 11, no. 1 (April 1972).

Minor, Hubbard T. "I Am Getting a Good Education . . . : An Unpublished Diary by a Cadet at the Confederate Naval Academy." Part 1. *Civil War Times Illustrated* 13, no. 7 (November 1974).

____. "Diary of a Confederate Naval Cadet." Part 2. *Civil War Times Illustrated* 13, no. 8 (December 1974).

Moebs, Thomas Truxton, ed. *Confederate States Navy Research Guide*. Williamsburg, Va.: Moebs Publishing, 1991.

Morgan, James M. "A Most Realistic War College." *Naval Institute Proceedings*, March–April 1916.

New York Times, April 9, 1865.

Official Records of the Union and Confederate Armies in the War of the Rebellion. Washington, D.C.: Government Printing Office, 1880–1901.

Official Records of the Union and Confederate Navies in the War of the Rebellion. Washington, D.C.: Government Printing Office, 1894–1927.

Ordnance Instructions for the Confederate States Navy. London: Saunders, Otley & Co., 1864.

Parker, William H. "The Conferate Navy." *Confederate Military History.* Clement A. Evans, ed. 12 vols. Atlanta: Confederate Publishing Co., 1895.

____. *Elements of Seamanship. Prepared as a Textbook for the Midshipmen of the C.S. Navy.* Richmond: Macfarlane & Fergusson, 1864.

____. *Questions on Practical Seamanship; Together With Harbor Routine and Evolutions.* Richmond: Macfarlane & Fergusson, 1863.

____. *Recollections of a Naval Officer 1841–1865.* New York: Scribners, 1883; reprint, Annapolis: Naval Institute Press, 1985.

____. "The Gold and Silver in the Confederate States Treasury." *Southern Historical Society Papers* 21 (January-December 1893).

Register of Officers of the Confederate States Navy 1861–1865. Mattituck, N.Y.: J. M. Carroll, 1983.

Regulations for the Confederate States School-ship Patrick Henry. July 23, 1863; microfilm at Yale University Library, film B2102, reel 15, n. 883.

Regulations for the Interior Police of the Confederate States School-Ship Patrick Henry. N.p.: n.d; microfilm at Yale University Library, film B2102, reel 15, n. 886.

Regulations for the Navy of the Confederate States. Richmond, Va.: Macfarlane & Fergusson, 1862.

Richmond *Daily Dispatch*, February 17, 1864.

Robbins, Peggy. "By Land and by Sea." *Civil War Times Illustrated* 37, no. 1 (March 1998).

Rochelle, James H. "The Confederate Steamship 'Patrick Henry.'" *Southern Historical Society Papers* 14 (1886).

Rutherford, Phillip. "The New Bern Raid." *Civil War Times Illustrated* 20, no. 9 (January 1982).

Scharf, John T. *History of the Confederate States Navy.* New York: Fairfax Press, 1977.

Shingleton, Royce G. *John Taylor Wood: Sea Ghost of the Confederacy.* Athens: University of Georgia Press, 1979.

Stiles, John C. "The Confederate States Naval Academy." *Confederate Veteran,* September 1915.

Still, William N., Jr., ed. *The Confederate Navy: Its Ships, Men and Organization, 1861–1865.* Annapolis: Naval Institute Press, 1997.

"The Confederate Treasure—Statement of Paymaster John H. Wheless." *Southern Historical Society Papers* 10, no. 3 (March 1882).

Truxton, Thomas. "A Short Account of the Several General Duties of Officers of Ships of War; From An Admiral, Down to the Most Inferior Officer." Available at Naval Historical Center web site, www.history.navy.mil/faqs/faq59–2.htm #intro.

Uniform and Dress of the Navy of the Confederate States. Richmond: Chas. H. Wynne, 1861; reprint, New Hope, Pa.: River House, 1952.

Vandiver, Frank E., ed. *The Civil War Diary of General Josiah Gorgas.* Tuscaloosa: University of Alabama Press, 1947.

Secondary Sources

Altman, James David. "The Charleston Marine School." *South Carolina Historical Magazine* 88, no. 2 (April 1987).

Averill, J. H. "The Evacuation of the City and the Days Preceding It." *Southern Historical Society Papers* 25 (December 1897).

Baker, Gary R. *Cadets in Gray.* Columbia, S.C.: Palmetto Bookworks, 1989.

Beach, Edward L. *The United States Navy: A 200 Year History.* Boston: Houghton Mifflin, 1986.

Bohannon, Keith. "Cadets, Drillmasters, Draft Dodgers, and Soldiers: The Georgia Military Institute During the Civil War." *The Georgia Historical Quarterly* 74, no. 1 (Spring 1995).

Civil War Naval Chronology 1861–1865. Washington, D.C.: Government Printing Office, 1971.

Conrad, Daniel B. "The Capture of the CS Ram *Tennessee* in Mobile Bay, August 1864." *Southern Historical Society Papers* 19 (1891).

Conrad, James Lee. *The Young Lions: Confederate Cadets at War.* Mechanicsburg, Pa.: Stackpole Books, 1997.

CSS *Neuse* homepage:www.ah.dcr.state.nc.us/sections/hs/neuse/neuse.htm.

Davis, Burke. *The Long Surrender.* New York: Random House, 1985.

Davis, Varina. *Jefferson Davis Ex-President of the Confederate States: A Memoir by His Wife.* New York: Belford, 1890.

Donnelly, Ralph W. "Blacks in the Confederate Navy." Unpublished paper. Richmond National Battlefield Park, Richmond, Va.

___. "Personnel of the Confederate Navy." *Civil War Times Illustrated* 13, no. 9 (January 1975).

___. *The Confederate States Marine Corps: The Rebel Leathernecks.* Shippensburg, Pa.: White Mane Publishing, 1989.

"Drummers and Fifers University Need in War of '61, Letter Shows." *Birmingham Age Herald*, November 4, 1934.

Dudley, William S. *Going South: U. S. Navy Officer Resignations & Dismissals On The Eve Of The Civil War*. Washington, DC: Naval Historical Foundation, 1981.

Durkin, J. T. *Stephen R. Mallory: Confederate Navy Chief.* Columbia, S.C.: University of South Carolina Press, 1987.

Horn, Stanley F. *Gallant Rebel: The Famous Cruise of the CSS Shenandoah*. New Brunswick, N.J.: n.p., 1947.

Instructions for the Guidance of the Medical Officers of The Navy of the Confederate States. Richmond: Macfarlane & Fergusson, 1864.

Kemp, Peter, ed. *The Oxford Companion to Ships and the Sea.* Oxford, U.K.: Oxford University Press, 1988.

Kennington, John. "Clothing, Pay and Provisions for the Savannah River Squadron 1861–1864." Navy and Marine Living History web site, www.navymarine.org/uniforms.

Lavery, Brian. *Nelson's Navy: The Ships, Men and Organisation 1793–1815.* Annapolis: Naval Institute Press, 1989.

Lee, C. H. *The Judge Advocate's Vade Mecum: Embracing a General View of Military Law, and the Practice Before Courts-Martial of the Army and Navy, With An Epitome of the Law of Evidence, As Applicable to Military and Naval Trials.* Richmond: West & Johnson, 1864.

Long, James C. "The Poorest Ironclad in the Confederacy: An Officer's Opinion of the *Albemarle.*" *Civil War Times Illustrated* 13, no. 9 (January 1975).

Lowry, Thomas P. *The Story the Soldiers Wouldn't Tell: Sex in the Civil War*. Mechanicsburg, Pa.: Stackpole Books, 1997.

Martin, Tyrone G. "North Carolina's Ironclad." *Naval History* 10, no. 4 (July–August 1996).

Melton, Maurice. "The First and Last Cruise of the CSS *Atlanta*." *Civil War Times Illustrated* 10, no. 7 (November 1971).

Putnam, Sallie Brock. *Richmond During the War: Four Years of Personal Observation.* New York: G. W. Carleton, 1867; reprint, Lincoln, Neb.: University of Nebraska Press, 1996.

Rafuse, Ethan S. "Save the Constitution." *Civil War Times Illustrated* 36, no. 2 (May 1997).

Report of the Engineer of the James River Improvement, for the Year Ending December 31st, 1872. Collection of William S. Craghead, Richmond Civil War Roundtable.

Rodger, N. A. M. *The Wooden World: An Anatomy of the Georgian Navy.* New York: Norton, 1996.

Rye, Scott. "Murder on the *Sumter.*" *Civil War Times Illustrated* 36, no. 5 (October 1997).

Savas, Theodore P. "Last Clash of the Ironclads." *Civil War* 16 (1989).

Semmes, Raphael. *Memoirs of Service Afloat.* Secaucus, N.J.: Blue & Gray Press, 1987.

Still, William N., Jr. *Iron Afloat: The Story of the Confederate Armorclads.* Nashville, Tenn.: Vanderbilt University Press, 1971.

Sullivan, David M. "From Hampton Roads to Appomattox: Virginia and the Confederate States Marine Corps." *Virginia Country's Civil War Quarterly* 8 (March 1987).

United States Naval Academy. "A Brief History of the United States Naval Academy." U.S. Naval Academy web site, www.usna.edu/VirtualTour/150years.

Williams, Scott K. "Black Confederates Fact Page." Geocities web site, www.geocities.com/BourbonStreet/Delta/3843/blackconfed.htm.

Unpublished Sources

Abstract from the logbook of Battery Brooke. Record Group 45, National Archives.

Brooke, John Mercer. Letter to Hon. J. L. M. Curry, November 30, 1863. Eleanor S. Brockenbrough Library, Museum of the Confederacy, Richmond, Virginia.

Brooke, St. George T. 1907. "Autobiography of St. George Tucker Brooke, Written for His Children." Library of Virginia, Richmond, Virginia.

Dabney, Robert. Robert Dabney Minor Papers. Minor Family Papers. Virginia Historical Society, Richmond, Virginia.

1863 Roster of Midshipmen. Virginia Confederate Rosters, vol. 19, reel 9. Library of Virginia, Richmond, Virginia.

Fleming, Robert H. "List of Midshipmen C.S. Steamer *Patrick Henry,* 1864–1865." Record Group 45, file NE, National Archives.

Harrison, James O., Papers. Library of Congress, Manuscripts Division.

Kell, John. John McIntosh Kell Papers. Rare Book, Manuscript, and Special Collections Library, Duke University, Durham, North Carolina.

Mayer, John F. Letter to Mrs. F. Powell Hardenstern, August 30, 1915. Eleanor S. Brockenbrough Library, Museum of the Confederacy, Richmond, Virginia.

"Miscellaneous Letters Sent, Office of Ordnance and Hydrography, Navy Dept. November 1864 to Mar 1865." Record Group 109, Chapter 7, v. 292, National Archives, Washington, D.C.

National Archives, Washington, D.C. Record Group 45: M260, Roll 5, "Records Relating to Confederate Naval and Marine Personnel"; File NE, "Drills, Training, and Education"; File NJ, "Discipline (Minor) and Minor Delinquencies"; Roll 15, File ME, "Medical"; Roll 15, File MM, "Medical"; Record Group 45, Roll 19, File NR, "Recruiting and Enlistments."

———. Record Group 109, Miscellaneous File, "Record for the Board for Examining Midshipmen, 1861–1862."

Semmes, Raphael. *Raphael Semmes Family Papers*. Alabama Department of Archives and History, Montgomery, Alabama.

United States. "Extract from Regulations of Navy School." *Navy Department Circular*. December 15, 1863. Tyre Glen Papers, Rare Books, Manuscripts, and Special Collections Library, Duke University, Durham, North Carolina.

Wilson, Beverly E., ed. "Willie Wilson's War 1861–1865: An Account of Some of the Experiences of Midshipman W F Wilson, C S Navy." Typescript (1969). Nimitz Library, United States Naval Academy.

Wilson, John A. "Notes on the War of 1861–62." Record Group 45, Notes of Midshipman John A. Wilson, CSN, On His Services During the Civil War, 1861–1865." National Archives.

Index

Sept. - 2004